A Century of Spin

A Century of Spin

How Public Relations Became the Cutting Edge of Corporate Power

DAVID MILLER and WILLIAM DINAN

Pluto Press

LONDON • ANN ARBOR, MI

First published 2008 by Pluto Press
345 Archway Road, London N6 5AA
and 839 Greene Street, Ann Arbor, MI 48106

www.plutobooks.com

British Library Cataloguing in Publication Data
A catalogue record for this book is available from the British Library

Hardback
ISBN-13   978 0 7453 2689 4
ISBN-10   0 7453 2689 7

Paperback
ISBN-13   978 0 7453 2688 7
ISBN-10   0 7453 2688 9

Library of Congress Cataloging in Publication Data applied for

This book is printed on paper suitable for recycling and made
from fully managed and sustained forest sources. Logging, pulping
and manufacturing processes are expected to conform to the
environmental regulations of the country of origin.

10   9   8   7   6   5   4   3   2   1

Designed and produced for Pluto Press by
Chase Publishing Services Ltd, Fortescue, Sidmouth, EX10 9QG, England
Typeset from disk by Stanford DTP Services, Northampton, England
Printed and bound in the European Union by
CPI Antony Rowe Ltd, Chippenham and Eastbourne, England

Contents

List of Abbreviations

AEI	American Enterprise Institute
AFL	American Federation of Labor
Aims	Aims of Industry
AISI	American Iron and Steel Institute
APPC	Association of Professional Political Consultants
ASI	Adam Smith Institute
BAP	British American Project
BCSD	Business Council for Sustainable Development
BCU	British Commonwealth Union
BEU	British Empire Union
BF	British Fascists
B-M	Burson-Marsteller
BRT	Business Roundtable
BYC	British Youth Council
CBI	Confederation of British Industry
CEO	chief executive officer
CER	Centre for European Reform
CFR	Council on Foreign Relations
CIA	Central Intelligence Agency
CIO	Congress of Industrial Organizations
CIPR	Chartered Institute of Public Relations
CND	Campaign for Nuclear Disarmament
CPS	Centre for Policy Studies
CSR	corporate social responsibility
EEF	Engineering Employers Federation
ERT	European Round Table of Industrialists
FBI	Federation of British Industries
GATS	General Agreement on Trade in Services
GATT	General Agreement on Tariffs and Trade
GDP	gross domestic product
GE	General Electric
H&K	Hill & Knowlton
HMC	Hobsbawm Macaulay Communications
ICC	International Chamber of Commerce
ICFTU	International Congress of Free Trade Unions
IEA	Institute of Economic Affairs

IMF	International Monetary Fund
IPPR	Institute for Public Policy Research
IRA	Irish Republican Army
IRD	Information Research Department
ISC	Institute for the Study of Conflict
LFIG	Labour Finance and Industry Group
LSE	London School of Economics
MoD	Ministry of Defence
MPS	Mont Pelerin Society
NAFF	National Association for Freedom (later known as the Freedom Association)
NAFTA	North American Free Trade Agreement
NAM	National Association of Manufacturers
NATO	North Atlantic Treaty Organisation
NGOs	non-governmental organisations
NICB	National Industrial Conference Board
NUM	National Union of Miners
OPA	Office of Price Administration
ORC	Opinion Research Corporation
PR	public relations
PRCA	Public Relations Consultants Association
PTA	Popular Television Association
RIIA	Royal Institute of International Affairs
RV	Rancheros Vistadores
SDA	Social Democratic Alliance
SDP	Social Democratic Party
SMC	Science Media Centre
SMEs	small and medium enterprises
TABD	TransAtlantic Business Dialogue
TNCs	transnational corporations
TUCETU	Trade Union Committee for European and Transatlantic Understanding
WBCSD	World Business Council for Sustainable Development
WEF	World Economic Forum
WTO	World Trade Organisation

Acknowledgements

This book emerged as we began to write a small historical chapter for a monograph on corporate public relations in the contemporary period. We felt the need to contextualise modern day PR and found ourselves chasing up obscure leads and biographical details on figures largely forgotten in the historical record. The result was that the historical chapter soon became a section of the planned book, and on the advice of the editorial term at Pluto, a book in its own right. The research underpinning this book stretches back over a decade and we acknowledge the support of the Economic and Social Research Council (ESRC) for this endeavour ('Corporate Public Relations in British and Multinational Companies', ESRC grant R000238993) which opened up the area of corporate PR for us and aroused our curiosity about the history outlined in this book.

This book has had a long gestation and is part of a wider collaboration between a number of people and organisations. We are grateful for the encouragement of our co-directors at Spinwatch, Andy Rowell and Eveline Lubbers, and the various contributors to the Spinwatch initiative, including Muhammad Idrees Ahmad, Billy Clark, Suzanne Garnham, Michael Greenwell, Claire Harkins, Tor Justad, Tommy Kane, Jonathan Matthews, Peter McQuade, Mat Pringle, Paul De Rooij and Bill Stevens. Special thanks are due to Julie-Ann Davis, Lynn Hill, Oliver Howard and Tracey Day for help with different parts of the manuscript.

There are many individuals who have helped, advised and inspired us in producing this book, including: Matthias Beck, Sharon Beder, Mark Brown, Bob Burton, Bill Carroll, John Casey, Colin Clark, David Collison, Paul deClerk, Aeron Davis, David Deacon, John Eldridge, Stuart Ewen, Bob Franklin, Des Freedman, Tim Gopsill, Ed Herman, Olivier Hoedeman, Mark Hollingsworth, Oyvind Ihlen, Nick Jones, Justin Kenrick, Alastair Macintosh, Stephanie and Steve Marriott, Robert McChesney, Niall Meehan, Uli Mueller, Brian Murphy, Greg Philo, John Pilger, Dieter Plewhe, Sheldon Rampton, Patrick Ring, Danny Schechter, Ken Silverstein, Jean Shaoul, Eric Shaw, Leslie Sklair, Tore Slatta, John Stauber, Gerry Sussman, Mark Thomas, Hilary Wainwright, Andrew Watterson, Kay Weaver, Erik Wesselius, Barry White, Dave Whyte, Granville Williams, and Kevin Williams.

We would also like to thank our colleagues and postgraduate students at the Department of Geography and Sociology at the University of Strathclyde for their support, and former colleagues at the Glasgow Media Group and Stirling Media Research Institute. We also want to say thanks to the good folks at Pluto for publishing this book and their continued support. The enthusiasm and assistance of Anne Beech, Melanie Patrick, Robert Webb and Mary Myers was crucial to this project. Thanks are also due to Rob Lilly, Helen Costello, Patsy and Bert Huegenin for their hospitality during our research trips to London and to Marina and James Lindsay for hosting our lengthy writing sessions within sight of Loch Achray. On a personal note we sincerely thank Emma Miller and Catie and Lewis Miller, Carol Clydesdale and Ciara and Niamh Dinan for their support and for tolerating the absences as we tried to break the back of this book and get it to the finishing line.

DM and WD
Glasgow, September 2007

1

The Cutting Edge of Corporate Power

I have no patience with those who try and attribute insidious and mysterious powers to public relations. Such ideas are wholly fanciful and without basis in fact.

John Hill, founder of PR firm Hill & Knowlton[1]

This book is about the power of public relations. It is about how corporations invented public relations and used its skills and techniques to impose business interests on public policy and limit the responsiveness of the political system to the preferences and opinions of the masses. The powers of public relations are mysterious in the sense that they are not well known. They are shrouded in secrecy and deception, which often enables PR operatives and PR firms to pursue their objectives undetected. The efficacy of corporate PR has, in fact, been largely suppressed from the historical record. This book is an attempt to reassess some of the history of popular democracy in the twentieth century by looking at how corporations have used public relations – propaganda – to secure their interests.

We argue that PR has played a very significant role in the course of popular democracy over the last century. The powers of PR are not mysterious in the sense that they are magical or superhuman. They are all too human, the products of diligence, hard work, planning and conscious ideological warfare. They result in the institutional political corruption so obvious in neo-liberal societies, where governments are much more responsive to the concerns of big business and the powerful than any other section of society. The result of corporate propaganda can be seen in the contemporary 'common sense' that what is good for business must be good for society. This kind of thinking is fostered as a means to protect the corporations and their allies from the possibility of democratic government.

This book sets out to remove the shroud of mystery and show how and why public relations originated, how it is implicated in processes of globalisation, and most seriously, how it has aided and abetted the rise to power of the global corporations and the consequent withering of democracy. This book examines how, since the dawn of representative democracy, corporations and political elites have used public relations and lobbying to subvert and subdue democracy. It shows how every serious prospect of advancing democracy has met a backlash from corporations, hard at work trying to manage and manipulate public opinion, the media, policy makers and anything else that might stand in their way.

SPIN AND PR

Spin has become the ubiquitous term for public relations tactics. It was initially applied to the news management techniques of political parties and the image-polishing of politicians, particularly during election campaigns, but spin has recently come to be used in relation to corporate and government activity. Spin is generally thought of as manipulative or deceptive communications. But the power of the corporations to manage the public agenda – which we examine in this book – is much more substantial than the popular notion of spin allows. This is because, first, the processes we examine are not limited to questions of communications alone. The attempts by the corporations to tame democracy and pursue their interests have to be accomplished by putting words and ideas into action. This can mean direct political action including dirty tricks, spying, burglary, agents provocateurs and even violence, a historical catalogue to which we devote some attention in a later chapter. But, equally, the notion of spin does not really capture the way in which the transformation of western societies towards the free market has been put in place by lobbying and public relations.

WHAT IS PR?

Much of the writing on PR focuses narrowly on what is often called the 'profession' of public relations. Sometimes this appears to include lobbyists and sometimes not. Rarely does it consider the wider ramifications of degraded and deceptive communications on public culture and society's institutions. While the PR industry expends considerable effort lauding and legitimating itself and its 'best practice', and many academics specialising in PR attend to the often apolitical technicalities of PR practice, the broader issues of what evasion, deception and manipulative communications are doing to democratic structures are avoided or neglected.

Across the globe PR agencies have a mixed reputation for ethical conduct. Perhaps the one thing that unites PR critics and PR apologists is the recognition that PR itself has a poor image.[2] Yet here is a real rupture between the PR industry's self-conception and how it is seen by critics outside. The profession of public relations likes to see itself as a force for good, promoting mutual understanding, positive relationships between publics and wider benefits for society. Yet this does not tally with the understandings of public relations that are current in popular culture. As we have detailed elsewhere, the popular representations of spin doctors usually involve depictions of Machiavellian schemers and fixers.[3]

Few of these portrayals manage to get beyond a rather one-dimensional pastiche of the spin doctor as behind-the-scenes bad guy. A notable exception is Kurt Vonnegut's modern classic, *Player Piano*, which takes the social consequences of the dominance of corporate culture as its central theme, and touches on the power of PR and how this is exploited on behalf of business. This book was said to have been inspired by Vonnegut's time working as a public relations executive in General Electric, one of the corporate leviathans of the post-war era. One can guess from Vonnegut's references to PR that he loathed the job – one of the minor characters in the novel prefers to turn to prostitution than have her husband work in public relations. The main protagonist is a captain of industry who has misgivings about the alleged benefits of private enterprise and the American way of life. One passage neatly captures the scope of this book and how the inventions of public relations seep into popular culture and consciousness.

The crusading spirit of the managers and engineers, the idea of designing and manufacturing and distributing being sort of a holy war: all that folklore was cooked up by public relations and advertising men hired by managers and engineers to make big business popular in the old days, which it certainly wasn't in the beginning. Now, the engineers and managers believe with all their hearts the glorious things their forebears hired people to say about them. Yesterday's snow job becomes today's sermon.[4]

Vonnegut also offers a definition of public relations which, despite the satire, arguably gets closer to the essence of PR than the volumes of academic theories and industry apologia on spin: 'that profession specialising in the cultivation, by applied psychology in mass communication media, of favourable public opinion with regard to controversial issues and institutions, without being offensive to anyone of importance, and with the continued stability of the economy and society its primary goal'.[5]

While Vonnegut's take on PR was well ahead of its time, the reach and influence of corporate PR have unquestionably increased dramatically since the 1950s. We have a wider focus on all the activities used by corporations to win the battle of ideas. This means their lobbying and their media manipulation, but it also means their philanthropy and the good works often undertaken under the title 'Corporate Social Responsibility'. It means their involvement with local communities and activist groups, their 'community engagement' and their dialogue with critics. We also include corporate funded think tanks and policy groups as well as deceptive front groups and 'institutes'. The lobbying and networking of senior management in peak business associations and corporate/elite social and networking clubs are also important, as are corporate intelligence and spying. Corporations do not see these as separate from their 'proper' public relations and nor should we.

We have sought to examine a wide range of activities in which corporations engage because it makes no sense to see PR professionals as divorced from corporate strategies. Nor does it make sense to draw an arbitrary line between the array of strategies corporations pursue to gain advantage in the battle of ideas. The most important reason for having this expansive definition of public relations and spin is to broaden the debate about spin and PR out from its narrow confines which relate to manipulating journalists and media agendas and operating simply in the sphere of ideas rather than seeing the battle of ideas as inextricably linked to questions of action and decision, and their consequences.

SPIN OR PROPAGANDA?

As a result we don't think that terms like 'spin' or 'public relations' are able to capture the full magnitude of what we are describing. Spin might suggest distortion and misinformation, but it does not really capture that strategic use of information intended to undermine the morale of opponents. Although 'public relations' as an industry has a poor reputation, the term itself suggests a kind of consensual process, with some level of mutuality. In reality public relations as developed by the corporations is a set of techniques for pursuing corporate interests rather than promoting common interests. Of course as any decent historian of PR will tell you, the term was invented specifically as a piece of spin as a means of re-labelling the activities previously known as 'propaganda'. As Edward Bernays, one of the founders of 'public relations' put it: 'propaganda got to be a bad word because of the Germans... using it [in 1914–18]. So what I did was to try to find some other words. So we found the words Counsel on Public Relations.'[6]

We think that propaganda is a better term than spin or public relations because it also implies the unity of communication and action. It is communication for a purpose. What we are examining is the rise of propaganda and its harnessing to the interests of great power. Yet, today propaganda sounds like a quaintly old-fashioned term which is perhaps more relevant to communication in times of war, if it has any remaining purchase at all. On the contrary, we contend that one of the many victories of corporate propaganda is that the term is no longer used to describe the activities we uncover in this book. In media and popular debate as well as in the field of academia, those who discuss lobbying or public relations or marketing or spin, do so in terminology which bears the mark of successful propaganda manipulation.

So we refer to the activities outlined in this book interchangeably as propaganda, spin, public relations, but we are always conscious that the terms are both contested and themselves the subject of propaganda. Because we recognise that the use of propaganda techniques is about the pursuit of interests we also see this as a question of the manufacture of consent. That is, we contend that the genesis of the PR industry itself, as well as its operation today, constitutes a huge apparatus for legitimating the interests of the few at the expense of the many.

MANUFACTURING COMPLIANCE

An important feature of our argument, however, is that spin, public relations and lobbying are not only about the 'engineering of consent'. To win the consent of the public might be desirable for the rulers of the world, but it is not always necessary. The key is to ensure public and political compliance. It is not that the public or decision makers actively agree and support the policy ideas promulgated by business lobbies and the corporations. What is critical is that they do not actively and aggressively oppose them. This is what makes the melding of ideology and action so powerful. In other words the aim and effect of much corporate propaganda is the manufacture of compliance.

There are two important elements to corporate engagement in the battle for ideas. The first of these is the attempt to manage public opinion and sentiment. To engineer consent, certainly, but also, at a minimum, to ensure compliance. The second element is to manage action. All of the networking, planning and policy discussion detailed in this book helps to build alliances amongst different corporate factions and to ensure that corporate and political elites are able to think and act with considerable unity. We think that both of these elements are important for the exercise of corporate power. This means that we do not see the question of 'consent' – meaning the consent of the governed – as the only question worth examining. We also think that elite unity is an important question and that it explains much about the conduct of politics in neo-liberal times. Given the progressively declining opportunity for most people to have any meaningful input into the democratic process, it should be clear to all that the political process is increasingly about managing elite consensus.

One cannot fail to notice that big business, the transnational corporations, have a structural advantage in terms of political activism under the conditions of liberal democracy. They have the resources, interest and opportunities to engage in politics and governance.[7] Yet, it is not simply an issue of corporations being able to throw more money at politics and politicians than any other faction of society (significant as this is). It is critically a question of how resources are targeted and marshalled. Cooperation rather than competition is arguably the hallmark of corporate political activism. To be sure different corporations will have different interests and at times will act alone or against each other. However, corporations' lobbying against one another does appear to be the exception rather than the rule, and 'corporate pluralism' is simply no substitute for proper public participation in democratic decision making.[8]

Nor is neo-corporatism or social partnership. Much of the analysis of corporatist policy making is now outdated, given the declining power of organised labour in the last few decades, and the massively increased power of capital. Under contemporary conditions, where business has taken a more prominent and proactive role in governance, it is difficult to see how trade unions or other social partners can easily act as countervailing forces to business power. This is why the struggles for democratic renewal and participation are critically important. This also explains why corporate propaganda is not simply trained on governments and public servants, but on civil society too. This is where the next challenge to business dominance is likely to come from.

CORPORATE POLITICAL ACTION AND NETWORKS OF POWER

The management of consensus by our rulers is done in identifiable ways by identifiable people. There is a long history stretching back at least 50 years of social scientists examining power networks. This is most famously associated with the work of C. Wright Mills and his 1956 book *The Power Elite*.[9] *A Century of Spin* aspires to stand in that tradition of examining interlocking power networks. Our focus on the battle of ideas and how this interacts with, on the one hand corporate board interlocks, and on the other corporate lobby and policy planning groups, suggests not simply that power elites 'have' power, but shows how that power is reproduced and enacted. Our argument is that this is done by the unity of communication and action in concrete circumstances. This seems to us a new approach to the relations between power and communication and we return to it in the conclusion in our consideration of communication and power and in particular the use of the concept of hegemony.

THE THREE WAVES OF CORPORATE POLITICAL ACTION

This book reveals how the free market system which underlies the most important challenges facing humanity today (war, poverty, environmental catastrophe and the withering of democracy) were put in place by concerted lobbying and political action by business interests over the last century. The book begins by tracing the involvement of public relations and propaganda at the most important political events of the last 100 years. Like the lead character Zelig in the Woody Allen film, PR practitioners seemed to be present behind the scenes at almost every event of importance. The next chapter deals with the first of what we refer to as the three waves of corporate political activism. The rise of corporate political activism started before the dawn of the modern democratic era in around 1920. In fact it was a response to the threat posed by democracy – the threat that the privilege and power held by the corporations and their owners in the upper classes would be dissipated once universal suffrage was introduced. So the corporations began working single-mindedly to defend their privileges, with the crucial period being between 1916 and 1926. In both the US and UK class-wide propaganda organisations emerged at this time and the business classes cut their teeth on secretive political activities. In both the UK and US 1919 was the decisive year in which the threat of revolution was seen off. In the UK a lesser but nonetheless significant threat was posed by the General Strike in 1926; a threat faced and defeated.

The second wave of political activism by the corporations followed the Wall Street Crash and the rise of the New Deal in the US. This extended period of class warfare lasted until well after the 1939–45 war and resulted in a huge increase in organised class-wide political activism and propaganda from corporate elites. In the UK the second wave started in the early 1940s with the rising threat of reform of industry and social welfare from an incoming Labour government after the war. UK business activists were not as successful as their US counterparts, but did manage to defend themselves against some significant reforms planned by the post-war government.

At first (in the period up until the 1950s), the corporations were only able to slow the march of progress. Democracy campaigners did win significant victories such as the New Deal in the US and the introduction of the NHS and the welfare state in the UK. But latterly, and with renewed vigour from the 1940s, the corporations started to go on the offensive, both in terms of the 'battle of ideas' and, critically, the on-the-ground struggles and strategies to put their ideas into practice. This ushered in the third wave of business activism from about 1968 to 1980, which we discuss in Chapter 5.

The decisive victories won by the corporations included the electoral successes of Thatcher and Reagan in 1979/80 and following on from these, the wholesale neo-liberal revolution which has progressively opened markets and transferred resources and industries once held in common into private hands. The result has been ever increasing class polarisation and inequality on the one hand and the looming environmental crisis on the other. We argue that the cutting edge of this campaign has been the battle of ideas – how ideas in the service of great power have been crucial to the project of bringing democracy to heel. Chapter 6 tells the story of the increasingly global dimension of corporate political activism and propaganda. The elite policy planning groups and networking meetings are places for the new global business elite to hammer out compromises and to construct a unity of purpose. The emergence of the global elite was both a consequence of and accomplished by the necessity to take the battle of ideas to the global level. Organisations like the Bilderberg Group, the World Economic Forum and the Trilateral Commission have helped to put in place the architecture of global neo-liberal governance. But this has also needed practical day-to-day implementation through the ever increasing networks of free market think tanks and the global spread of the PR industry, which we examine in Chapter 7.

The remainder of the book examines the final elements of the corporate campaign to remove the threat posed by democracy. This involved the long term process of undermining the Labour Party in the UK, which had survived the three waves of corporate political activism in a way that the Democrats in the US did not. Chapter 8 examines the first part of this process – the pulling of Labour's teeth. This began long before Tony Blair became party leader. We pick up the story in 1945 and chart the attempts by corporate activists and their allies in American government to undermine the Labour Party. The campaign picked up momentum during the third wave of corporate activism with the creation of the SDP, which split the left vote, but it really made decisive steps with the active assault on the power of organised labour starting with the Grunwick dispute in 1977 and culminating in the miners' strike of 1984/85. Throughout this period, we show the crucial importance of the battle of ideas and of propaganda, used in close harmony with other forms of political and economic action.

After the defeat of the left, the next step was to turn Labour into a party of big business. Chapter 9 tells the story of how the Labour Party under Kinnock, Smith and Blair changed so much that it could command the confidence of the transnational corporations. By that stage, we argue, the real content of democratic politics had effectively disappeared.

Chapter 10 brings the story up to date by focusing on the links between corporate and neo-conservative activists and the Conservative Party under David Cameron. Our argument about the importance of public relations to corporate power is more than borne out in the networks around Cameron – and we might say in the fact that Cameron is himself a public relations operative by trade.

We conclude the book with an account of where the relationship between the corporations and public relations is heading now. But we also raise some issues about how to understand the relationship between public relations, propaganda and power. These issues are a little more abstract and perhaps arcane than much of the material in the rest of the book. The argument engages with debates about the power of ideas and the importance of seeing ideas as fundamentally linked to the historical circumstances in which they emerge as well as in relation to the interests of those who produce and use them. Faint hearted readers might like to skip this section! Nevertheless, we think it is important to show how the ideas in this book connect with other academic debates and we want to suggest a framework for understanding corporate political activism and contemporary history. Such analytical framing suggests ways of thinking, seeing and acting in the world today, which we believe will be of interest and relevance to those engaged in activism and the new social movements of this era which confront corporate power, namely those campaigns for human rights, social justice and ecological sustainability.

PR BENEATH THE RADAR

Most people would struggle to name the biggest PR companies in the world. The world's most notorious corporations are well recognised from Bhutan to Belize, Belfast to Bujumbura: Coca-Cola, Nestlé, McDonald's, Monsanto, British American Tobacco, Nike, Shell, BP, Exxon. But the businesses, consultants and hirelings engaged in pursuing the interests of these corporations remain much more obscure. Our wider conceptualisation of the persuasive techniques of corporate PR has led us to identify PR agencies and lobbying firms as some of the key agents of this form of propaganda.

During the long process of researching and writing this book, which started properly in 2000, but whose genesis goes back a lot further, we have been attending conferences and seminars run by PR agencies, lobbying consultancies, corporations and think tanks. When we have been asked by colleagues and friends about our research and what we were doing, we have tended to explain our research by talking about how corporations influence society and public policy through the use of PR and lobbying. We have often had the feeling that our explanations about the political dimensions to PR have surprised or bemused. This may be in part because it requires a mental leap from thinking about PR as the showy, the staged and the phoney so often associated with political spin or celebrity puff, to thinking about PR, and corporate propaganda in particular, as direct domestic political manipulation. So the necessity of translating our concerns and research means we end up posing the problem in a fairly direct way: how is it that democracy appears to work so badly, and that corporations are able to get away with their crimes against humanity and the planet?

The urgency of this question was intensified because of the historical period in which we did the research, starting with the 'Battle of Seattle' in 1999 and progressing through the 9/11 attacks, the rise of the anti-war movement against the attacks on Afghanistan and Iraq and the flowering of the World Social Forum (and the associated European Social Forums) as a response to the corporate World Economic Forum. At a more local level we were also absorbed by the possibilities for democratic renewal in Scotland as New Labour devolved some powers from London to Edinburgh. This constitutional change was popularly understood as a significant opportunity for participatory governance, and the dawn of an open, transparent and responsive political culture.

We struggled with how best to present and explain all of this and we grappled with what it all meant. This book is our attempt to try to tell the story of what we found and to put it into an intelligible context. In the end we felt we had to go back to the beginning of all this to explain how it emerged in the first place. This book is therefore an attempt to tell the story of the rise of corporate propaganda and PR.

So this book is our attempt to try to explain how the 'insidious' and 'mysterious' power of PR works to undermine democracy – the very opposite of what its chief exponents claim that it does. Before we can work out how to tackle vested interests and concentrated corporate power, we need to understand how it works. We think that PR and lobbying are critical components of corporate power and we hope that this book contributes to wider public knowledge about them as a prelude to effective action against them and the corporate power which they represent.

2
Public Relations: The Zelig Complex

In his film *Zelig*, Woody Allen paints a picture of Leonard Zelig, the human chameleon, as impossibly or improbably present at every major historical event. Played by Allen, 'Zelig is a man first noticed at a party by F. Scott Fitzgerald, who has the ability to turn into other people when surrounded by them. For example, if he is among doctors, he transforms into a doctor', notes one account. 'I shouldn't say it's an ability, it's more of a coping mechanism for Zelig. As he admits in psychiatric care, he wants to fit in so badly that he literally becomes whoever he is with.'[1] This might stand as a decent description of PR operatives. Always present, often unnoticed or forgotten at important historical events.

This chapter gives a tour through the unauthorised history of the PR industry. This is an account which the industry does not want to become common knowledge, but which we have assembled from the public record.

Perhaps the place to start is with a suicide in Rome in early 2005. Edward von Kloberg III, 63, an American lobbyist, flung himself from the Castel Sant'Angelo in Rome. As one report noted, this was appropriately enough the 'site of Tosca's suicide in the Puccini opera'. 'Italian newspapers said he had been depressed after a failed attempt at reconciliation with his Lithuanian homosexual lover'.[2] Von Kloberg was described as the 'tyrants' lobbyist' after he died because of his unashamed representation of the world's worst dictators. But his credit was still good with the global elite. He was a confidant of successive American presidents. Indeed 'among items found on his body was an American magazine cover with a picture of him meeting the first President George Bush'.[3] Typically flamboyant, he died as he lived; a hanger-on of the global elite.

His voice, said one friend, was marked by an 'almost Rooseveltian, high-class accent.' He drove enormous black cars and draped foreign medals (Zaire's Order of the Leopard among them) across his tuxedo. At night, he sported one of two favorite black capes: one with red lining, the other with prints of doves. As was said of the Bloomsbury diarist Violet Trefusis, a writer he admired, von Kloberg had a 'taste for outmoded splendors.' He believed such flourishes were essential to conducting business with world leaders, the kings and presidents for life whose presence he relished. When they listened to his advice, it was 'very invigorating', he said.[4]

Von Kloberg was born Edward Joseph Kloberg and added the 'von' when Arnaud de Borchgrave, the CIA connected journalist and propagandist, 'told him it sounded more distinguished'.[5]

Kloberg's view was that no client was beyond the pale. 'Lawyers represent both guilty and innocent clients. Why should a different standard be applied to public relations and government affairs counsel?' he asked. But his list of clients reads like a roll call of western supported dictators. These included President Mobuto of Zaire, the military dictatorships of Guatemala and Burma, Samuel Doe of Liberia, and Saddam Hussein. Saddam Hussein? Kloberg represented the Iraqi dictator when he was gassing the Kurds at Halabja. He said he was 'utterly fascinated' by the Iraqi leader and returned to Washington to 'propagandize why they were gassing the Kurds'.[6] At the time, as Kloberg himself pointed out in his own defence, Hussein was an ally of the West. Asked if he was ashamed to represent killers and thieves, he responded: 'Shame is for sissies.' The *Washington Post* obituary also recalled the 'most outrageous and lasting public impression of von Kloberg', which

came from a notorious 'sting' operation by *Spy* magazine. For a story the satirical journal titled 'Washington's Most Shameless Lobbyist,' a staff writer posed as a Nazi sympathizer whose causes included halting immigration to the 'fatherland' and calling for the German annexation of Poland. According to the magazine, von Kloberg expressed sympathy for the fake client – and her $1 million offer. And then he was drubbed in print. Shortly afterward, he showed up at the opening of *Spy*'s Washington office with a first-aid kit and sported a trench helmet, 'so I can take the flak,' he announced. Friends of von Kloberg saw the article as a revolting caricature of a man whose grace and charm were displayed at intimate dinner parties he threw to unite disparate voices – 3,500 dinners, each with 12 guests, he estimated.[7]

Von Kloberg's larger than life persona is perhaps atypical of the industry, but his proximity to the powerful is not. In the US and the UK the involvement of PR people in key moments of crisis is not often a prominent part of the historical record. This is just how the PR people like it – covert, subterranean, in the dark. PR operatives are technicians in the back room ensuring that corporations and governments are able to pursue their interests, just so long as no light is cast into the shadows.

It is often imagined that propaganda was the offspring of total war, that it was something only latterly and reluctantly taken up in peace time. Tracing the development of corporate spin shows this to be a mistaken view. In both the US and UK, government and business propaganda was already emerging.

In 1914 Ivy Lee, one of the pioneers of corporate propaganda, attempted to reshape the image of the greatest industrialist of the age, John D. Rockefeller. Rockefeller had been responsible for the Ludlow massacre in which 19 miners and their families (including 12 children) were killed. Lee's publicity sheet claimed that the massacre was carried out by 'well-paid agitators sent out by the union' and that legendary union organiser Mother Jones (then 82) was 'a prostitute and the keeper of a house of prostitution'.[8] Both stories were entirely false, the former being the precise opposite of the truth; the killings were carried out by forces called in by Rockefeller's company. As Lee put it:

It is not facts alone that strike the popular mind, but the way in which they take place and in which they are published that kindle the imagination... Besides, what is a fact? The effort to state an absolute fact is simply an attempt to... give you my interpretation of the facts.[9]

Facts were flexible and minds malleable. The presentation of events, processes and information was of the greatest importance – a philosophy well suited to the idea that history could be presented and re-presented and that it could therefore be controlled by 'educated' and 'enlightened' elites. The philosophy suited the role of the new propagandists too as they moved in influential circles, working their magic and moving on to the next issue.

Perhaps the PR pioneer who best suited this role was Edward Bernays, whose role in the making and breaking of reputations was almost as significant as his own self-publicity. He advised the rich, famous and powerful, acting as manipulator extraordinaire. In so doing, he pioneered the development of public relations as an industry.

Bernays worked for the tobacco industry for much of his career. He is infamously credited with breaking the taboo against women smoking in public through a carefully choreographed and remarkably successful PR stunt. He instructed his own secretary Bertha Hunt to invite young debutantes drawn from a list supplied by a Bernays contact at *Vogue* magazine (at that time a client of Bernays) to join her in striking a blow for sexual equality. The instructions were clear: no actresses and none looking too 'model-ey'.[10] Ten young women paraded down Fifth Avenue in New York on Easter Sunday 1929, proudly smoking their 'Torches of Freedom'. They were not told that they were bit players in a PR stunt for the tobacco industry, nor that it was set up by Bernays. The 'demonstration' was captured by the photographer Bernays had laid on, and news and images of the Torches of Freedom protest spread quickly across America, just as Bernays had intended.

Bernays, who lived to be 103, dominates the history of propaganda and public relations, appearing like Zelig in the shadows at major world events. Stuart Ewen recounts his visit to Bernays' home in 1990, when the propaganda pioneer was 99 years old:

He led me through a dark room off the landing. Its walls were covered with scores of framed black and white photographs, many of them inscribed. Wordlessly, yet eloquently, the pictures placed my ancient host close to the heartbeat of a century. Bernays on his way to the Paris Peace conference, 1919. Bernays standing with Enrique Caruso, Bernays and Henry Ford. Bernays and Thomas Edison. Bernays and Dwight David Eisenhower. An inscribed photo portrait of his uncle Freud, was also conspicuous. Bernays with the 'great men' at the 'great events' of the twentieth century.[11]

WAR AND PROPAGANDA

When the 1914–18 war came the US government recruited already existing propagandists together with journalists. Along with Bernays were the journalist and PR theorist Walter Lippmann and PR operatives Carl Byoir and Arthur W. Page. Ivy Lee joined President Wilson's Red Cross War Council in 1917 to direct publicity, though he was keen to leave by 1918. His reasoning was revealed in a telegram to John D. Rockefeller: 'my service to the Red Cross has not been of great expense directly, but has been the cause of losing considerable business I might have had'.[12] Both Lippmann and Bernays were present in Paris when President Wilson was acclaimed by thousands of Parisians as he arrived for the Versailles peace conference. Both were impressed by the power of propaganda in creating mass adulation for Wilson. 'When I came back to the United States, I decided', said Bernays, 'that if you could use propaganda for war, you could certainly use it for peace.'[13]

Less well known perhaps is the role of British propagandists before, during and after the First World War. In many ways the British were pioneers of propaganda, which is unsurprising given Britain's colonial history and the close links between propaganda and conflict. The present day British Ministry of Defence 15 (UK) Psychological Operations Group, for example, traces its origins back to the Boer War in the late nineteenth century.[14] The British government were not averse to using propaganda before the First World War, and many of those who would later work in the War Propaganda Board had already undertaken domestic propaganda for the National Insurance Commission.[15] The battle against the Irish republican movement in 1920 saw British intelligence agents pioneering black propaganda efforts.[16] In the period after the Great War and the partition of Ireland in 1921, many of these operatives turned up in the PR industry or in other propaganda roles.

Some of the key figures working in propaganda and spin in the UK at this time included Basil Clarke, Sydney Walton and H.B.C. Pollard. Clarke was a former war correspondent for the *Daily Mail* (1914–18), director of 'Special Intelligence' for the Ministry of Reconstruction in 1918, and was appointed to the Ministry of Health on its creation in 1919 with responsibility for 'stimulating public opinion' which mainly involved, according to one account, 'the insertion of articles in the press'.[17] In 1920 he was appointed Director of Public Information at Dublin Castle, directing the British propaganda operation against the Irish republican movement, for which he was knighted. It was in this role that Clarke developed his ideas and tactics on 'propaganda by news'. The key quality of the propaganda was, as Clarke put it, 'verisimilitude' – having the air of truth. According to Clarke's own account, the routine 'issue of news gives us a hold over the press... [journalists] take *our version* of the facts... and they believe all I tell them' (emphasis in original). The service 'must look true and it must look complete and candid or its "credit" is gone'.[18]

The British policy was, as Brian Murphy's detailed research shows, to disseminate lies and half truths which gave the appearance of truth. As Major Street, another of the propagandists in Ireland noted: 'in order that it may be rendered capable of being swallowed', propaganda 'must be dissolved in some fluid which the patient will readily assimilate'.[19] In 1924 Clarke left government and set up perhaps the first PR agency in the UK. By the end of the 1920s Editorial Services, as it was called, was a significant operation with 60 staff. In the late 1920s and early 1930s Clarke worked as a PR consultant for the Conservative Party and by 1933 Editorial Services had handled more than 400 accounts.[20]

Among the accounts was work for the beer industry. The brewers were closely involved in the creation of the first class-wide propaganda agency in 1919 (National Propaganda, on which see Chapter 3) and later hired Clarke. Clement Shaw, the chief PR man for the Brewers Society, wrote that in the early days Clarke 'reigned as undisputed monarch of PR'. Clarke was centrally involved in pushing corporate interests such as those of H.J. Heinz for whom he promoted canned foods, by attacking the non-canned competition; and in extending the concept of home ownership for the Halifax Building Society. He also wrote speeches for King George V. The King reportedly approved of these because they stopped him appearing 'too bloody pompous'. His son, Alan Clarke – who also went on to become a PR operative and who worked at Editorial Services – testifies that it 'tended, at one time, to be a clearing house for all kinds of people needing a job'.[21]

Sydney Walton was another key operative in business and government propaganda during this period. Walton, a former undercover agent, ran secret propaganda campaigns for the coalition government of Lloyd George and the organisational network around the British Commonwealth Union (a corporate funded lobby and propaganda group set up in 1916). In 1922 he set himself up in business as a PR consultant, one of the first in Britain. He was hired by the Conservative Party in 1926 to run their 'information fund' or propaganda campaign against the General Strike with a budget of £10,000. Walton spent over £25,000 on propaganda during the five months of the 1926 miners' strike.[22]

Hugh Pollard was another notable figure in the emergence of militant business activism in the UK. He was active in intelligence work during the 1914–18 war as a staff officer in the intelligence section of the War Office (1916–18). He later worked in Ireland as a press officer of the Police Authority's information section, liaising with Basil Thomson, head of Special Branch in London. Pollard was a racist ideologue. Among his views on those who resisted the British empire in Ireland was the following: 'there is nothing fine about a group of moral decadents [the IRA] leading a superstitious minority into an epidemic of murder and violent crime... The Irish problem is a problem of the Irish race, and it is rooted in the racial characteristics of the people themselves.'[23] The Irish he thought were 'racially disposed to crime', have 'two psychical and fundamental abnormalities... moral insensibility and want of foresight' which 'are the basic characteristic of criminal psychology'.

Colonel Hugh Pollard, as he later became, turned up again in right wing 'diehard' circles in 1936 when he flew from Croydon airport on a Dragon Rapide light aircraft to the Canary Islands. He and his collaborators were on a mission in which they picked up General Francisco Franco in the Canary Islands, and flew him to Spain to launch his murderous coup against the republican government. Accompanying him was Toby O'Brien, a leading lobbyist and Conservative Party spin doctor in the post-1945 period.[24] At Central Office O'Brien was involved in lobbying for the introduction of commercial television.

PROPAGANDA AND NAZI GERMANY

Before Hitler and Goebbels confirmed the bad name that propaganda had started to attract with the 'evil deeds' of the 'Hun' in the First World War, there was little ambivalence amongst corporate activists about the use of the term. They used it regularly and with no embarrassment. After the 1914–18 war some of their most developed thinkers started the process of reconsideration and introduced the term 'public relations'. Both Ivy Lee and Edward Bernays claimed to be the first to use it, but it is clear that it was from the start a propaganda term.[25]

Since the creation of the term public relations it has been a key part of the work of propaganda to pretend that PR and propaganda are separate with the former largely undertaken by 'us' and the latter largely by authorised enemies or in extremis. But contrary to the authorised version of propaganda history, the early activists and writers on PR did not learn their trade from the Germans... it was the other way around.

In 1933 Karl von Wiegand, a foreign correspondent for the US Hearst newspapers visited Goebbels and on being given a tour of his library discovered Bernays' *Crystallizing Public Opinion* on the shelves. Bernays' book was being used by Goebbels 'as a basis for his destructive campaign against the Jews'.[26] 'I was shocked', Bernays later wrote. 'Obviously the attack on the Jews of Germany was no emotional outburst of the Nazis, but a deliberate, planned campaign.'[27] Bernays was first told of this in 1933 by Wiegand himself, but was 'savvy enough' not to repeat the story until the publication of his autobiography in 1965.[28]

Both Hitler and Goebbels (and a variety of other Nazi ministers) were also familiar with the work of Ivy Lee having separately met him in Germany, when he was contracted by I.G. Farben, one of the biggest companies in Germany. Lee's services were secured at a retainer of $29,000 a year in 1934. Farben wanted Lee to advise on 'what could be done to improve [German–American] relations... continuously'.[29] Lee's contact at Farben, Managing Director Dr Max Illgner, arranged the introductions. At his 'half hour or so' meeting with Hitler, Lee said he would 'like to understand him better'.[30] Goebbels assured Lee that the Nazi government 'did not want to interfere within the United States'.[31]

Lee's view on Hitler, as confided to John D. Rockefeller, was apparently that 'Hitler would do much to restore German confidence, and that a confident and successful Germany was a prerequisite to a healthy Western economy'.[32] Lee 'conceded that the advice he had offered his client was ultimately intended to guide the German government in its public relations in the United States'.[33] Amongst Lee's advice was the suggestion that Foreign Minister von Ribbentrop (later hanged for war crimes at Nuremberg) 'should visit the US to explain Germany's position' to the president and 'also to enlighten the Foreign Policy Association and the Council on Foreign Relations'.[34] This would help, wrote Lee, to gain American understanding that Germany wanted to re-arm only because the 'government is left with no choice except to demand an equality of armament'.[35] He went further, advising the Nazis to claim that their storm troops were 'well trained and disciplined, but not armed, not prepared for war, and organised only for the purpose of preventing for all time the return of the communist peril'.[36] Lee was so deeply implicated in PR advice for the Third Reich that the US ambassador to Berlin, William Dodd, on meeting him declared him 'an advocate of fascism'.[37]

Lee's meeting with Goebbels was longer than that with the Fuhrer. Lee reported his meeting to the US ambassador who recorded in his diary that Lee 'warned Goebbels to cease propaganda in the United States, urged him to see the foreign press people often and learn how to get along with them'. Goebbels met with foreign diplomats (including Ambassador Dodd) a month later. 'At an appropriate moment', wrote Dodd, 'Goebbels arose and read a somewhat conciliatory speech to the diplomats and the foreign press.' 'It was plain', Dodd wrote in his diary, 'he was trying to apply the advice which Ivy Lee urged upon him a month ago.'[38]

In 1933 another PR pioneer, Carl Byoir, took on the account of the German Tourist Information Office, landing it with the help of the well known Nazi sympathiser, George Sylvester Viereck. Byoir employee Carl Dickey travelled to Germany with Viereck and reportedly interviewed 'Hitler, Goering, Goebbels... and most of the other Nazi dignitaries'.[39] Byoir then opened an office in Berlin and their contract was increased to $6,000 per month.

In 1934 both Lee and Dickey were called before the House Un-American Activities Committee to explain their relations with the Nazis. Lee claimed – in a classic spin manoeuvre – that he had not engaged in any propaganda in the US. But he had of course advised the Nazi government how to conduct its propaganda and had, as he conceded to the committee, briefed US journalists in Berlin on behalf of the Nazis. The committee concluded that both companies had 'sold their services for express propaganda purposes'.[40] Lee's reputation was compromised by the Un-American Activities Committee, shortly after which, in November 1934, he died.

Worse was to come. After the war Lee was named in an indictment at the Nuremberg war crimes tribunal. Lee was 'retained', stated the indictment, 'to devise methods for countering the boycotts and organising pro-German propaganda'. 'The propaganda was', said Deputy Chief Counsel Josiah Du Bois, Jr., 'indispensable to German preparation for, and waging of, aggressive war.' Aggressive war as determined at Nuremberg was the supreme war crime, containing within it all the other war crimes.

Historians of PR bend over backwards to convince themselves that Lee was only giving 'standard public relations advice', 'along the same lines' as his US clients and that he was at worst naïve.[41] They, and the industry for which they are apologists, prefer not to face the fact that there are more similarities between 'standard PR' and Nazi 'propaganda' than they would like to admit.

ZELIG THE FAKER

Taking a lead from Bernays' stunt to promote smoking amongst women, was PR pioneer Carl Byoir. Byoir, whose eponymous company became a leading PR firm before the 1939–45 war, made extended use of front groups a trademark of his style of spin. In the 1930s chain stores were spreading across the US, often driving local and independent traders out of business. At the time a New Deal proposal meant that new legislation to tax chain stores was in the offing.

Byoir's firm, working for the chain store company A&P, created a raft of fake groups to pretend that the public supported the chain stores. The fake groups included the National Consumers' Tax Council, the Emergency Consumers' Tax Council and the Property Owners Inc., a group so well camouflaged that even Byoir's clients were unaware it was a fake. The proposed federal tax was defeated in 1940. Byoir crowed in 1949: 'From that time until today we have opposed 247 anti-chain store bills, introduced in the state legislatures. Only six passed. In the past eight years not a single anti-chain bill has become law.'[42] Both Byoir and A&P were indicted for using fake front groups or what the judge called 'devious manipulations'.[43] Byoir's firm was fined $5,000, but gained more clients as a result of the publicity around the case.

Front groups are a classic strategy for keeping PR in the dark, for pretending to the media, the public, politicians and regulators that corporate interests are popular. They are extensively used today by the biggest PR firms. Byoir's firm itself is still in existence, now owned by communications giant WPP. Disguising the source of information, masking and carefully 'positioning' the corporate interest have been perennial practices of PR since its inception. Ivy Lee recognised the spin and lobbying advantages of forming trade associations to speak on behalf of business interests to both the government and the public. Lee was instrumental in the creation of the American Petroleum Institute (1919), copying the success of the American Iron and Steel Institute (1908). Trade and industry associations, which on the surface appear dull and unimportant, are now key players in political lobbying and advocacy across the globe. They function to coordinate policy positions, maintain the discipline of member companies and to represent them in the corridors of power and the court of public opinion.

PR operatives managed the transition from war to peace in 1945 with relative ease. Many of those employed in propaganda and intelligence activities during the war moved seamlessly into professional public relations in the post-war period, including several of the luminaries of the industry who lend their names to the major PR company brands of today. Dan Edelman, founder of Edelman PR, now the biggest independent PR firm in the world, worked in the US Psychological Warfare Division writing a nightly analysis of German propaganda.[44] Alfred Fleishman (of Fleishman Hillard, now owned by communications conglomerate Omnicom) was a Pentagon-based public information officer, and Harold Burson did a stint as an Army reporter for American Forces Network, covering the Nuremberg trial, before returning to civilian life and co-founding Burson-Marsteller, now one of the biggest PR firms in the world, a subsidiary of WPP.[45]

Burson notes that 'World War II was the second great catalyst for forming public relations firms. Scores of demobilized public information officers, many former newsmen, started their own firms.'[46] This growth in the PR industry is reflected also in the foundation of both the Public Relations Society of America and the Institute of Public Relations (in the UK) in 1948.

POST-WAR PROSPERITY: PR GOES GLOBAL

Soon PR people developed more of a taste for travel, popping up all over the world. Marion Nestle cites the example of the banana company Chiquita, formerly known as United Fruit, which 'has an exceptionally rich history of influence over the US government'.[47] Perhaps its most famous lobbying effort was its persuasion of the CIA to support a coup against the democratically elected Arbenz government in Guatemala. In 1954, the Arbenz administration expropriated land owned by United Fruit for redistribution to the poor.[48] Bernays persuaded his employers, United Fruit, that the government should be subverted, since it threatened the interests of the company. This was done by a campaign of propaganda in the US which resulted in the CIA backed military coup in Guatemala, described by Bernays as an 'army of liberation'. The company became the American government's de facto beachhead against communism in Latin America.[49] As *Boston Globe* journalist Larry Tye puts it: 'most analysts agree that United Fruit was the most important force in toppling Arbenz and that Bernays was the fruit company's most effective propagandist'.[50] This lobbying adventure cost around 150,000 Guatemalan lives.

But Bernays was not the only influencer working the political channels for United Fruit. They engaged a range of movers and shakers in Washington to press their case. Perhaps the most significant was Thomas 'The Cork' Corcoran, a former New Deal adviser in Roosevelt's 'brains trust', who left government to become a highly influential commercial lobbyist. The scale and strategy of the political campaign to effect regime change in Guatemala anticipates what would perhaps now be recognised as 'best practice' in contemporary lobbying. All the critical decision makers and audiences were catered for. While

Eddie Bernays would later fix the press and public opinion in the US, Tommy the Cork had for a number of years been lobbying to fix the politics. Corcoran was retained by United Fruit in 1949 as a lobbyist and legal adviser. He facilitated United Fruit's access to business and political elites in America, soliciting campaign contributions for Roosevelt and introducing the company president Sam 'the Banana Man' Zemurray to business luminaries like Nelson Rockefeller.

Even before Arbenz was elected in 1950, Corcoran had suggested to the US State Department that they should assist a US friendly moderate to come to power in Guatemala. He also brought in the newly formed CIA, who were prepared to help. Corcoran coordinated the campaign to overthrow Arbenz between United Fruit, the CIA, and the State Department. Importantly, Corcoran also had a strategy for the post-coup scenario. He advised United Fruit to donate 100,000 acres of land to Guatemalan peasants, thereby ensuring that the return of the remainder of expropriated lands to the company was made more palatable for the Guatemalan people. He also placed former director of the CIA Walter Bedell Smith on the company board, over-ruling reservations about Smith's business knowledge: 'For Chrissakes,' he argued, 'your problem is not bananas... you've got to handle your political problem.'[51] Likewise, Bernays did not neglect the post-conflict scenario. He advised a concerted effort to build goodwill with the people of Guatemala through the creation of a tourist information office, a letter writing campaign by American students learning Spanish to pen-pals in Guatemala, and using private American foundations to sponsor medical aid and training programmes for Guatemalan doctors.[52]

Throughout the next decades Zelig-like PR operatives were on hand at the conflicts and controversies that defined the age, supporting and promoting the interests of corporations and governments. The international PR firm Hill & Knowlton was to prove a very useful front for the CIA. Robert T. Crowley, who spent much of his career soliciting cover from American businesses for CIA activities across the globe, remarked 'Hill & Knowlton's overseas offices were the perfect "cover" for the... CIA. Unlike other cover jobs being a public relations specialist did not require technical training for CIA officers.'[53] Leading Washington PR operator Robert Gray, who was with Hill & Knowlton for 20 years, also had close links with intelligence circles. He was implicated in the Iran-Contra affair though his associations with William Casey, then Director of Central Intelligence. Gray and Casey had worked together on the Reagan campaign in 1979–80. Gray's colourful and controversial career is meticulously documented by Susan Trento, who links him and his firm Gray & Company to a variety of espionage and clandestine activities, including Korean spying and lobbying in Washington (using US funds!), representing Haitian dictator 'Baby Doc' Duvalier, as well as influencing democratic deliberation in Spain on membership of NATO, while nominally working for the Spanish nuclear industry. 'Fighting communism was their idealistic cover. The chance to make money was their reward', notes Trento. 'The conservative movement that helped elect Ronald Reagan and George Bush went worldwide in the 1980s.'[54]

As conflicts broke out across Africa in the post-colonial reordering of that ravaged continent, Zelig was again on hand. In the 1960s the case of oil rich Nigeria is notable. Several established PR agencies represented one side or the other in the civil war, seeking to influence international sentiment on the conflict. Burson-Marsteller for example was retained to discredit claims of genocide by the Nigerian government. These PR firms opened doors in Washington and London to politicians, business elites and editors, or they managed to attract favourable publicity for their clients. They did little to resolve the war, or promote mutual understanding. Rather, PR becomes an adjunct to and in some ways an enabler of conflict: 'under most competitive conditions', notes Morris Davis, the author of a study of this episode, 'the introduction of public relations skills is more likely to increase strife than diminish it... Nigerian/Biafran use of overseas public relations cannot be said to have improved prospects of an early settlement... the techniques merely enhanced both sides' politico-military capabilities'.[55]

PR stalks conflicts. The apologist use of PR techniques to disguise or 'soften' torture and human rights abuses is a damning indictment of the business of public relations. The image of the military junta in Argentina in the 1970s was actively polished by global PR firm Burson-Marsteller (B-M). During this period, an estimated 35,000 people 'disappeared'. Some of the torture techniques used included *el submarino* (holding a person's head under water or excrement until near drowning), *la picana* (an electric prod applied to the most sensitive parts of the body), or rape. Little wonder the junta of General Videla needed some perception management magic from B-M, who themselves benefited from a steady stream of business working for various dictators and authoritarian regimes. Romanian tyrant Nicolae Ceaucescu was a client and the agency was also credited with representing the CIA/Apartheid backed UNITA during the Angolan civil war, white-washing South Korea's deplorable human rights record and working with Indonesia at the time when it was accused of genocide in East Timor.[56] This kind of work is not simply done by a 'few bad apples'. The publication of *The Torturers' Lobby* in 1992 illustrated how widespread such practices were. Leading PR firms, lobbyists and lawyers – many closely connected with government – were earning $30 million per annum representing serial human rights abusers.[57]

But this rogues gallery isn't simply confined to governments and despots. Corporate clients provide most of the work and money for the PR industry. So, not only did a company like B-M work for the worst offenders against democracy and human dignity in this period, they also actively represented the worst polluters and offenders against the environment and public safety too. B-M did public relations for Babcock & Wilcox after the Three Mile Island nuclear accident in 1979 and continued their dubious work on environmental issues during the 1980s and 1990s by helping to manage the Bhopal crisis for Union Carbide. Other clients with image and regulatory problems include Philip Morris and the tobacco industry, biotech firms like Monsanto, and clients across the energy sector.[58] Like many of their leading competitors, B-M have a notable track record in discrediting the environmental movement on behalf of industry, creating deceptive front groups to promote pro-corporate messages on environmental and public health issues,[59] and managing the threats to business profitability posed by environmental regulation. Burson-Marsteller worked on behalf of the Business Council for Sustainable Development (BCSD) in the lead up to the first Earth Summit in Rio de Janeiro in 1992. The key achievement of the BCSD was to keep regulation of the environmental impact of corporations off the agenda, thereby ensuring that important decisions about pollution and energy consumption were delayed. The World Business Council for Sustainable Development (WBCSD) repeated this trick at the second Earth Summit in Johannesburg in 2002.

Needless to say the PR industry is deeply ambivalent about this historical sketch. On the one hand it will deny and divert and dissemble. On the other, sometimes PR people will blurt out the truth. Often this will be in convivial settings where they imagine they are among friends. But sometimes purveyors of the corporate line seem to have a constitutional need to tell the truth about what they do and then to try to justify it.

MONEY TALKS

Picture the scene, in the small Swiss town of Lucerne, overlooking the lake around which the town was constructed. The ancient tower which rises up out of the lake was used in times gone by to incarcerate 'witches' – those whose messages were unwelcome to the powers that be. The tower is now a pretty tourist attraction. Inside the town's arts centre the Swiss School of Journalism has convened a conference, 'A Complicated, Antagonistic and Symbiotic Affair', to which one of us delivers an account of PR rehearsing some of the material in this chapter on Ivy Lee and Edward Bernays. The audience contains a number of PR executives, some of whom shift nervously in their seats but don't ask any questions, polite or otherwise. Instead, the view of PR as a conspiracy against democracy is challenged by James Grunig from the University of Maryland. Grunig is the leading academic apologist for the PR industry. He along with the other official historians of PR likes to pretend that PR might have been a bit rough around the edges when it started but that it is better now.[60] One recent example is the case of a book on international PR with the title *Towards the Common Good*.[61] It is hard to imagine a less appropriate description for the PR industry.

Grunig made the response that, although he wasn't an expert on Lee, he thought some historians had a different version of Lee's role. Indeed this is true. Furthermore he noted that the list of Lippmann, Lee, Bernays and Byoir, left out some of the ethical pioneers – in particular he mentioned Earl Newsom and Arthur W. Page.[62]

So let's have a look at them. Among Earl Newsom's clients in the 1940s and 1950s were Ford, Standard Oil, CBS, Eli Lilly, Campbell Soup and Macy's. He is credited with transforming the reputation of Henry Ford II from a 'rather inconsequential young man' associated with Nazism and anti-Semitism (by virtue of accepting an honour from Hitler's government), to an industrial '"statesman" of undeniable appeal'. He is said to have accomplished the same for Standard Oil in relation to its links with the German corporation I.G. Farben in 1929. He crafted a 'long and cleverly written presentation' to Congress, which argued that the links with I.G. Farben 'were of great help' to the US war effort. Needless to say, this was at best a distortion, but as a result, 'Standard was off the hook'.[63]

Or we can look at the career of Arthur W. Page. Page served as a propagandist in the US military during the 1914–18 war and became the first PR vice-president of AT&T in 1927. Even if we depend on the account given in the hagiographical biography written by Noel Griese, a less than wholesome portrait emerges. Page wrote the press statement announcing the dropping of the atomic bomb on Hiroshima for President Truman in 1945. He was also involved in subverting trade union demands for improved conditions in Chile in 1946.[64] From 1946 to 1960 Page became strongly involved in anti-communist propaganda and played a major role in developing the CIA's Radio Free Europe. His crusade for freedom was, in the 1950s, run with the support of the Heritage Foundation and the Advertising Council, both corporate funded free market think tanks, which feature later in this book.[65] The truth is that the phrase 'ethical PR' is an oxymoron.

Some defenders of the industry are less guarded. Later that morning in Lucerne the conference heard from PR man Klaus Kocks. 'As a spin doctor,' he said, 'I'm strongly opposed to discriminating against lying.' Kocks stated his view that 'the development of capitalism needed a "doppelmoral" – double standards – right from the beginning'.[66] It is only, says Kocks, 'a neurotic obsession of Calvinistic witch hunters' to 'discriminate against' and 'delegitimise' lying. Perhaps Kocks was imagining spin doctors being consigned to the tower in the middle of Lucerne's lake. Kocks is former spin doctor for Volkswagen and for the Herstelle und Betriebs der Atomkraftwerke in Deutschland, the body responsible for building and running all Germany's 19 nuclear power plants.

Kocks pushes a relativist case arguing that 'spin doctoring is a privately financed public service provided by communication professionals to support markets that are in need of storytelling to enhance somebody's business or the economy as a whole'.

There is, he says, 'no such thing as story-free markets'. If you don't believe him you are possibly a victim of the 'facts and figures myth' which is 'quite popular with scholars'. In reality, says Kocks, there are only varying stories. Of course his whole relativist house of cards starts to shake, if we ask whether the view that there are really only stories is true, or just another story.[67]

For Kocks, corporate governance is simply a case of 'keeping up appearances'. The most important rule is 'don't get caught'. The PR industry has trouble with shoot from the lip practitioners like Kocks and often tries to find ways to show that they are an unethical minority. One of Britain's most colourful PR men is Max Clifford, who has often acknowledged that he lies on behalf of his celebrity and political clients. He happily admits: 'I've been telling lies on behalf of people, businessmen, politicians and countries for 40 years. It shouldn't be necessary, but it is. I'd rather be honest, but I cannot be all the time... All PROs at all levels lie through their teeth.'[68]

His insouciance riles some elements in the PR industry. Simon Cohen, founder of allegedly 'ethical' PR agency Global Tolerance, says Clifford's views are 'deeply worrying... It's bad PR to say you're in PR now.'[69] Clifford has been challenged to debate his views in public on more than one occasion. In 1994 he debated with Quentin Bell of the Quentin Bell Organisation (now owned by Chime Communications) and in early 2007 Clifford was called upon to debate the motion that 'PR has a duty to tell the truth', against PR industry stalwarts.[70] On both occasions Clifford won the vote at the end of the debate.

Most spin doctors are more reticent than Kocks or Clifford. They dissemble, they pretend, they act concerned. They will say and do anything if it will serve the interests of their clients and they think they can get away with it. They will even act ethical if needed – they are the chameleons of the business world. But the response of the trade journal *PR Week* to the debate on truth in early 2007 was noteworthy because the paper editorialised in favour of deception as a sign of integrity. 'The fact that PR people admit they need to lie occasionally is a sign of growing honesty and confidence in what they do', wrote the editor.[71]

From the very beginning of the PR industry, public relations practitioners have engaged in deception, trickery and other techniques designed to foster vested private interests. There is no company that the industry as a whole will not represent. There is no dictator or war criminal considered beyond the pale. The Zeligs of PR flit from page to page of the history books trying to leave no trace and trying to ensure that the interests of their clients prevail against the interests of humanity and the planet.

3
The Hidden History of
Corporate Propaganda, 1911–30

A few minutes' walk from the Houses of Parliament, immediately behind Westminster Abbey, is an open square, called Dean's Yard. It was here in early 1919 that the leading and most class-conscious representatives of British industry met to set up the first cross-industry public relations body in the UK. The meeting took place in offices owned by the brewery owners lobbying organisation, the National Publicity Agency.

Passing the front of the Abbey to gain entrance through the narrow arch which hides this tranquil square in the midst of the hustle and bustle of Whitehall and Westminster were some of the most important figures in the development of corporate political action in Britain. The meeting had been called by a pivotal figure, the newly elected MP for West Derby, Reginald Hall. Better known as Rear Admiral Reggie 'Blinker' Hall, the MP had been elected officially as a member of the Conservative and Unionist Party at the 1918 election, the first election under expanded suffrage. Also attending the meeting were Evan Williams, chairman of the Mining Association, Cuthbert Laws, director of the Shipping Federation, Major John Gretton, a Tory MP (and chairman of Bass Brewery), Arthur Balfour, the Sheffield steel manufacturer, Major Richard Kelly (director of the National Publicity Agency) and Sir Allan Smith of the powerful Engineering Employers Federation. By the end of the meeting a new organisation had been agreed. It was unblushingly titled 'National Propaganda' and its function was to counter 'subversion in industry'.

National Propaganda was funded by contributions from industry and became the pre-eminent corporate propaganda organisation of the inter-war period. Yet it is little known. Indeed those historical references to National Propaganda which do exist are fragmentary and sometimes contradictory. The organisation has been almost entirely forgotten in the history books. No commentator on PR in Britain mentions the existence or importance of this organisation or the network of corporate propaganda bodies surrounding it. In fact some claim that there was 'relatively little' corporate PR in the UK prior to 1945.[1] We will return to look in some detail at the activities of National Propaganda later in this chapter, but first we need to flesh out aspects of the political climate in the UK and US which gives context to this form of pro-business activism.

THE THREAT OF DEMOCRACY

What were the leaders of industry afraid of? Nothing less, they said, than a violent workers' revolt. The Bolshevik Revolution in Russia and the rise of militant labour did animate government, business and intelligence circles. The Lord Privy Seal, Bonar Law, reported to Prime Minister Lloyd George the views of George V: 'the King is in a funk about the labour situation and is talking about the danger of a revolution'.[2] But it is clear that what they feared most was the potential of universal suffrage to produce an elected government which might attempt to move against the interests of business. What really exercised them, according to Basil Thomson – then head of Special Branch and very close to Blinker Hall and National Propaganda – was a 'democratic revolution'.[3]

The mounting worries of 1919 marked an intensification of attempts by big business to organise collectively to pursue their interests. Well before either the Bolshevik Revolution or the First World War there emerged a dense web of business lobby groups which were closely intertwined with government, police and intelligence agencies. The necessity to set up such lobby groups was well captured by Allan Smith, director of the Engineering Employers Federation, the most politically significant business lobby group at the time. 'The political developments which are taking place', he noted, 'and the probable large increase in the strength of the Labour Party [at the 1918 General Election] makes such an action appear to be a necessary development.'[4] The worry, in essence, was the possibility that in the first election in which universal suffrage obtained (for men and women under 30), the forces of Bolshevism and pacifism (as the mildly reformist Labour Party was characterised) might triumph.

THE INTELLECTUALS AND DEMOCRACY

The threat of democracy troubled some leading intellectuals as well as politicians and business lobbyists. In the US this manifested in a concern about how society's elites might cope with the potential consequences of the extended franchise. 'The crowd is enthroned', as PR pioneer Ivy Lee put it in 1914.[5] Lee believed in the necessity of 'courtiers' to 'flatter and caress' the crowd. The courtiers were the professional propagandists. It was essential, wrote Walter Lippmann, the most important US theorist of the trend, that 'the public be put in its place' so that 'each of us may live free of the trampling and the roar of a bewildered herd'.[6] The fear of the irrational crowd 'became an insistent note among leading intellectuals'. At the end of the nineteenth century Gustav Le Bon had sounded the alarm in his influential book *The Crowd*. Le Bon argued that 'a crowd thinks in images' and 'an orator in intimate communication with the crowd can evoke images by which it will be seduced... The powerlessness of crowds to reason prevents them displaying any trace of the critical spirit of discerning truth from error.'[7] Le Bon's work was developed by Gabriel Tarde, who distinguished between the 'crowd' and the 'public'. For Tarde, the 'crowd' was the power of the past. Now, with new means of mass communication such as the telegraph, printing press and railway, a collective 'public' was created even though people were not physically present in the same place and time – 'a dispersion of individuals who are physically separated and whose cohesion is entirely mental'. 'The crowd is the social group of the past', Tarde wrote. 'Whatever its forms, standing or seated, immobile or on the march, it is incapable of extension beyond a limited area; when its leaders cease to keep it in hand, when the crowd no longer hears their voices, it breaks loose... But the public can be extended indefinitely.'[8] In his view the public was both more affected and less of a threat than the crowd. More affected in the sense that newspapers distribute through time and space information and ideas which impinge on, implicate and influence countless thousands – 'even those who don't read papers, but who talking to those who do, are forced to follow the groove of their borrowed thoughts. One pen suffices to set off a million tongues.'[9] This power is a potential threat to society – the socialist or anarchist state of mind did not 'amount to anything' before 'a few famous publicists, Karl Marx, Kropotkin and others, expressed them and put them into circulation'.[10] But the political dangers posed by the public are less pressing than those of the crowd.

Tarde gave the example of 'feminine publics', made up of 'readers of popular novels or fashionable poetry, fashion magazines, feminist journals and the like'. These he says 'scarcely resemble' feminine crowds and have a 'more inoffensive nature'. Women assembled together on the street though, 'are always appalling in their extraordinary excitability and ferocity'.[11] The geographical and social distribution of the public meant new strategies for communicating with the masses were required. The management of public communication was becoming a practical and political imperative for elites and intellectuals. Tarde concluded his essay on the public and the crowd with a ringing challenge to intellectuals to win the battle of ideas with the public in order to maintain elite power in the face of the rise of the public:

What will preserve the intellectual and artistic summits of humanity from democratic levelling will not, I fear, be recognition of the good that the world owes them, the just esteem for their discoveries. What then? I should like to think that it will be the force of their resistance. Let them beware if they should separate.[12]

In both the US and Britain a number of writers and thinkers responded to these new circumstances by working together to resist democracy. Many of this group shared a fascination with the possibilities of social control and the management of consent.

Walter Lippmann was the most influential of all the theorists of propaganda-managed democracy. Lippmann's view was that the 'manufacture of consent' was both necessary and possible. 'Within the life of the generation now in control of affairs, persuasion has become a self conscious art and a regular organ of popular government.'[13] Edward Bernays, as one of the most influential early PR practitioners, tried putting Lippmann's ideas into practice. Both his first two books (*Crystallizing Public Opinion* (1923) and *Propaganda* (1928)) were published a year after Lippmann's interventions (*Public Opinion* (1922) and *The Phantom Public* (1927)). Bernays argued that:

The conscious and intelligent manipulation of the organised habits and opinions of the masses is an important element in democratic society. Those who manipulate this unseen mechanism of society constitute an invisible government which is the true ruling power of our country.[14]

The manipulation could only take place because the mass public was conceived as irrational and responded not to facts but to feelings or prejudices. Bernays' thinking was influenced by some of the early social psychologists such as Le Bon and Tarde, but also by his uncle Sigmund Freud. Bernays later had Freud's works translated and published in the US and personally promoted them. But it was not only nephew Edward that Freud influenced in the 1920s. Both Ivy Lee and Walter Lippmann had become interested in his work. 'I have found', Lee told an interviewer in 1921, 'the Freudian theories concerning the psychology of the subconscious mind of great interest... Publicity is essentially a matter of mass psychology. We must remember that people are guided more by sentiment than by mind.'[15] Lippmann too had come across Freud, but much earlier. In one of those curious twists of fate Lippmann wrote his first book in a cabin in the backwoods of Maine in the company of his friend from Harvard, Alfred Kuttner, who was at that moment translating Freud's *Interpretation of Dreams* into English under the direction of one of the early US psychoanalysts, A.A. Brill. As a result Lippmann studied Freud with, as he wrote to Graham Wallas, 'a great deal of enthusiasm'. The result was that Lippmann's book, *A Preface to Politics* (1913), was replete with Freudian terms.[16]

In the United States the threat of democracy was created by the extension of the franchise from 15 to 50 per cent of adults between 1880 and 1920.[17] This was accompanied by rising antagonism to the power of business, expressed succinctly in the label 'robber barons', which was given to corporate leaders and the super-rich at the time, including Henry Ford, J.P. Morgan, Andrew Carnegie and perhaps most famously, John D. Rockefeller. Rockefeller and his Standard Oil company had provided an object lesson in how big business might accumulate and retain power. By 1885 the company 'had its own network of agents throughout the world, and its own espionage service, to forestall the initiatives of rival companies or governments'.[18] Despite this, the rise of organised labour and the attacks on business from investigative and campaigning journalism led to a backlash against corporate power and the rich. As a result anti-trust legislation was introduced to prohibit cartels and anti-competitive business practices. This meant that some of the biggest corporations in America were broken up. Standard Oil was divided into numerous smaller corporations, creating in the process some of the most important oil companies of the twentieth century such as Exxon, Amoco, Mobil and Chevron.

The corporations – individually and collectively – increasingly adopted public relations, propaganda and lobbying techniques to resist the encroachment of popular government or to counter attack to win new sectional concessions. The defence of their interests was accomplished by hiring their own public relations personnel, by banding together in class-wide lobby groups and by creating policy planning groups to try to exert influence on public policy questions.

In 1906 J.P. Morgan and Company hired Ivy Lee to defend them against anti-trust moves by the government. In 1907 Lee was asked to do a similar job for the Pennsylvania Railroad. Vice-president M.J.B. Thayer noted this was because they had 'come to the conclusion… that the time had come when we must take "offensive" measures as it were, to place our "case" before the public'.[19] Corporations also tried to go on the offensive by using the new techniques to re-engineer perceptions. Leaders in this area were AT&T, Eastman Kodak, General Electric, General Motors, Ford, Goodyear Rubber, National Cash Register and Standard Oil.[20] These were the first few steps along the road to the branding and corporate governance practices of today. They attempted to humanise the corporation. 'The word corporation is cold, impersonal and subject to misunderstanding and distrust', wrote Alfred Swayne of the Institutional Advertising Committee in advice to General Motors.[21] Over at AT&T, advertising executive Bruce Barton wanted more than a vague positive feeling. People no longer feared the big corporations – at most they would 'only tolerate them'. But even though the public did not 'fully understand', 'fully trust' or even 'love' the corporations, it was felt corporate propagandists should try to create such sentiment.[22]

The National Association of Manufacturers was created in 1895. In 1903 an internal leadership 'coup' transformed NAM from 'an international trade organization into a virulent anti-union one'.[23] Its activities included hiring an employee of the House of Representatives as a spy; making campaign contributions to sympathetic Congressional candidates; creating a front group called the Workingmen's Protective Association to campaign for Republican candidates; paying operatives to waylay Congressmen on the way to the chamber so they would miss important votes; marshalling a disguised propaganda campaign through newspaper syndicates; distributing significant amounts of propaganda to schools, colleges and civil society organisations. This was all revealed at the first Congressional inquiry into lobbying in 1913. The inquiry concluded that:

The correspondence between officials and employees of the association laid before your committee and placed in evidence shows it to have been an organization having purposes and aspirations along industrial, commercial, legislative, and other lines so vast and far-reaching as to excite at once admiration and fear – admiration for the genius which conceived them, and fear for the ultimate effects which the successful accomplishments of all these ambitions might have on a government such as ours.[24]

Corporate leaders also formed a new policy planning group called the National Industrial Conference Board. According to its own account it was 'born out of a crisis in industry in 1916. Declining public confidence in business and rising labor unrest had become severe threats to economic growth and stability.' It was 'an entirely new type of organization. Not another trade association. Not a propaganda machine. But a respected, not-for-profit, nonpartisan organization that would bring leaders together to find solutions to common problems and objectively examine major issues having an impact on business and society.'[25] The concern to find solutions was tested in 1919 when the NICB was one of three representatives of business summoned by President Woodrow Wilson, partially in the hope of averting the then looming steel strike, to a 'National Industrial Conference' to discuss methods

of bringing capital and labor into close co-operation, and to canvass every relevant feature of the present industrial situation, for the purpose of enabling us to work out, if possible, in [a] genuine spirit of co-operation a practicable method of association based upon a real community of interest which will redound to the welfare of all our people.[26]

The 'management participants refused to accept any type of collective bargaining', thus making progress impossible and showing the real role of the Conference Board as a corporate policy planning and lobby group.[27] The NICB was set up by four corporate bosses, three of whom have been described as 'professional militants' who had made careers out of promoting corporate interests.[28] All four 'enjoyed some notoriety during their active careers only to pass largely unnoticed into the silence of history'. The Conference Board (as it later became) was in other words formed out of a desire by corporate leaders to 'unite American employers' into a class-wide organisation.[29]

According to some accounts 'The "dollar decade" of the 1920s temporarily put to rest the nation's fears of the power of business.'[30] But clearly this was accomplished in part by the use of techniques to manufacture consent. These activities – the 'deliberate use of propaganda' as Bernays put it – transformed the political fortunes of big business from 'ogres' to 'friendly giants' by the mid 1920s.[31]

Shortly before the war... the newspapers of New York took a census of the press agents who were regularly employed and regularly accredited and found that there were about twelve hundred of them. How many there are now [1919] I do not pretend to know. But what I do know is that many of the direct channels of news have been closed and the information for the public is first filtered through publicity agents. The great corporations have them, the banks have them, the railroads have them, all the organisations of business and social and political activity have them.[32]

But even this growth in publicity does not account for the full range of techniques used. The key moment which saved the day for the corporations in the 1920s was the pioneering of techniques for strike-breaking which welded the new propaganda techniques together with intimidation, harassment and violence. The decisive period was 1919–21. In 1919 more than 4 million workers were involved in industrial disputes, four times the number in the previous year. Beginning in 1919 almost 400,000 miners went on strike, sparking one of the longest-running industrial disputes in the US which resulted in the destruction of the miners' unions. Ivy Lee was retained to defend the strike-breaking activities of the Logan County Coal Operators Association in October 1921. They hired armed Pinkerton and Baldwin-Felts 'detectives' and were authorised to sign up their own 'deputy-Sheriffs' to crush a miners' march in Logan and Mingo Counties, assembled to protest police brutality against union organisers: 'In pitched battles over 6 days that became known as the battle of Blair Mountain, some 70 miners were killed.'[33] In the face of an influx of state police, national guards and federal troops ordered in by the President, the defeat of the miners was inevitable. Lee's job was to justify the strike-breaking tactics. He quickly issued a series of Miner's Lamp and Coal Facts bulletins and a number of pamphlets full of 'false and exaggerated information' about the dispute. This information came from the mine operators and was 'published as truth' by Lee. The pamphlets were purportedly published by the 'Logan District Mines Information Bureau', a fake front group set up by Lee for his client. In the Great Steel Strike of 1919 the same new propaganda tactics were used in alliance with the traditional harassment and intimidation (20 people lost their lives in the strike).

Five days after the strike began the steel corporations launched a campaign of full-page advertisements which urged the strikers to return to work, denounced their leaders as 'trying to establish the red rule of anarchy and bolshevism' and the strike as 'Un American' and even suggested that 'the Huns had a hand in fomenting the strike'.[34]

Louis Post, the Secretary of Labour at the time, complained that intense corporate propaganda 'produced an anti-red hysteria about an invented plan by workers and their leaders to overthrow the government'.[35] The Interchurch World Movement concluded that the strike was defeated by 'the strike breaking methods of the steel companies and their effective mobilisation of public opinion against the strikers through charges of radicalism, bolshevism and the closed shop. None of which was justified by the facts.'[36]

As a result, trade union power was decisively defeated during the 1920s. 'Civil liberties were left prostrate, the labour movement was badly mauled, the position of capital was greatly enhanced and complete antipathy towards reform was enthroned', wrote historian Robert Murray.[37] In addition, 'the Communist Party had been shattered and gone underground... institutions of police repression had been installed and the United States had been made safe for business', as historian and activist Joel Kovel has put it.[38] The role of the early propaganda experts in this transformation was central. As *Editor and Publisher* summed up the transformation of the reputation of Rockefeller on his death in 1937:

It must be admitted without a grudge, that Ivy Ledbetter Lee did a swell job of press-agentry in not only removing the stigma of commercial pirate that the old gentleman wore for so many years, but actually substituting it for a saintly halo... He [Rockefeller] paid little attention to newspaper comment until the Colorado mine massacre turned the big Eastern papers loose at him and invested 26 Broadway with a howling mob of protesting pickets. Then the suave Lee entered the picture, gave the Rockefeller press relationships the guise of candour, played no favourites and succeeded, it must be admitted, in more than once turning merited public anger toward approval.[39]

'Among the nations of the earth today', wrote one observer in 1921, 'America stands for one idea: Business.'[40] The 'robber barons' were not transformed simply by the manipulation of words and ideas, but by the use of new techniques of press management in alliance with older coercive practices.

MANAGING DEMOCRACY IN THE UK

In the UK the threat of democracy was a pressing concern to the business, political and intellectual classes. The intellectual case was advanced by figures formerly associated with the reformist left. Lippmann was a young student member of the Socialist Party in 1910 when he first met the British academic Graham Wallas, himself a former Fabian. Wallas published *Human Nature in Politics* in 1908, which gave renewed currency to the paternalist notion that the ignorance of the general public meant that democracy was impossible. Wallas was a significant modern theorist of the democratic incompetence of the masses whose legacy to ideas of a 'propaganda-managed democracy' is largely forgotten.

Wallas argued in *Human Nature in Politics* that 'human intellectual limitations' created the possibility of the 'manipulation of the popular impulse' and therefore that the realisation of popular democracy was difficult, if not impossible.[41] Wallas propounded the view that democracy should avoid 'those questions... which cause the holders of wealth and industrial power to make full use of their opportunities'. If they did so, 'the art of using skill for the production of emotion and opinion has so advanced, that the whole condition of contests would be changed for the future'.[42] This work profoundly influenced Lippmann who was exposed to it when Wallas lectured in the US in 1910. While Lippmann is widely recognised today as an important intellectual progenitor of the theory and justification of propaganda-managed democracy, Wallas's contribution is acknowledged less often. There is little awareness that the concerted movement to, as Alex Carey memorably put it, 'take the risk out of democracy'[43] also happened in Britain.

PREPARING THE (IDEOLOGICAL) GROUND

When Wallas travelled to the US to lecture at Harvard in 1910 he met Lippmann and they became firm friends. Lippmann acknowledges his debt to Wallas, 'the man who diverted me more than anyone else' away from socialism.[44] Wallas was clearly impressed by the young Lippmann and dedicated his next book, *The Great Society* (first published in 1914) to him.[45] Concern with the necessity of enlightened elites guiding the masses was current in Britain as well as the US. The experience of the 1914–18 war popularised this self-interested paternalism among the British political elite. Charles Higham was one of the earliest practitioners of corporate propaganda in the UK. Higham was an advertising executive recruited as a government propagandist in the 1914–18 war. A publisher's notice in 1920 referred to him as 'the super advertising man who taught the British Government how to harness the immense power of scientific publicity to the chariot of war'.[46] One of only two advertising personnel knighted for services to

British propaganda after the war, he has been described as 'probably the most articulate... on the subject of propaganda' of the advertising men recruited by Government.[47]

Higham's views show striking parallels with those PR pioneers who worked to influence US opinion on entry into the first world war for the Committee on Public Information (also known as the Creel Committee). These included Lippmann, Edward Bernays and Carl Byoir – all of whom were key figures in the development of public relations and corporate propaganda. Higham agreed with Wallas that the problem of democracy was the 'amazing ignorance' of the people[48] which resulted from the 'limit to one's capacity for imbibing knowledge'.[49] Public opinion, therefore, needed to be 'educated' to ensure that the people were enlightened. The problem for government was that no sufficient propaganda apparatus existed: 'Suppose a grave revolution broke out tomorrow and the Government wanted to call upon the latent good sense in the public, to, as it were, electrify them with the message – Stop and Think.'[50]

To do this required that propaganda appeals 'turn them from cold reason... to emotion'. If people are 'spoon-fed with well watered facts', Higham wrote, 'they merely suffer the monotony of semi-military control' in war time. 'None of us will ever forget the emotion that inspired us all in the first few weeks... of the war', but to rekindle that there should be 'a deliberate recharging of the atmosphere by invoking a renewal of the original state of mind... The most idealistic emotion peters out unless it is fed, recreated, continually galvanised.'[51] Higham concludes that 'there is no good habit or lofty idea that could not be inculcated in a people in a few short years if the right methods were used... we can move human energy in any direction by organised and public persuasion'.[52] Higham went on to advise Government for several years after the war, entered Parliament as a Unionist MP in 1918 and also became a leading advertising executive. His own attempts at mass 'education' did not always find favour, though, as when he attracted controversy for his role in 1920 of 'marshalling advertising to recruit members of the Royal Irish Constabulary, the "Black and Tans" hated for their brutality and atrocities against the Irish in the war of independence'.[53]

THE PRACTICAL CAMPAIGN TO SIDELINE DEMOCRACY

The views of Higham and Wallas in the UK and of Lee, Bernays and Lippmann in the US were shared in the business classes, particularly amongst some of the biggest industrialists. The British business classes were already positioning themselves against democracy by the late nineteenth century. The Engineering Employers Federation (EEF) was a key capitalist lobby group set up in 1896. By 1911 a hugely important and now largely forgotten activist for big business, Dudley Docker, was organising corporate propaganda outfits known as 'Business Leagues' under the slogan *'pro patria imperium in imperio'* – For our country; a government within a government.[54] In other words, business rule. 'If our League spreads', wrote Docker in 1911, 'politics would be done for. This is my object.'[55]

In 1916 Docker was Founding President of the Federation of British Industries (FBI). The FBI was a cross-industry body and acted as a broker for varying interests, meaning that it couldn't get involved in political campaigning on issues where its membership was divided, particularly over free trade versus protectionism. Although much of British manufacturing was protectionist, there were significant currents for whom free trade was in their interests.

Thus there was a network of other overlapping and interlocking propaganda, campaigning and front groups. The British Commonwealth Union (BCU) was set up with the explicit aim of promoting 'a powerful industrial party in the House of Commons'.[56] The intent of the business activists can be gauged from the names they gave themselves – the 'London Imperialists' and the 'die-hards'. The die-hards tried to link up with the FBI, meeting nine of their executive in March 1917. Eight of the FBI members went over to the BCU, but the ninth, Docker, although enthusiastic, hung back. He became involved the following year after the FBI formally rejected the BCU advance.[57]

It was Docker who suggested that the BCU run candidates in the 1918 elections. They fielded 24 covert candidates, whose ostensible party allegiance was a cover for business loyalties: 'It shall be clearly understood that the political label of the candidate takes second place following upon his clearly defined duty to the Union.'[58] On election day 18 of their candidates were successful and became MPs, including Christabel Pankhurst.[59]

NATIONAL PROPAGANDA

The next year the BCU launched a powerful new organisation whose name unblushingly revealed its purpose: 'National Propaganda.' It was based at 25 Victoria Street – an address shared by a cluster of anti-democratic organisations such as the Union Defence League, the Employers Parliamentary Council and the Property Defence League. Its own propaganda identified its connections with various radical right groups such as the British Empire Union and the National Citizens' Union. In 1921 National Propaganda absorbed another minor anti-Bolshevik organisation, the Liberty League, after 'its treasurer absconded with its funds'.[60] It was significant largely for the fact that it had been set up in 1920 by the well known authors, Rudyard Kipling (author of *The Jungle Book*) and H. Ryder Haggard (author of *King Solomon's Mines*), and Lord Sydenham, later a prominent member of the British Union of Fascists, as were a number of other National Propaganda activists.[61]

Lloyd George and the coalition government became increasingly interested in propaganda during peace time. Higham, the advertising king, dedicated his book on mass publicity to Lloyd George as the 'first Prime Minister to appreciate the value of educational publicity'. Tory ministers in the cabinet also appealed to newspaper editors to show their good sense 'by refraining from attacks on the capitalist class'.[62] In 1919, after the railway strikes, Lloyd George was involved in secret meetings with business leaders associated with National Propaganda to discuss 'educational propaganda'. Docker was present as was Douglas Vickers of the BCU and Sir Vincent Caillard of the EEF, FBI and BCU. The sum of £100,000 was eventually forthcoming from National Propaganda members to run the campaign 'concerned with anti-Bolshevism and increased production propaganda'. The campaign was run by former undercover agent Sidney Walton. Walton's 'information service' was granted unrestricted access to Special Branch files on left wing activists. '[From] 1922 the network expanded, with MPs and journalists on the payroll, and a variety of notables including even the Lord Chancellor, until Walton claimed to be able to put "authoritative signed articles" in over 1,200 newspapers.'[63] Walton's aim was to use the press as 'a vast college of simple economics' by means of what has been described as 'bribery on a substantial scale'.[64] The production and planning of authoritative articles were lubricated by payment. By 1921, according to some accounts, the government was contributing to the propaganda fund and Walton was able to budget for up to £100,000 a week if needed.[65] This seems to have been a separate effort to that run by Blinker Hall through National Propaganda, which had a budget in this period of some £250,000.[66] Walton's propaganda organisation was eventually merged with the Industrial League, run by Lord Burnham the newspaper proprietor.

The BCU changed strategy in 1922 and chose to concentrate exclusively on propaganda, rather than organise as a political party in the constituencies.[67] However, in 1925 the BCU was wound up. Its propaganda activities, largely focused on National Propaganda, were reorganised through a series of regional groups, 14 of which were created by 1924, each of which used the name 'Economic League'. National Propaganda itself was renamed the Economic League in 1925.

ECONOMIC LEAGUE

In early propaganda material circulated to its members the League described its mission as follows:

What is required is some years of propaganda for capitalism as the finest system that human ingenuity can devise, to counteract forty years of propaganda for Socialism.[68]

The League was unusual in its positive approach to propaganda, which it later called a 'crusade for Capitalism'.[69] It sought to challenge collectivist ideas head on, taking the battle to the factory gate. The League paid a large number of speakers to take the message throughout the country. According to the League's own account:

Speakers were selected not only because of their aptitude for discussing economic problems in simple terms but also for their ability to make themselves heard and deal with violent opposition. They were big men in every sense of the word, tough, well able to look after themselves, and with plenty of physical and moral courage. Most of them had come to the League straight from the services.[70]

There can be little doubt that this was not a campaign based on arguments and ideas alone. This was a struggle against popular democracy which used violence and intimidation alongside persuasion and propaganda. The propaganda was simply an element of the strategy which also involved intrigue, subversion, bribery and spying.

The network of organisations connected to and coordinated by National Propaganda was significant. It absorbed groups like the British Empire Union and the National Citizens' Union and integrated their activities. Amongst these was the operation of a private intelligence service, often with the active cooperation of the Special Branch and the police. The British Empire Union in particular had an estimated membership of around 10,000 and from 1917 was engaged in anti-German agitation. The BEU was implicated in the anti-Jewish riots of 1917 and attempted to disrupt 'meetings of pacifist and civil libertarian organisations' not stopping 'short of violence and threats'. In Liverpool, its secretary, John McGurk Hughes, together with associates, 'broke into premises, stole and forged documents and behaved as agents provocateurs'.[71] According to John McGurk Hughes in one of his reports to the shipping companies, 'we have the complete confidence and help of Scotland Yard'.[72] McGurk Hughes himself was also an agent of MI5.[73]

National Propaganda was set up not only to 'fight subversion relentlessly and ruthlessly' but also to 'replace it by constructive thought and ideas, by what, for want of a better term, is known as simple economics'.[74] This account, written by the League itself, indicates how closely intertwined were the propaganda and private intelligence and spying work of National Propaganda. The early involvement of National Propaganda in attempts to target active socialists, trade unionists and others perceived as a threat to class power was an enduring part of the League's activities which were formalised after 1945.

The best historical survey of the period remarks that 'it is hard to exaggerate the intensity or scope of such propaganda or its resources'.[75] Contrary to many available accounts their principal role in this period was propaganda intended to undermine the democratic process and the labour and trade union movements. The history of this tendency in the UK has been almost entirely written out of the UK political record.[76] The threat that they faced was the possibility of popular rule. No longer would it be sufficient to rely on government to defend elite interests. With voting, governments could change. Instead it was necessary to find ways to ensure that power could be defended, whatever government was in power. As Mike Hughes has put it, 'it was no longer enough to protect government from the people, the machinery of the state had to be protected from government'.[77] This was the origin of the long and involved attempts by the secret state and key corporations to defend their interests from democratic decision making; the campaign, in other words, to ensure that democracy did not work.

THREE KEY PLAYERS IN EARLY
CORPORATE PROPAGANDA IN BRITAIN

Dudley Docker

Docker was an important corporate activist at the forefront of attempting to roll back democratic reforms. He was a successful businessman from Birmingham and was amongst the earliest corporate warriors in Britain. In 1910 he said: 'I can... imagine a community... doing itself remarkably well under a really able and powerful tyrant; only this I should insist upon – that he must be a first-rate businessman.'[78]

Docker became a newspaper proprietor in 1914 with the purchase of *The Globe*. He used it to promote his allies in politics. 'A newspaper in London is a source of political power', wrote his contemporary D.A. Thomas, echoing Docker's views. 'My object being to influence opinions not so much of the man in the street, but those of Parliament and Clubland.' This was made explicit in the first editorial after Docker took over:

> Deeply concerned in the maintenance of our national supremacy, [we] are disturbed... by the setting of class against class for purely political ends... [we] intend to uphold the real interests of the country... It will be our policy to urge unflinchingly that the control of the business affairs of the nation be placed in the hands of businessmen.[79]

Needless to say Docker was an involved proprietor, 'the choice of lead stories, as much as the editorial comment... reflected Docker's wishes'.[80]

Docker saw politics simply as a means of advancing corporate concerns: the general interest and business interests were essentially the same thing. 'Politics often come between masters and men', he wrote in 1911. 'Business – a common interest – can only bring us closer together.'[81] He thought that socialist ideas were not deep rooted: 'the men do not act on intellectual impulse, and [that] the doctrines they parade are mainly catchwords'. With the exception of a small number of socialist theorists and 'the type of labour agitator who is a mere iconoclast', militancy was 'essentially a reaction against... individual remoteness from the employer'. 'I doubt if any man who is on nodding terms with his Managing Director ever becomes a willing striker.' Yet Docker was not content just to have management moving freely about the factory. It was also 'an elementary business proposition that industrial success is impossible unless the employer studies and trains the sentiments of his workpeople with the same efficiency that he equips his... machinery'.[82]

To pursue such goals Docker created Business Leagues in 1910 and 1911. His obsession was the formation of 'a business government with business men in the cabinet'. This was a theme he returned to again and again, arguing with all comers on the need for an Industrial Party. He told a meeting of the Wednesbury Business League in 1912 that as few as 20 'hard headed business men' in the House of Commons 'who knew really what they wanted' could revolutionise politics.[83] He was instrumental in the creation and development of a series of business propaganda and lobby groups including the Federation of British Industries (the forerunner of today's Confederation of British Industry), the British Commonwealth Union in 1916, the British Manufacturers Association (later the National Union of

▶

Manufacturers) in 1915 and other 'die-hard' lobby groups.[84] He was intimately involved in the establishment of National Propaganda and is – as many of the pioneers of corporate propaganda – a rather neglected figure in historical accounts of the period.

Reginald 'Blinker' Hall

William Reginald Hall, known as 'Reggie to his many friends, "Blinker" to the rest of the Navy'. Hall's nickname 'came from his habit of constantly blinking his eyes, something his daughter ascribes, together with a chronically weak chest, to the appalling food at his preparatory school, where the boys had to creep out at night to get turnips from the fields to fill their little bellies'.[85] A typical product of the public school system Blinker Hall was a disciplinarian with a ruthless nature and a cruel sense of humour.[86] Hall enjoyed recounting the tale of his retribution against a judge he perceived as handing down a 'light' sentence to a German spy. Mr Justice Bray had commented in his judgment that the information passed by the spy related to 'targets of no military importance'. In response Hall 'took care to send back a report to Germany, in the spy's name, which gave the position of the judge's country house' as a target. Not long afterwards Hall found himself seated next to Bray at dinner. The judge bemoaned the fact that his house had been bombed by German Zeppelins and that he had narrowly escaped with his life. 'Hall's delighted rejoinder was "Well, it was not a target of any military importance, was it?"'[87]

On entering the world of intelligence Hall 'instinctively and immediately threw himself into "The Great Game", using all the weapons of deception, disinformation, double agents, bribery, blackmail and general skull-duggery' associated with intelligence.[88] Hall was one of those men 'who never made the mistake of confusing patriotism with loyalty to elected governments'. He was closely involved in the capture of Roger Casement in Tralee Bay two days before the Easter rising in Ireland. Hall ensured that Casement was not put into the hands of Dublin Castle (headed by the despised liberal, Birrell) but transferred directly to London where Hall, and his friend Basil Thomson, the head of Special Branch, personally interrogated him. Hall sealed Casement's fate by circulating his 'black diaries',[89] to the press and the US ambassador, thus ensuring his execution. 'It was all very gratifying; an object lesson in secret service power which Hall… was never to forget.'[90] His deputy, William 'Bubbles' James, noted that Hall 'would not stand aside when a traitor might escape his just fate through emotional appeals of people who did not know the gravity of the offences'.[91]

When Blinker Hall left the Navy in February 1919 he put these enthusiasms to extensive use. Within a few months Hall was immersed in the creation of 'National Propaganda' and other business front groups such as the British Commonwealth Union. He was chairman of National Propaganda in its early years and coordinated the Economic Study Clubs from an office in London.[92]

Hall's dislike for democratic governance was again evident through his involvement with the leaking of the Zinoviev letter, which was an attempt to sabotage the election chances of the Labour Party in 1924. He had been appointed as principal agent of the Conservative Party in 1923 and on the eve of polling day he secretly conspired with the head of MI6 to pass the forged letter to the *Daily Mail*:

▶

'this was a "document" supposedly written by Gregory Zinoviev, president of the Communist International, instructing British Communists to use their sympathisers in the Labour Party to prepare for revolution'. The letter was published in the *Mail* four days before the election under the headline 'Moscow Orders to our Reds – Great Plot Disclosed' and 'effectively brought down the Labour Government'.[93] This affair earned the *Daily Mail* the enduring sobriquet 'the Forger's Gazette'.

Hall later resigned as chair of the Economic League, but remained a supporter – taking up the role of general manager of the strike-breakers' daily propaganda sheet *British Gazette*. His enthusiasm for the great game and his dislike of democratic politics ensured he remained connected to intelligence matters as well as to the misinformation and propaganda that go hand in hand with them. He died in 1943 at the age of 73.

John Baker White

White became head of the Economic League in 1926, steering it through almost half a century of subversion. Upon leaving college in 1920 (when he was 18) until his death, 'his career encompassed a range of organisations which have played important roles in the development of the secret state'. He was soon drawn into the world of spooks and subversion when he was recruited by his stepfather, a Special Branch officer, to deliver a secret letter to IRA leader Michael Collins. Later he joined a private intelligence agency connected to the secret service, for which he spied on communists and 'obtained inside knowledge to use against them'.[94] White decided early on that 'fighting communism' would be his profession: 'I saw Bolshevism as a manifestation of the anti-Christ and from that sprang dedication.' Later in the early 1920s he took up the role of publicity officer for the Mining Association, the mine-owners' propaganda body. After taking a hands-on role in strike-breaking in the General Strike, he was appointed Director General of the Economic League in 1926. In the 1930s White became an admirer of Hitler as well as the British Fascists (a forerunner of the British Union of Fascists). He notes that he had visited the British Fascists' headquarters in 1923. His 'mother was a close friend of Nesta Webster, the intellectual doyenne of the BF, and had collaborated with her in writing *The Communist Menace*, and White, too, seems to have been friends with the Lintorn Ormans, the movement's founders. White admired the BF for meeting "the Communists on their own ground and [fighting] them with their own methods... in many bloody and sometimes considerable battles at street corners and in public halls".'[95] Rotha Lintorn Orman, he declared, 'was one of the bravest people I have ever met in my life... [whose] bravery was by no means purely physical'. White believed that had she been 'gifted with greater political judgement... [and] with the backing of funds, and had she been able to formulate a more constructive policy, the movement might have become an important factor in the political life of Britain'. That aside, however, White was convinced that the BF had 'achieved an end for which it has never been credited. It forced the Communist Party to abandon much of its militant activity....'[96] Baker White's fascism was his political touchstone and he was given to anti-Semitic outbursts in his writing. He penned an admiring book about Germany in which he noted how Hitler 'looks, speaks and behaves like a national leader, using the word in its highest sense, and

▶

he has great natural dignity... he is without question a very great man'.[97] Perhaps unsurprisingly Baker White left this book – alone among his nine volumes – out of his Who's Who entry.

White played an active role in the war though with postings in MI7 as head of Radio Propaganda, in the Ministry of Information. In 1941 he was promoted to Lieutenant-Colonel and recruited to the Political Intelligence Department in the Foreign Office, the forerunner and cover name for the Political Warfare Executive, which ran British black propaganda activities during the war.[98] White later wrote an account of this period in his book *The Big Lie* (1955).

White was Director of the Economic League for 19 years and publicity adviser for another 25. He stood down as Director to become a Conservative MP (for Canterbury 1945–53) and was later chair of a Freedom Association branch in Kent.[99] White died in 1988 having devoted most of his life to fighting against the possibility of democracy. His story, as with so many others we review in this book, encapsulates the close link between propaganda and wider intelligence and political action in defence of elite interests.

Together these three men were at the forefront of the development of propaganda and PR in the UK. They are almost entirely forgotten today, despite playing crucial parts in developing the 'great game' of power politics in response to challenges from below, notably those posed by organised labour, and popular democracy. Surprisingly, critical and radical histories of the period fail to mention their concrete and significant role.

THE GENERAL STRIKE

The mettle of the propaganda and intelligence networks operating on behalf of manufacturing industry was tested within the decade by the General Strike of 1926. Despite Labour forming its first coalition administration, the Central Council of the Economic League reported to its members in 1924 that the democratically elected government was the primary target of their work.

The fact that there were found five and a half million British citizens willing to place in power as well as in office a body of men plunged in uneconomics, pledged to the nationalisation of industry, and plighted in troth to subsidise Russian Bolshevism with British savings, is a measure of the education work that remains to be done.[100]

By this stage the League had between 150 and 200 corporate members, and 'a considerably more diverse and sophisticated [intelligence] operation than the state's own... the most co-ordinated anti-Labour machine this country has ever seen'.[101]

When the General Strike came in 1926, it started with the miners, but their strike was precipitated by the coal owners who 'adopted an attitude of self-righteous determination'. The miners 'must be brought to heel'.[102] The Economic League played a significant role in the strike and collaborated closely with the Federation of British Industries and with the government in propaganda and strike-breaking – ensuring they recruited 'volunteers' to do the jobs of the strikers. The failure of the General Strike 'considerably weakened' the trade union movement.

The strike fundamentally changed the relationship between employer and employed in Britain by reinforcing the corporatist argument that employees' best interests were served by satisfying the interests of the employer.[103]

According to the League's own account its activities helped in both strike-breaking in the General Strike and the defeat of the miners who stayed on strike. The League despatched a 'flying squad' to do 'constitutional work' to support a breakaway union in the Nottingham coalfields. The aim was to 'get the miners back to work'. They engaged in the by now tried and trusted tactics of using speakers 'equipped with vans and leaflets'. Both experienced and new recruits were despatched including at least two former Black and Tans in a 'rough and tough' campaign which, according to the League, 'accelerated the return to work and the eventual collapse of the strike'.[104]

The role and importance of the assorted business lobbyists and propagandists in this period is downplayed by a number of historians, claiming it is difficult to tell how successful the propaganda was or doubting the success of such activity simply by dint of the apparently unsubtle or unpleasant methods deployed. But the success of coercive propaganda is not measured in the wholesale conversion of the working class to capital, but in the creation of structures capable of effectively pursuing the interests of capital. This is precisely what the intelligence and propaganda operation amounted to, with its direct sabotage of left political organisations. By decisively undermining the willingness of the labour movement to continue with the strike, by making it seem unwinnable, and by portraying the strike as the choice between 'class warfare and the collapse of capitalist society on one hand and industrial harmony on the other',[105] the Economic League were pursuing the classic propaganda strategy of making the enemy feel that resistance is hopeless. The propaganda was not something divorced from the interests and strategies of the corporate propagandists but integral to it. It is certainly the case that corporate interests were under threat from the advance of democracy, and for much of the period between 1918 and 1979 their interests were at least potentially under challenge. But they managed in the General Strike, and later in the post-war period, to sabotage all but the most limited forms of effective democratic reform.

The Economic League continued its activities throughout the 1930s and 1940s, engaging in propaganda, and gathering intelligence on the left. The League tried to work closely with trade unions against the left, largely covertly. Throughout this period they continued to collaborate closely with the police, Special Branch and MI5.

The first wave of business activism was not a resounding success. It had achieved victories, including sabotaging the first Labour government and ensuring that democratic reform was slowed. But the pressure for change built up dramatically once again in the US and Britain following the catastrophic effects of the 1929 Wall Street Crash. Contrary to the picture painted by many historians and other analysts, and accepted in much public debate, corporate propaganda was not something that emerged in the US and was then exported to Britain. It emerged independently in Britain in the same period and for the same reasons, though, as we have shown, there was some cross-fertilisation of ideas and practice.

4

The Second Wave of Corporate Propaganda, 1936–50

The second wave of corporate activism started in the US well in advance of the UK. It was prompted by the political aftermath of the Wall Street Crash, the resulting depression and the consequent movement against big business as expressed in the New Deal. Corporate power – indeed the whole capitalist system – was increasingly questioned. In the US this swept Franklin D. Roosevelt to power in 1932 and returned him with a landslide in 1936. The launch of the second wave of business activism was occasioned in particular by Roosevelt's second presidential election victory. On the campaign trail Roosevelt had noted 'I should like to have it said of my first administration that in it the forces of selfishness and of lust for power met their match. I should like to have it said of my second administration that in it these forces meet their master.'[1] This represented a serious challenge to business; one they did not shy away from. Utilising the full range of economic and political, legal and illegal tools at their disposal, the corporations launched unprecedented propaganda campaigns to defend the system and their interests.

The emergence of corporate propaganda in the UK saw organised business joining the battle of ideas. Activists in the social movement for capitalism had their successes, not least in preventing the fuller development of democratic decision making. But some of the flow of history in the period from the turn of the century until about 1930 offered the prospect of significant social change through the redistribution of wealth, underpinned by extended suffrage. By the 1930s, with the rise of fascism, it was fashionable to counter-pose ideas of liberalism against those of 'totalitarianism', a move that positioned economic liberalism on one side and fascism and communism on the other. The devotees of economic liberalism were, however, still concerned about the travails of the rich. Although the organisations of the right had managed to repulse radical change in Britain following the introduction of universal suffrage, they could see the writing on the wall for the defence of class privilege. In the US the New Deal ushered in an era of big government rather than big business, meaning that corporate interests suffered in the cause of reducing injustice and inequality. As a result US capitalists and their corporations were quicker to launch a counter attack than were their UK counterparts, whose interests were not so directly threatened in the 1930s. In the US, at the vanguard of the propaganda campaign was the National Association of Manufacturers (NAM), who engaged in a political struggle to preserve capitalism as a system.[2] In a re-run of the first wave of business political activism, business did not win the 'battle of ideas' in the abstract but also in concrete terms involving cracked heads, the destruction of popular morale and the transfer of power and resources from one part of society to another.

RESPONSE TO THE NEW DEAL

The New Deal and the unparalleled political opposition to monopoly and oligopoly capitalism forced corporate leaders to plan a strategy to defend their interests collectively. The National Association of Manufacturers was the vehicle for this, but it had first to be taken over by a small group of class-conscious business leaders who had been meeting privately at a dinner group they themselves dubbed the 'brass hats'. The NAM old guard were edged out in December 1931 and one of the 'brass hats' installed as president. This followed the pattern of the previous wave of activism when a similar coup in NAM was staged in 1903, transforming the trade association into a crusading anti-union organisation (see Chapter 3). In 1933, only months into the first term of the Roosevelt administration one of the new guard, Robert Lund, penned a memo which stressed the need for 'public relations', and 'effective publicity' in order to launch 'an active campaign of education' to tackle the 'general misinformation of our industrial economy' brought about by 'selfish groups' including labour, socialists and 'the radicals'. NAM would remain at the forefront of the campaign to defend big business throughout the next decade.

THE MOHAWK VALLEY FORMULA

The positive campaign to promote the capitalist system also depended on the development of propaganda techniques to break the capacity of the unions to take effective industrial action. Yet again the novelty of the methods should not distract us from the intimate relation between propaganda and coercion.

The wave of industrial unrest was essentially about the right of the unions to organise and to engage in collective bargaining – a fundamental human right and one enshrined under the New Deal by the National Labor Act (The Wagner Act) of 1935. The employers would not accept this and sought, in the words of the official commission of enquiry, a 'new alignment of forces', meaning the introduction of new propaganda methods to mobilise public opinion.[3] These were pioneered by James Rand, the boss of the Remington Rand company which manufactured typewriters and early calculators. Rand was a notorious anti-union boss with a history of brutality and deception. The 1936–37 strike by an American Federation of Labor (AFL) affiliate was novel for the degree of brutality shown against the strikers, but also for the development of propaganda tactics as part of the strategy to defeat the strike. The dispute is notorious for spawning the 'Mohawk Valley formula', so named after the location of the Remington Rand factory in Illion in the Mohawk Valley in New York State. The nine-point formula was devised by James Rand, Jr. (see box, below). The US Department of Labor summarised the strategy as follows:

The formula included discrediting union leaders by calling them 'agitators', threatening to move the plant, raising the banner of 'law and order' to mobilize the community against the union, and actively engaging police in strike-breaking activity, then organizing a back-to-work movement of pro-company employees. While the National Association of Manufacturers enthusiastically published the plan, the National Labor Relations Board called it a battle plan for industrial war.[4]

The National Association of Manufacturers distributed the formula to members in the June 1936 issue of the NAM's *Labor Relations Bulletin* immortalising the 'Mohawk Valley formula' as a classic blueprint for union busting. The aim, as one contemporary observer put it, 'envisages a public opinion aroused to the point where it will tolerate the often outrageous use of force by police or vigilantes to break the strike'.[5]

But the formula was really put to the test in the following year by the National Association of Manufacturers in alliance with the Iron and Steel Institute in the Johnstown steel strike of 1937. The dispute was between the Congress of Industrial Organizations (CIO) and the Bethlehem Steel plant in Johnstown, Pennsylvania. Bethlehem Steel was owned by 'Little Steel' (which also owned a series of other steel companies) who were able to call on the support of NAM, the

---

The Mohawk Valley formula

1. When a strike is threatened, label the union leaders as 'agitators' to discredit them with the public and their own followers. Conduct balloting under the foremen to ascertain the strength of the union and to make possible misrepresentation of the strikers as a small minority. Exert economic pressure through threats to move the plant, align bankers, real estate owners and businessmen into a 'Citizens' Committee'.
2. Raise high the banner of 'law and order', thereby causing the community to mass legal and police weapons against imagined violence and to forget that employees have equal right with others in the community.
3. Call a 'mass meeting' to coordinate public sentiment against the strike and strengthen the Citizens' Committee.
4. Form a large police force to intimidate the strikers and exert a psychological effect. Utilize local police, state police, vigilantes and special deputies chosen, if possible, from other neighborhoods.
5. Convince the strikers their cause is hopeless with a 'back-to-work' movement by a puppet association of so-called 'loyal employees' secretly organized by the employer.
6. When enough applications are on hand, set a date for opening the plant by having such opening requested by the puppet 'back-to-work' association.
7. Stage the 'opening' theatrically by throwing open the gates and having the employees march in a mass protected by squads of armed police so as to dramatize and exaggerate the opening and heighten the demoralizing effect.
8. Demoralize the strikers with a continuing show of force. If necessary turn the locality into a warlike camp and barricade it from the outside world.
9. Close the publicity barrage on the theme that the plant is in full operation and the strikers are merely a minority attempting to interfere with the 'right to work'. With this, the campaign is over – the employer has broken the strike.[6]

National Industrial Council (a front group for the NAM) and the Iron and Steel Institute (an organisation set up in 1908 as one of the first trade associations with the intent of shaping opinion rather than just representing their members). The reorganised NAM had by this stage created two propaganda divisions, the Public Relations Committee and the National Industrial Information Committee, founded in 1934 and 1935 respectively. James Rand sat on the latter organisation and NAM did all it could to support strike-breaking and spread the Mohawk Valley formula. The response to the strike by the employers also involved a huge investment in propaganda operations, bringing together some of the pioneers of the US public relations industry to promote and defend the industry, bent on managing and coercing public opinion and action. The campaign was one of the first challenges for John Hill and his new firm Hill &

Knowlton, who offered close support to the industry. The National Association of Manufacturers' propaganda adviser was James Selvage. Bethlehem Steel's PR operative, John Price Jones, drafted in a copy agency to help the publicity effort, led by George Ketchum. Hill, Selvage and Ketchum were the principals in early PR firms which still exist today.[7]

The innovations in propaganda policy involved, in particular, smearing the strikers as communist; engaging large numbers of private police to attack the strikers; and, most significantly, the creation and funding of 'citizens' committees' to attempt to foster and manage public opposition to the strike. At the time the citizens' committees and the 'Steel Workers Committee' – described by Cutlip as a 'paper' organisation – posed as independent manifestations of popular opinion. In reality they were founded and run by the corporations, with Bethlehem Steel paying $25,000 to the citizens' committee in June 1937.[8] NAM, under the guidance of James Selvage, hired Hill & Knowlton to help with the communication aspects of the strike-breaking. H&K was also hired by the American Iron and Steel Institute and by member companies like Republic Steel, who in turn increased contributions to both AISI and NAM under Hill's influence in the years 1933–37.[9] NAM itself increased its spending on propaganda dramatically from $36,500 in 1934 (7.2 per cent of their income) to $793,043 in 1937 (55.1 per cent of their income).[10] The industry campaign involved the release of selective information and the intimidation of local communities via the 'citizens' committees'. One tactic was revealed in the subsequent La Follette Committee inquiry discovery of internal memoranda from Hill & Knowlton. An H&K staffer had written that the steel company should mobilise the local business community to pressure the local newspaper publisher. The memo also suggested that 'some pressure might also be judiciously exerted through the advertisers in Birmingham'. This was later referred to by Hill as 'wholly innocent'. He also falsely stated that the Committee had given H&K 'no chance to clarify the memorandum' or to 'refute' the 'interpretation' of it.[11] Hill also hired a journalist, George Sokolsky, to write material about the industry for his columns in the press. Unsurprisingly this was done covertly and Sokolsky's relations with the companies were not disclosed until after the strike. Sokolsky received $28,000 from the steel industry between June 1936 and February 1938. As *Time* described it, the subtlest performer for Hill & Knowlton was George Ephraim Sokolsky, author, lecturer, industrial consultant. Some of Mr. Sokolsky's lecturing was done at 'civic progress meetings' arranged and paid for by local employers but publicly sponsored by 'neutral' groups.[12]

In conclusion *Time* noted: 'Mr. Sokolsky's philosophy: "I do not like coercion in any form. I prefer spontaneous enthusiasms"' – meaning spontaneous in appearance only. The integration of the citizens' committees and the paid 'independent' journalist, together with management of the local press and 'judiciously exerted' pressure on advertising revenues as a means of manipulating community responses amounts to more than education or even to the use of 'persuasion'. It amounts to a systematic attempt at coercion. In the context of the use of espionage and the hiring of armed detectives, there can be little doubt that this form of propaganda is itself a form of coercion.

The inquiry which followed the Little Steel strike was one of the first to examine the tactics of a PR company. The La Follette Committee did not like what it found, castigating the NAM claim that it was simply involved in 'educating' the public. Its campaign 'cannot be said by any stretch of argument to contribute to a better understanding of our "Industrial Economic Society"... They asked not what the weaknesses and abuses of the economic structure had been and how they could be corrected, but instead paid millions to tell the public that nothing was wrong. The association considered its propaganda material an effective weapon in its fight against labor unions.'[13] Even the historian Richard Tedlow (whose sympathetic study of the PR industry concludes that the rise of PR is 'an indication of the health of American Democracy'), writes of this episode that, 'the corporate public relation apparatus had indeed sought to quell labor unionism, and it had been used in tandem with the most vicious anti-union tactics in order to protect the public opinion flank of the conservative corporation'.[14]

Hill, described in various places as a 'convinced conservative', remained devoted to smears and deceptions all his life, writing – falsely – in his autobiography that the 1919 steel strike was 'communist inspired' and that the Johnstown Memorial Day Massacre in which ten demonstrators were shot dead by police had been organised by 'Communist agitators'.[15] Later Hill maintained that the La Follette Committee which had investigated and condemned NAM and Hill & Knowlton's handiwork in the strike had been acknowledged by

La Follette himself to have been 'unfair' and that the committee staff had been 'dominated by communists'.[16] This was typical Hill, unable or unwilling to tell the truth if it was not in his interests.

After the Remington Rand strike, the originator of this coercive form of industrial relations, James Rand, declared in an address to the 'Citizens' Committee': 'Two million businessmen have been looking for a formula like this and business has hoped for, dreamed of, and prayed for such an example as you have set.' An example, he concluded, that would 'go down in history as the Mohawk Valley Formula'.[17]

The strike was politically significant because it meant that the growing power of the unions was halted. The formula, which is rarely mentioned in most histories of the development of propaganda and PR, was widely used by the US business classes.[18] In 1950 it was noted that since 1936 'these "scientific" methods of strike breaking have been applied in every major strike in the country'.[19] As we will see, the techniques were also used to great effect more than 50 years later in the showdown which broke the power of the unions in the UK in the 1984/85 miners' strike.[20]

BUSINESS FINDS ITS VOICE

The second wave of business activism was significant in shaping not only industrial relations, but public relations too. It represented a critical shift in the strategy and the stakes of corporate propaganda. 'The entire project was original. Business men had sold goods and services; they had sold individual companies, or industries, or even specific ideas (like the idea that the private ownership of utilities is best); but they had never before undertaken to sell business as a whole.'[21] From the mid 1930s NAM launched a two decade long campaign to 'identify the free enterprise system with every cherished value, and identify interventionist governments and strong unions (the only agencies capable of checking the complete domination of society by the corporations), with tyranny, oppression and even subversion'.[22] Robert Lund, the 'brass hat' leader of NAM, set out his vision:

Industry must educate public opinion... We must come back to the fundamental fact that unless we reach the people, others will, and the prejudice they create is more than likely to be injurious.[23]

By the end of the 1930s the corporations thought they were turning the corner. Lund stated in 1938 that 'this program, five years ago initiated a new formula in public contact by industry, that in volume of publicity the campaign has totalled more than all other similar programs combined... millions of our people believe today in these principles who did not five years ago'.[24]

The next task, according to a NAM PR strategy document in 1939, was to 'link free enterprise in the public consciousness with free speech, free press and free religion as integral parts of democracy'.[25] The Second World War delayed the execution of this idea but NAM launched a massive propaganda campaign at the end of the war. 'All available media were used to arouse the general public', noted one account, 'to insist that the country replace bureaucratic control with free competition.' The sociologist Daniel Bell wrote that 'the apparatus itself is prodigious: 1,600 business periodicals, 577 commercial and financial digests, 2,500 advertising agencies, 500 public relations counselors, 4,000 corporate public relations departments and more than 6,500 "house organs" with a combined circulation of more than 70 million'.[26]

The National Association of Manufacturers was not the only class-wide propaganda body in existence at this time. The US Chambers of Commerce were also active distributing more than a million copies of their pamphlet on 'Communist Infiltration' in 1946 alone.[27] This social movement to defend capitalism was joined during the war years by a body set up to defend the mass consumer society. The Advertising Council was originally created as the War Advertising Council in 1942. In 1947 it received 'unprecedented amounts of money' from business toward the $100 million economic education campaign to 'sell' the 'American economic system to the public, including large donations from General Foods, General Electric, General Motors, IBM, Johnson and Johnson, Procter and Gamble, Goodrich, and Republic Steel'.[28] Daniel Bell described the output of the campaign as 'staggering':

The Advertising Council alone, in 1950, inspired 7 million lines of newspaper advertising stressing free enterprise, 400,000 car cards, 2,500,000,000 radio impressions... By all odds it adds up to the most intensive 'sales' campaign in the history of industry.[29]

The campaign was premised 'on the assumption that if Americans were taught to think correctly about the free enterprise system then they would approve of business activities and not call for government regulation of them'.[30]

Organisations such as the Opinion Research Corporation (ORC) did studies to prove that Americans were ignorant of economics and the fundamentals of the American economic system and needed economic 'education'. However these studies were essentially surveys of how strongly business values were held in the community. Many students erroneously thought that owners got too much profit and gained most from new machinery. Worst of all, from a business point of view, over half of the students agreed with the Marxist statement: 'The fairest economic system is one that "takes from each according to his ability" and gives to each "according to his needs."' This was even though most teachers disagreed with the statement. The failure of students 'to see through this Marxist doctrine' was taken to be evidence of 'how little high school seniors comprehend the fundamentals of our system.'...

The ORC argued that 'ignorance and lack of understanding of how the business system works go hand in hand with a willingness to vote for measures that undermine the system.' Clearly it was best to correct such ignorance at school. School children, it found, were more likely to view regulation of business and government control of prices favourably but this could be corrected with simple 'education'. [31]

Adults too were found to be malleable if they were provided with misleading propaganda by business. The attack by the corporations on the Office of Price Administration offers one example. The OPA was a federal agency set up during the war to control prices and inflation. The notion of price ceilings was of course anathema to business and it quickly set about undermining the organisation. The NAM campaign against the OPA was denounced by then President Truman who also quoted opinion poll figures showing that the proportion of people who believed the OPA was necessary declined from 85 per cent before the NAM onslaught, to 26 per cent by November 1946. The OPA was first cut and then destroyed by Congress as a result. Business won its objective and the OPA was disbanded, allowing prices to soar in the latter half of 1946.[32]

As Carey notes, 'apart from the years affected by the Korean War, the American labour movement was never again able to increase the (low) proportion of the workforce it had organized'.[33] By the end of the 1950s, writes Elizabeth Fones-Wolf, 'the business community could point to favourable results. Liberal hopes for a fully articulated welfare state had been crushed, while union representation of the work force had begun its long decline. Meanwhile the popular image of organized labor shifted from heroic defenders of the New Deal to just another special interest group.'[34]

THE SECOND WAVE IN THE UK

In Britain in the same period, the backlash against privilege gathered pace through the 1930s and the demand for public ownership of the 'commanding heights' of industry sounded a warning to the corporate lobbyists. In the middle of the war a new organisation called Aims of Industry was founded, dedicated to defending private interests against democratic reform and with the explicit aim of countering the emerging pressure for nationalisation of key industries.

In the post-1945 period the Economic League created a 'youth movement' taking propaganda into youth clubs and also targeting 'housewives'. The League continued to have a close relationship with the FBI, and nurtured one with Aims of Industry (Aims). The rationale was that after the heroic sacrifices of the British public during the Second World War they should be able to enjoy a greater share of the nation's wealth. Much like the creation of National Propaganda, Aims was born at a meeting of leading businessmen. It was called by H.G. Starley of Champion Sparking Plugs and funded by Tate & Lyle and other corporations (such as Ford, Imperial Chemical Industries (later ICI), Rolls Royce). Aims took the lead in propaganda and publicity in the press and advertising media, while the League continued its direct propaganda tactics. As Labour Research described it in 1950: 'the FBI is the back room boy, the Economic League and Aims of Industry are the hot gospellers'.[35]

TATE AND STATE

The gospel they were hot for in the 1940s was that Britons should take the state out of Tate. In the 1940s UK sugar producers invented one of the most enduring pro-corporate logos in Mr Cube. Mr Cube, only recently retired, was invented as part of a campaign to defend the sugar industry, primarily Tate & Lyle, from being taken into public ownership.

Peter Runge, the company's campaign strategist, recalled how 'we were strongly advised to have a cartoon character who, if he caught the public's imagination, could say the most outrageous things and get away with it, and who could act as a buffer between the public and Tate and Lyle'. Brandishing his sword of free enterprise and protected by his T&L shield, Mr Cube would 'say sensible, cogent or outrageous things' with appropriate grimaces and gesticulations, allowing Tate to 'concentrate on attacking the Socialist policy in a somewhat more dignified manner.'[36]

From the end of July 1949 Mr Cube 'found his way on to millions of sugar packets on the nation's breakfast tables. Mr Cube's catchy slogans were analogous to Cold War sound bites, agitating some Government ministers... into near apoplexy. "Take the S out of State", urged Mr Cube; "state control will make a hole in your pocket and my packet". The simplest and most effective message was "Tate not State!"'[37]

The Mr Cube campaign was run by Aims of Industry. Crucial to Aims' early success was that it presented itself as a non-political body and registered as an educational charity. As an internal memo of the time notes, 'its strength lies in the fact that as a non-profit making no-party public relations organization it has access for propaganda work to factories and working men's clubs, the BBC and the press on a scale which would not be possible on a purely party basis'.[38] In the first six months of 1949 Aims of Industry speakers gave 41 broadcasts on BBC radio programmes.[39] An early internal report on the sugar issue noted that 'Members of Parliament showed a constant willingness to co-operate by putting questions in the House'.[40] Aims also borrowed credibility from the BBC by hiring the legendary BBC journalist, Richard Dimbleby (the father of prominent contemporary broadcasters Jonathan and David Dimbleby) to visit the Tate & Lyle refinery, and make 'an extensive recording of interviews with contented Tate and Lyle employees'. Eventually 'some 400 albums of six records each were used by Aims'.[41] Sugar remained in private hands:

Polling was heavy on election day, February 23rd, 1950. Towards dawn on election night, sitting in the Tate boardroom, Peter Runge of Tate and Lyle exclaimed 'By God we're going to beat the buggers'. Bearing in mind the obstacles stacked against Mr Cube in 1949, he was perhaps entitled to raise his glass – his chances of getting the company's name off the list [of companies to be nationalised] had seemed slender just nine months earlier.[42]

'We have... won the first round', boasted Lord Lyle at the 1951 AGM of Tate & Lyle.[43]

Aims of Industry also advised the British Medical Association and the medical profession as part of their campaign to resist the introduction of the National Health Service. In this they were unsuccessful. But they were extremely active. In 1948–49 according to their own account:

National and provincial newspapers published a total of 87,305 column inches of material... More than 300 newspapers and magazines are now publishing our editorial material regularly... It will be seen that our message is reaching not only the worker but his wife. In addition to this general campaign on behalf of free enterprise... [Aims] has launched a vigorous attack on the plans to nationalise sugar, steel, meat, wholesaling and importing, cement and water.[44]

Aims enjoyed the continued support of a wide variety of well known companies including Ford, Rank (later Rank, Hovis MacDougall), Tate & Lyle, Sir Robert McAlpine, Slough Estates, Eagle Star Insurance, Firestone Tyres. Its budget for the year 1948–49 was £150,000. 'Aims of Industry', reported the trade union funded Labour Research Department, 'are now well organised to carry out campaigns of a similar nature for any industry who may want to take protective action.'[45]

Many did. In the early 1950s Aims of Industry was to the fore of the successful campaign to introduce commercial television.[46] The Popular Television Association (PTA) was the vehicle for this deceptive lobby. According to Ronald Simms, the full-time secretary of the campaign, the Association was set up by 'a number of public spirited men'. 'I can categorically assure... that this Association is not "a cloak to cover the activities of an advertising medium"', wrote Simms in a letter to the press. The Association's vice-president, Lord Foley, claimed that its members had 'no direct interest' in what the Association called 'competitive television'.[47] In fact, the Association was set up at the instigation of Conservative Central Office, as was admitted by the Conservatives' head of propaganda Lord Woolton some six years later. Simms himself had been seconded from W.H. Gollings, the advertising agency which stood to rake in business from the introduction of commercial television. The campaign was funded by the members of the PTA, whose identities were kept secret, though the bulk of contributions were acknowledged to have come from the 'radio/television manufacturers'.[48] The campaign was run with the assistance of Aims of Industry, which provided two staff on secondment, paid for by the Association. One of them, Gordon McIvor, took over as secretary when Simms went to work as a spin doctor at Conservative Central Office.

Aims distributed propaganda material, news stories, films and 'made available their panel of "freelance lecturers"', who were 'now billed as experts on television' and appeared before 'chambers of commerce, Young Conservative clubs and Rotary Clubs' throughout the country.[49] Their message was that advertising would appear at the beginning and end of programmes but that 'there would never be any interruptions' – a straightforward falsehood. But the techniques for delivering the message were also deceptive and included a campaign of letter writing from 'fake persuaders', identical letters published in the local press throughout the country from citizens with very similar names. The US academic H.H. Wilson was able to trace one identical letter in 22 different papers signed variously: M. Awan; M.A. Warr; M. Adam; M. Swan; M. Ardan – all with the same address.[50] Articles penned by Aims and the PTA were sent to the press and appeared in newspapers throughout the country often with 'no indication of its source'. Only a few papers refused to cooperate. *The Aldershot News* was one and referred to 'pages and pages of foolscap publicity material written under names famous in the entertainment world' appearing 'every week' for the 'last six months'.[51]

In 1957 Aims of Industry conducted a successful campaign against the re-nationalisation of the steel industry: 'Thousands of industrial employees found propaganda leaflets and messages inserted in their wage packets, some of them straightforwardly warning of the dire consequences of re-nationalisation on their conditions and wages. Others contained more subtle personal appeals from company directors and managers for loyalty and support.'[52]

Much of this is conveniently consigned to the memory hole by historians. The companies involved pretend they are at the mercy of public scepticism sometimes whipped up by 'political vote-catching propaganda and the pens and voices of the middle class intelligentsia':

Profits; Failure to work in the public interest; inefficiency; bigness. These are the lines of attack and, because the attackers of business are many and its defenders few and not so ready to take up cudgels, the public assumes an attitude of doubt, if not actual hostility and distrust.

So claimed B.W. Galvin Wright, the publicity controller of ICI, in a speech on 'Industrial Statesmanship', in Heidelberg in the early 1960s.[53] Typically this is the polar opposite of the truth of corporate propaganda, which, as we have seen in this chapter, was ever keen to take up cudgels both literally and metaphorically. ICI was, of course, a major funder of both the Economic League and Aims of Industry.

BUSINESS GOES ON THE OFFENSIVE

The first and second wave of campaigns to defend free enterprise and halt the advance of organised labour and democratic decision making, which ran up to the 1950s, were essentially defensive. They had their successes but as the 1939–45 war loomed there was a widespread worry amongst intellectuals that despite particular victories, the overall battle of ideas was being lost. The need to go on the offensive against democratic thinking, against social democracy, against democratic planning and against Keynesian policies was plain to a number of those who supported the free market. In Britain an Austrian émigré in the Economics Department of the London School of Economics (LSE) was worrying over how best to roll back ideas about democracy and collective planning which had become mainstream following the 1914–18 war and the Bolshevik Revolution. Friedrich von Hayek, one of the most influential thinkers of the twentieth century, had been appointed at the LSE in 1931. He visited Paris in 1938 to participate in a five day colloquium in honour of Walter Lippmann. Lippmann, who attended the meeting as guest of honour, had earlier made what his biographer calls a 'sweeping bow' to Hayek in his book *The Good Society* published in 1937.[54]

'Lippmann's book', writes John Bellamy Foster, 'marked an intellectual turning point in the development of neoliberalism.' The colloque met only once, interrupted by the war, but from this 'arose some of the main ideas' for Hayek's *Road to Serfdom* (1944). It also provided the 'initial stimulus' for the creation, under the guidance of Hayek, of the Mont Pelerin Society (MPS), in 1947.[55] The MPS performed a key role in the renovation of the case for capitalism.[56] Between 1937 and 1947, though, the corporations and their advocates amongst the intellectuals did not rest. While large numbers of professional corporate publicists got involved in war propaganda activities, there were those at home who set about creating new free enterprise organisations. In the US the lines of development for the latter half of the twentieth century were being set. The American Enterprise Institute (1943) and the Foundation for Economic Education (1946) were both created in this period.

The American Enterprise Institute (AEI) was created by the American Enterprise Association, a business lobby group founded in New York in 1938. According to its own account, the Association was horrified when, in 1943 'in Congress there was talk of making wartime price and production controls permanent to prevent another Depression when peace finally arrived'.[57] It resolved to open a Washington office, which, in effect, established the Institute (although it was still called the Association for some years after its creation). The AEI was 'a partnership of top executives of leading business and financial firms (Bristol-Myers, General Mills, Chemical Bank) and prominent policy intellectuals (Roscoe Pound of the Harvard Law School, economic journalist Henry Hazlitt, and disillusioned New Dealer Raymond Moley)'.[58] The AEI's own account makes clear that:

From the beginning, however, the Association's spirit was libertarian and conservative rather than simply 'pro-business'. Its founding mission statement would still serve well: to promote 'greater public knowledge and understanding of the social and economic advantages accruing to the American people through the maintenance of the system of free, competitive enterprise.'[59]

According to some accounts, though, the AEI remained 'invisible' for its first decade.[60] But the AEI is important for three reasons. First, it provides a link between the business activists of the second wave of activism and the third wave, not least through the involvement of Henry Hazlitt. Second, it was one of the first think tanks, involved in the production of research and policy activity (aimed exclusively at elites) rather than mass propaganda. Third, it was important because of what it became – a leading light of the neo-conservative movement in the 1970s and beyond.

The Foundation for Economic Education also involved the ubiquitous Henry Hazlitt. It was set up by Leonard Read, general manager of the Los Angeles Chamber of Commerce, who invited Henry Hazlitt, then a journalist at the *New York Times*, to become one of the original trustees. Hazlitt played a leading role in popularising the work of Hayek and of his mentor Ludwig von Mises in the US in the post-1945 period. It is said that the Foundation was at least part of the inspiration for the creation by Hayek himself of the Mont Pelerin Society the next year. Hazlitt was also at the founding meeting.

THE CASE FOR CAPITALISM: THE MONT PELERIN SOCIETY

The ideological backlash against Keynesian economics and big government began on the slopes of Mont Pelerin, above Lake Geneva in Switzerland in 1947. In company with a 'tiny band of economists, philosophers and historians' the Mont Pelerin Society was founded. It had the 'war aim' of reversing 'the tide of collectivism sweeping across Europe after 1945 from the Soviet Union westward to Britain already being converted into a socialist laboratory', as one if its British acolytes Ralph (Lord) Harris put it.[61] Their intent was the same as those who had met in Dean's Yard in 1919, namely to undermine popular democracy in the corporate interest. Their intellectual bellwether, Friedrich von Hayek, declared 'We must make the building of a free society once more an intellectual adventure, a deed of courage.' The strategy was not to convince the public, who in the view from Mont Pelerin were mere followers of their betters, but to convince the intellectuals of society who were perceived as won over by 'socialism'. 'Once the more active part of the intellectuals have been converted to a set of beliefs, the process by which these become generally accepted is almost automatic and irresistible.'[62]

The Mont Pelerin Society sought to assemble at 'agreeable' venues around the world a 'growing number of carefully vetted' members to meet in 'private conclave' every year or two.[63] Like contemporary professional lobbyists, these shock-troops in the battle for ideas 'eschewed publicity' preferring to work amongst the intellectuals and through sympathetic institutes and other backroom methods. The result, over time, was the creation of a remarkable number of think tanks across the world. In the UK one of its early manifestations was the creation of the Institute of Economic Affairs (IEA) in 1955. The decision to refrain from overt propaganda or direct political action was taken at the first meeting of the MPS:

The group does not aspire to conduct propaganda. It seeks to establish no meticulous and hampering orthodoxy, it aligns itself with no particular party. Its object is solely, by facilitating the exchange of views among minds inspired by certain ideals and broad conceptions held in common, to contribute to the preservation and improvement of the free society.[64]

THE INSTITUTE OF ECONOMIC AFFAIRS

Anthony Fisher was a chicken farmer. He went to the US and discovered battery farming. With the money he made introducing it to the UK he intended to go into politics. But after reading *The Road to Serfdom*, and discovering that Hayek worked at the LSE, he promptly made contact. Hayek inducted Fisher into the Mont Pelerin Society and advised a different course. According to Fisher's daughter, 'Hayek said "don't go into politics. You have to alter public opinion. It will take a long time. You do it through the intellectuals."' So Fisher set up the Institute of Economic Affairs and, at a Conservative Party meeting in East Grinstead, met Ralph Harris who would run the new organisation. Harris was joined by another economist, Arthur Seldon, and they began the task of countering social democracy. They started in a single 'cramped' office. Although they had a breakthrough when they organised the 1959 Mont Pelerin Society conference at Oxford, enabling access to an international network of potential authors,[65] they gained their most valuable allies over a decade later in 1966 when they met William Rees Mogg, the newly appointed editor of *The Times*. Mogg, in turn, asked Peter Jay, then a civil servant at the Treasury, to become a journalist. Jay was sent to Washington and there he came across the Chicago School of (Mont Pelerin affiliated) economists, including Milton Friedman. Jay was converted to economic liberalism and *The Times* under Rees Mogg became a key propaganda outlet for market fundamentalism.[66] But before the political shift to the right came the events of 1968: the student uprising in France and the demonstrations against the Vietnam War in Britain. Revolution and change were in the air and the corporations and their intellectual vanguard were once again on the defensive.

5
The Case for Capitalism –
the Third Wave, to the 1980s

The influence of the Mont Pelerin Society has been extremely significant. Within a generation their ideas had been adopted by right-wing political movements everywhere and a further 10–15 years later they had also successfully neutralised the remnants of parties founded to represent the common interest. On her election in 1979 Margaret Thatcher elevated the head of the IEA to the House of Lords. 'It was primarily your foundation work', wrote Thatcher in a letter of thanks, 'which enabled us to rebuild the philosophy upon which our Party succeeded in the past.'[1] The IEA was the first UK instance of what would eventually become a network of more than 100 free market think tanks around the world.[2]

POST-1968 BLUES AND THE RISE OF THATCHER

Even before the 1968 wave of protests, Aims of Industry was lamenting that 'capitalism in Britain has, for many years, been intellectually on the defensive'.[3] In the aftermath of the student revolt of 1968 and the rise of radicalism in the UK and across the West, the established propaganda organisations of capital in Britain – the Economic League and Aims of Industry – were joined by other subversive groups. This period was the genesis of the third wave of corporate political activism and was mirrored in the US at almost exactly the same time. In the UK the Institute for the Study of Conflict (ISC) was created in 1970 with money from, amongst others, the CIA. A pamphlet in 1972 focused on 'Subversion in British Industry'. Its author was one Nigel Lawson, a former editor of the *Spectator*, later to be Chancellor of the Exchequer under Thatcher. Lawson was approached to write the pamphlet by Brian Crozier, director of the ISC, who had been impressed by a Lawson opinion piece in *The Times* which in Crozier's view 'showed he understood the situation'.[4] They printed only 30 copies as 'the report was not for the wider public: the target audience was industry itself'. With help from the Economic League and Aims of Industry one of Crozier's 'converts' was John Whitehorn of the

CBI. Whitehorn penned a memo appealing for more business support for the ISC and its collaborators, which also included extreme anti-democratic organisations like Common Cause Ltd and Industrial Research and Information Services Ltd.[5]

During 1971 the President and Director General of the CBI had talks with a number of heads of companies who are worried about subversive influences in British Industry... they have also been in touch with a number of organisations which seek in their different ways to improve matters... Their objectives and methods naturally vary; and we see no strong case to streamline them or bring them together more closely than is done by their present loose links and mutual co-operation.[6]

Appealing for the necessary funding from business, the memo noted that the ISC 'plans to take an increasing interest in the study of subversion at home, and has a research project on the drawing board on conflict in British industry to be carried out, if finance is forthcoming, through case studies of conflicts in the docks, shipbuilding, motor industry, and construction'.[7]

The money was forthcoming and the ISC produced a special report on 'Sources of Conflict in British Industry', published just before the 1974 election. Naturally this was not presented as a report funded by business when published with what Crozier describes as 'unprecedented publicity' in the *Observer*. The report was yet another attempt by corporate and intelligence interests to interfere with the democratic process.[8] The ISC's partners in subversion, Aims of Industry, were also active in the 1974 election campaign, spending £500,000 on anti-Labour advertising – including one advertisement with Stalin behind a smiling mask.[9]

The ISC was joined by other radical right organisations in quick succession, from the Centre for Policy Studies (1974), the Freedom Association (1975), to the Adam Smith Institute (1976). The ferment of free market ideas and their networks were expanding. At the centre of this intellectual assault was the Hayekian obsession with restoring corporate power. The activists involved came from the circles nurtured by the Mont Pelerin Society.

THE PLOT AGAINST WILSON

The Freedom Association and the Institute for the Study of Conflict were, along with older groups like Aims of Industry and the Economic League, at the more activist and hands-on end of the ideological war on democratic reform. This meant active links with the intelligence services and dirty tricks operations. Since the creation of the Economic League – as we have seen – there had been traffic between government intelligence and police operatives and the business lobby groups. In the 1970s the concern of the business classes about defending their privileges was only part of a wider anxiety among the upper classes about the Wilson government. As is well documented, sections of the intelligence services had been involved in subversion of the elected governments led by Wilson and Heath. The plotters spread the idea that Wilson was a Soviet agent operating a communist cell within Downing Street and they planned to assemble secret armies in the event of a breakdown of law and order. Some even went as far as to sound out the royal family about heading a government of national unity in the event of a coup. As John Booth, writes:

Senior members of the armed forces, the aristocracy, business, the media, Cold Warriors, professional anti-Communists, the British security services and the CIA went about dirty work that could have resulted in a military coup. When troops and tanks suddenly appear at Heathrow, when private armies are being openly talked about and the support of the Royal Family is being canvassed, we are not far from the abyss.[10]

These conspiracies also involved business activists like the ISC, Ross McWhirter of the Freedom Association and Michael Ivens of Aims of Industry amongst others.[11] The business campaign against democracy was, in other words, supported by a faction of the ruling elite in Britain. Their unity and resolve illustrates that this was not simply a question of winning the battle of ideas but of putting ideas into practice. It is difficult to think of a set of actions more distant from purely ideological struggle than the planning of a military coup.

It is important to remember that this activity was the context of the work of the think tanks and that the personnel and funding came from overlapping sources with the rest of the activist right. In the midst of this ferment, the economic liberals given confidence by the Mont Pelerin Society and the Institute of Economic Affairs saw the next step as taking over the Conservative Party. The vehicle for this was to be the Centre for Policy Studies.

ENTER THE 'MAD MONK'

Keith Joseph is credited with being the politician who developed the ideas behind Thatcherism in the UK. He was instrumental in setting up the Centre for Policy Studies (CPS) in 1974, and unlike the IEA, Joseph's vision for the CPS was for it to be self-consciously political. As a result, contributions to the CPS were supposed to be declared as donations to the Conservatives.[12] At first the intention, as Joseph put it, was simple: 'My aim was to convert the Tory party.'[13] This phase ended with the election of Margaret Thatcher as party leader in February 1975. The second phase was to spread the gospel further. 'Research projects will be designed to prepare public opinion for specific policy decisions', noted an internal memo, 'rather than simply extend the boundaries of knowledge.'[14]

At the CPS John Hoskyns, a systems analyst, and Norman Strauss, a marketing executive for Unilever, joined Joseph. Hoskyns spent over a year figuring out what was wrong with Britain and representing it all in diagrammatic form. The problem was that everything seemed to be caused by everything else. Nevertheless Joseph introduced Hoskyns and Strauss to Thatcher, whose interest prompted them to do more work on their model. 'As they worked some of the things that Hoskyns had put in his diagram seemed to become more important than others. But one thing would come to dominate their thinking.' After all the scribbling, it turned out that the trade unions were ultimately to blame for all the ills of British society. They had to be defeated.[15]

The first round of the battle to defeat the trade unions was not long in coming and the forces of the right were already preparing. A new organisation, the National Association for Freedom (NAFF, later known as the Freedom Association), was set up by Colonel Juan Hobbs of the Conservative Party funding front group, the British United Industrialists, and Michael Ivens of Aims of Industry. This group emerged in what one of its founders, Norris McWhirter, called the 'dark days of 1975'. 'What was needed', noted McWhirter, 'was some kind of association which would defend our rights and liberties.'[16] The 'finest hour' of the NAFF came in 1977 when they took to the streets to break the strike at the Grunwick film processing plant in London.[17] 'The strikers first walked out when a worker was sacked after being forced to do a job he could not possibly do in the time alloted for it', wrote Sivanandan at the time. The workforce was predominantly Asian women and 'this was typical of the punitive, racist and degrading way in which the management treated the workforce'. The workers were advised to join a union by the local trades council and when they did, the owner of the plant, George Ward, refused to recognise the union and sacked all of those who had joined it.[18] This was the first time that the power of the unions had been challenged directly by the activists of the right and it gave them a taste of the battles to come. Described by Cockett quite correctly as 'Hayek's footsoldiers', this was strike-breaking as learnt in the 1926 General Strike, and at Mohawk Valley in New York in 1936.

The right was on the offensive. First of all they brought in lawyers and money to 'stiffen the resolve' of George Ward. But as the dispute mounted and post office workers came out in solidarity, the post on which Grunwick's mail-order business depended was halted. The tactics used at Grunwick are referred to by sympathetic chroniclers as 'military style' and involved street level confrontation. The decisive moment was reached when John Gouriet of the NAFF came up with the 'Operation Pony Express' plan which involved entering the Grunwick building in the middle of the night and removing all the blocked mailbags. These were then driven to a rendezvous in the country from where volunteers began to fan out across the country distributing the mail in a wide range of post boxes to avoid it being blocked by sympathetic post workers. Teresa Gorman (later a Conservative MP), who was involved, tells the tale from her perspective:

We saw ourselves as a kind of underground movement resisting the growth of socialism... we took them [the mail bags] down to a barn in deepest Shropshire or somewhere, where we all assembled, us rebels, us free-market people, in the dead of night, and stuck stamps on all these envelopes. We posted our consignment in different post boxes all over the land. And it was that little event which began the breakdown of the stranglehold of trade unionism in this country. It really did. It was very exciting to be a part of.[19]

The defeat at Grunwick was catalytic for the right. They had seen that they could take the unions on and win, and they would make sure that they were better prepared for the next big conflict.

THE THATCHERITE VICTORY

The intellectual battle between Keynesian principles and market fundamentalism intensified as the alleged threat from the left persisted. The IEA sponsored a new think tank, the Social Affairs Unit, run by Digby Anderson, the far right sociologist and Mont Pelerin member. Anderson had been encouraged by both Michael Ivens of Aims of Industry and Arthur Seldon of IEA. The emergence of the Social Affairs Unit between 1976 and 1980 marked the arrival of the last of the think tanks which were key to the promotion and 'practical implementation' of Thatcherite market fundamentalism.

A particular hub of neo-liberalism was the University of St Andrews in Scotland, the home of many middle-class students who didn't quite make it to Oxbridge, and middle-aged American golfers in bad checks. St Andrews had strong connections with the IEA (Ralph Harris had lectured there) and provided the impetus for the Adam Smith Institute (founded by Madsen Pirie, Eamonn Butler and his brother Stuart Butler, who were all students there, as was Alan Peacock). Among the new wave of Tory MPs in the 1980s, Christopher Chope, Michael Forsyth, Michael Fallon and Robert Jones were all St Andrews graduates and associated with the ASI. Michael Forsyth was typical of many of those who had multiple connections throughout the networks of the radical right. Elected as an MP for Stirling in 1983, Forsyth went on to become Scottish Secretary from 1994 to 1997 when he lost his seat, along with all the other Tory MPs in Scotland, as New Labour swept to power. Forsyth wrote two pamphlets for the ASI in 1980 and 1982 advocating privatisation and the contracting out of public services to the private sector. He set up his own PR firm to take advantage of the opportunities to advise firms which might win the competitive tendering contracts. But Forsyth had also been active in other radical right propaganda agencies such as Aims of Industry, writing their pamphlet *Barriers to Privatisation* in 1984.[20]

The import of all this was that on the one hand the free market right was becoming more confident and organised, better able to weld together an alliance that was broad enough to seek and win government power as well as to pursue their interests directly. They had won the battle of ideas, but, in our terms, this is understood not as winning majority support in popular opinion, but as creating a leadership bloc. The key things that they were able to do were first to work out what policies they wanted to pursue and second to raise morale on their side and amongst their supporters to give them confidence that they could carry them through.

In particular the policy that the CPS were agreed on, which was practically unthinkable in open politics at the time, was that they had to take on and smash the trade union movement. Although the Conservative Party 'formally supported the management during the Grunwick dispute, few had appreciated the significance of it. The CPS, however, did, and it was on the issue of trade union power – and how to curb it – that the CPS now began to take up a position far in advance' of the rest of the Party.[21] In highly confidential memos to

Thatcher in 1978, Alfred Sherman of the CPS pushed his view that taking on union power was not only necessary, it was practically achievable: 'What counts is that "do something about the unions" is again thinkable.'[22] It was the signal achievement of the CPS that they were able to give Thatcher the confidence to adopt this as a policy. The CPS had written a celebrated policy document for Keith Joseph following a discussion as far back as 1976. The document, *Stepping Stones*, outlined the steps that an incoming government would need to take. The attack on the trade unions became more and more important as the document was redrafted. It was eventually accepted by the Shadow Cabinet in March 1979 and Norman Strauss and John Hoskyns of the CPS got down to drawing up concrete plans for taking on the unions.[23]

THE UK/US NEXUS

In telling the story of how the neo-liberals won in the UK we should not forget political developments across the Atlantic. The process was again parallel for the same reasons it had been in 1942–50. In the 1970s though there was also – it seems – considerable interchange of personnel and collaborative activity. After leaving St Andrews University, the founders of the Adam Smith Institute – Madsen Pirie, Eamonn and Stuart Butler – all worked in the US with Edwin Feulner,[24] who was in 1974 to set up perhaps the most important new neo-liberal think tank of the 1970s, the Heritage Foundation, which along with the American Enterprise Institute (AEI) played a similar role in the Republican victory in 1980 as the IEA and CPS had done in the UK. Feulner had worked at the IEA in 1965. Indeed the cooperation and exchange between US and UK think tanks, including interchanging personnel, is unsurprising, 'guided as they were by the same economists and publicists of the Mont Pelerin Society'.[25]

THE BUSINESS ROUNDTABLE

The fight to restore corporate power in the UK entered a new stage after the emergence of the progressive new social movements of the 1960s. In the US too the business classes were anxious. Public sympathy for business was, according to one observer, 'in freefall'.[26] In August 1971 a chance conversation between the corporate lawyer and serial corporate board member, Lewis Powell, and his neighbour, a Chamber of Commerce activist, led to Powell setting his ideas for business strategy down on paper. His confidential memo on the 'Attack on the American free enterprise system' provided the blueprint for what Ted Nace describes as 'one of the most successful political counter-attacks in American history'.[27]

Powell's memo was important. Two months after he wrote it he was nominated to the Supreme Court by President Nixon, from where he could help implement his vision. But most important was its recommendations for action. It saw business as under 'massive assault' from all sides – from the environmental, consumer and student movements – not just by 'extremists of the left' but from 'perfectly respectable elements of society; from the college campus, the pulpit, the media, the intellectual and literary journals, the arts and sciences and from politicians'. 'Few elements of American society today', wrote Powell, 'have as little influence in government as American business.' That this statement was patently at odds with reality, then or now, matters not. It was certainly the case that big business had lost some ground to public health and environmental and consumer protection legislation. Powell's solution was a call to corporations to act as a class:

Strength lies in organization, in careful long range planning and implementation, in consistency of action over an indefinite period of years, in the scale of financing available only through joint effort, and in the political power available through united action and national organizations.[28]

The concerted response from big business began in 1972 with the founding of the Business Roundtable (BRT), made up of the CEOs of 200 of the largest companies in the US. By 1976 it was described as the 'most powerful' business lobby in Washington.[29] This perception is reinforced by the close integration and overlapping memberships between the BRT and other key business lobby groups such as the Business Council, the Committee for Economic Development and the Conference Board and the US Chapter of the International Chamber of Commerce. In the years between 1972 and 1979 the percentage of members of the BRT policy committee with links to one or more of the four groups just mentioned was never less than 86.8 per cent and in 1978 reached 100 per cent.[30] In its first few years it was credited as having played a largely 'defensive role' in blocking progressive legislation under the Ford and Carter administrations, including helping to abort the proposed Consumer Protection Agency.

The early 1970s witnessed the arrival of a wide range of business lobby groups in Washington. Just as in the UK at the same moment a glut of think tanks, interest groups, and PR initiatives for the free market emerged in a third great wave of business political activity. Amongst the signs of this was the dramatic increase in the use of lobbyists in Washington. Between 1968 and 1978 the number of corporations with lobbying offices in the capital increased from 100 to more than 500. Between 1971 and 1979 the number of corporations with registered lobbyists rose from 175 to 650.[31] The head of the Coors brewing family, Joseph Coors, was reportedly 'moved' by Powell's memo to donate $250,000 which was used to set up the Heritage Foundation in 1973. Amongst other parts of this venture was the creation of the Pacific Legal Foundation and the American Legislative Exchange Council set up with money from, among others, the wealthy US right-wing Olin Foundation and the Competitive Enterprise Institute. These were essentially class-wide organisations. A number of bodies specialising in particular issues also surfaced funded by the tobacco, food, oil, chemical and other industries under threat for damaging the environment or public health. In the years after the election of Reagan, the Business Roundtable and its constellation of allies (both old and new) went on the offensive. It latterly played the leading role in the campaign to pass the North American Free Trade Agreement (NAFTA) into law, thus ensuring that a key piece of the architecture of globalisation was put in place.[32]

The Business Roundtable was joined by a whole host of other organisations as part of the rise of what Sidney Blumenthal has called the 'Counter-Establishment'.[33] In particular we should note the role of the think tanks including the American Enterprise Institute and the Heritage Foundation and the role of the Mont Pelerin Society in the US. The AEI grew rapidly in influence in the US in the 1970s and corporate donations swelled partly as a result of Powell's memo. In 1977 about 200 corporations accounted for 25 per cent of the $5 million annual budget. By 1981 600 corporations were contributing 40 per cent of the budget of over $10 million per year.[34] Irving Kristol, grandfather of the neo-conservatives, takes up the story: 'AEI's views on economic policy appeal to the business community. It has been a citadel of free-market economics as the demand for AEI's kind of thinking began to expand. The business community suddenly woke up to the fact that it had enemies... Business leadership has become much more sophisticated and aggressive.'[35] The Heritage Foundation, created within a year of the Centre for Policy Studies, quickly established itself as a focal point for business activism and was operating with a budget of over $10 million by the mid 1980s.

Like the UK think tanks Heritage provided more than ideas. In Washington, according to one account from the 1980s, 'it serves as a meeting place for conservatives, with daily lectures, debates and briefings. Corporate representatives meet with government decision-makers through the Washington Policy Roundtable... A resource bank of scholars and policy experts around the nation has been compiled to provide the media and congressional hearings with conservative commentary.'[36] Like the CPS, the Heritage Foundation provided a blueprint for radical market reform. Before Reagan took up the presidency, it released its massive 'Mandate for Leadership' that was 'prepared before Reagan became the Republican nominee... Heritage later claimed that more than 60 per cent of its proposals had been adopted by the administration.'[37]

'The corporate politicization process shows business acting less as a collection of individual profit seekers and more as a class cognizant of general business interests.'[38] When Reagan became president the influence of the AEI could be seen by the fact that more than 30 AEI scholars and officials served in senior Reagan administration positions.[39] If there was a difference between the US and UK, it was in the status accorded to one member of the intellectual vanguard of the neo-liberal movement. Milton Friedman was at the first Mont Pelerin Society meeting in Switzerland and, according to Blumenthal, was the key figure 'responsible for reviving free-market ideas' in the US.

He was a one man think tank, author of numerous public policy proposals... who served both the American Enterprise Institute and the Hoover Institution... He joined Ronald Reagan and Alexander Solzhenitsyn as one of only three Honorary Fellows at the Hoover Institution; he starred in his own television series, *Free to Choose*, which with his wife, he adapted into a best selling book... In 1976 he won the Nobel Prize in Economics, thereby becoming a figure of worldwide renown and distinction. His advice has been sought by presidents and prime ministers – and even a Latin dictator.[40]

That dictator was General Augusto Pinochet of Chile, who had unleashed a murderous coup against the Allende government on 11 September 1973. Pinochet too was handed an economic blueprint, like those given to Thatcher and Reagan, by Chilean neo-liberal disciples of Friedman. They had been funded by the CIA and became the 'top advisers of the Junta'.[41] Friedman was invited to Chile by Pinochet and he went, advising on his theories of controlling the money supply. Friedman seemed unabashed at being entertained by the dictator. But in words betraying his political rather than his economic analysis he claimed that Allende 'brought the coup on himself'. 'Why should I have had qualms about going down there?' he stated. 'The military hadn't overthrown a democracy.' Except... that it had. Taken away from monetarist theory, Friedman's grasp of the difference between democracy and dictatorship was a little tenuous.

CAPITALISM IN THE ASCENDANT

The 'case for capitalism' had been made and had been put into practice. The next step was to govern in the interests of capital. This meant the wholesale abolition of the remnants of social democracy. It meant breaking trade union power in places like the UK where it was still significant, destroying manufacturing industry on the altar of the great god Money Supply, cutting back on public expenditure on welfare and transferring as much of the public sector as possible to the private sector. It also meant, crucially, putting in place the structures and taking the decisions that would free finance capital and allow the neo-liberal revolution to sweep the globe. The stage was set for the rise of the social movement for global capital. And the neo-liberal think tanks played their role in this, alongside the emerging global policy planning groups. Anthony Fisher, who had set up the IEA in 1955 went on to create the Atlas Economic Research Foundation in 1981 in order to, in the words of John Blundell of the Foundation, 'litter the world with free-market think tanks'. By 1991 Atlas claimed to have had a role in funding or advising 78 think tanks and to be on good relations with another 88. Since then the think tank explosion has not diminished. Today, Atlas is still active and lists nearly 500 free market think tanks in its online directory (though they don't claim to have been involved in creating or helping all of them).[42]

In order to complete their project the neo-liberals needed to evacuate any meaningful content that democracy might have. They say this quite openly. Ralph Harris, reflecting on the history of the Mont Pelerin Society and the subsequent founding of the Institute of Economic Affairs, spells it out: 'I now express our remaining war aim as being to deprive (misrepresentative) democracy of its unmerited halo.'[43]

6
The Real Rulers of the World

Christopher Meyer walked into the woods to relieve himself. For the British ambassador to the US, this was an extraordinary night. Meyer was impressed, perhaps overawed, by the circles in which he was mixing. The Redwoods of Northern California are not the usual place for British ambassadors to answer the call of nature, but this was not just any forest. He was among the trees of Bohemian Grove, the watering hole of the US elite. Meyer sensed others answering the call too. He looked one way and saw George H.W. Bush, the senior; he looked the other way and saw George W., the President of the US. Meyer almost died and went to heaven. He thought to himself: 'Mum, if you could see me now.'[1]

In his memoir of the period Meyer tells us how great an honour it is to be invited to the 'exclusive club' that is the Grove. Bohemian Grove is made up of self-organised 'camps', some of which have more 'lustre' than others. Meyer writes that invitations are 'highly prized', and, modesty aside, reveals that his hosts had 'access everywhere'. Meyer can barely conceal his excitement at attending a morning lecture by the notorious Henry Kissinger and climaxes at the 'epicurean dinner at which we drank jeroboams of Petrus 1962' in the company of the 'most distinguished member of my camp' – David Rockefeller.[2]

Christopher Meyer was the British ambassador to Washington during the post-9/11 period. In a previous existence he was the chief spin doctor for the Conservative Prime Minister John Major. No doubt Meyer's mother would have heard of the Bush boys and might be impressed by the toilet company he kept, but it's likely she would have been less familiar with the organisation whose gathering Meyer was attending.

Bohemian Grove is a social club for members of the ruling class in the US. It is one of the most unusual and central clubs amongst the US elite which runs a two week annual camp in its 2,700 acre Bohemian Grove just north of San Francisco. The club brings together political and business elites as well as celebrities and important outsiders, such as British ambassadors, who have been invited since at least 1947.[3] Among the events at the Grove are plays, concerts, lectures, together with shooting, canoeing, swimming and walking tours of the forest.

'The most memorable event', writes William Domhoff, the sociologist who did the first serious study of the club, 'is the opening ceremony, called the Cremation of Care. The ceremony takes place at the base of a 40 foot Owl shrine constructed out of poured concrete and made even more resplendent by the mottled forest mosses that cover most of it.' The ceremony involves the burning of an effigy named 'Dull Care' which 'symbolises the burdens and responsibilities that these busy Bohemians now wish to shed temporarily'. As Domhoff notes, the intention is 'to create a sense of cohesion and solidarity' amongst those present.[4] Successive Presidents from Hoover, through Nixon, Reagan, Bush the first, Clinton to Bush the second, have been among the attendees, often delivering off-the-record lakeside talks. Business elites are significantly represented at Bohemian Grove. In the 1970s 40 of the top 50 US corporations were represented there and participating directors were often from the 'inner circle' of corporations who also belonged to the key business lobby or policy planning groups such as the Business Council, the Conference Board, the Committee for Economic Development.[5]

Bohemian Grove is not the only US elite social club, but it is perhaps the best known and was a model for others. For example, in southern California there is the Rancheros Vistadores club (RV) set up in 1930 by 'a prototypical member of the American Upper Class', John J. Mitchell. The club for the upper classes of southern California involves a week of horse riding in May each year accompanied by rodeo, entertainment and other activities including 'great quantities of beer' and 'a whole floor' of a Santa Barbara hotel being set aside for the members of the club to visit prostitutes, bussed in specially for the week by RV members. Among the more famous members of the club were Walt Disney, who contributed cartoons of Donald Duck and Mickey Mouse sporting RV insignia, and Ronald Reagan, the former Governor of California and ex-President of the US, who was also a Bohemian Grove member.[6] Some corporations even formed their own clubs to foster cohesiveness amongst managers. General Electric, for example, ran a regular summer camp on the symbolically named 'Association Island'. The island, on Lake Ontario, was owned by GE, and was used from 1922 for camps for each of the five company divisions. 'No women were invited. The camps had the same aura that pervades college fraternities [and] exclusive men's clubs.' The camps served as a 'system of recruitment into the upper echelons of the company'. The camps were satirised by Kurt Vonnegut in *Player Piano*, based in part on his time as a PR operative for General

Electric. 'Attendance at the camps was a privilege for a select few', writes David Nye, who discovered the camps in photographs in the GE company archive. The photos were the only record he could find of what went on at the camps in apparent secrecy 'ensured in part by the adolescent and absurd nature of these activities. The camps became a sanctuary where regression to premarital male bonding was actively encouraged.'[7]

The function of Bohemian Grove and other similar retreats is pretty clear: it is to instil a sense of collective belonging in the attendees and to allow them to network and bond as a class. Bohemian Grove, along with a small number of other elite social clubs and policy planning groups is not widely known. Most of the elite clubs are shrouded in mystery and secrecy, often attempting to keep themselves out of the news. The Mont Pelerin Society, for example, consciously did not adopt a media strategy, preferring instead covert ideological war. Bohemian Grove operates to this day, as Christopher Meyer's anecdote at the beginning of this chapter testifies.

It is clear, however, that many of the other formal and informal organisations which bring together members of the ruling class perform a similar function to social clubs like Bohemian Grove. At every centre of governance there are similar networking and policy planning clubs which fulfil social as well as political and ideological functions. In Edinburgh the ruling class has the well-networked 'New Club' unobtrusively overlooking Edinburgh's main shopping thoroughfare, Princes Street. According to the New Club's website, and to journalists who have graced its premises, it has the best view in Edinburgh across Princes Street Gardens to the Castle.[8] The New Club brings together business elites and professionals with those in politics and the civil service.

The myriad of policy planning groups available for corporate executives performs similar but more directly political service. In particular, elite level corporate-wide groups function to unify interests and plan strategy.

ON CONSPIRACIES

Conspiracy: a secret plan to carry out an illegal or harmful act, esp. with political motivation; plot.[9]

As a result of secrecy, wild and sometimes conspiratorial stories about these organisations and their links abound, particularly on the internet. This or that group is the essential element of the 'Zionist World Government' or the 'Knights Templar' or world Jewish conspiracy. Such stories about alleged secret conspiracies running the world in conclave, without the knowledge of the organs of government, in effect short cut proper analysis of power structures and how they operate.

There is no single conspiracy running the world. On the contrary, the people who do run the world are engaged in many harmful activities against democracy. Although secrecy and covert operations are a central part of these plots, they can, in the end, be exposed, by virtue of investigation, yes, but most importantly by examining how any given organisation relates to others. In other words, by examining the cohesiveness with which varying elites act together, the extent to which they are networked and operating for the same ends. 'The conspiratorial view places power in the hands of only a few dozen or so people, often guided by one strong leader', notes William Domhoff, a distinguished US authority on power networks. In reality, he notes, 'there is a leadership group of many thousands for a set of wealth-owning families that numbers several million'.[10]

Most importantly, this means the structures of domination are largely visible, not hidden. The corporate boards and policy planning processes, the corporate social responsibility (CSR) ventures, the trade associations and lobby groups are all public and usually have their own websites. Yes, they plan and organise with each other, but no there is no secret conspiracy operating behind the visible front. The visible front does just what it says on the tin – it aims to run the world.

THE SOCIAL MOVEMENT FOR GLOBAL CAPITALISM

Christopher Meyer's piss in the woods illustrates the intimate relationship between UK and US elites. On one hand, the partial integration of UK elites into US ruling circles is evident in the 'war on terror' and especially in the invasion of Iraq. But it is telling that Meyer should be so impressed by his Bohemian chums. Can we imagine Paul Wolfowitz making similar comments about meeting Blair or any other British politician?

The shadow of US interests hangs heavy over British politics. The case for capitalism is sponsored not just by the corporations but by the military and political establishment in the UK and US. We saw in Chapter 3 that the rise of democracy galvanised the business and political elites to defend their interests by launching sustained propaganda campaigns and in Chapters 4 and 5 how they returned from what they regarded as the wilderness to re-establish corporate control through the neo-liberal revolution in the UK and US around 1979–80 and elsewhere across the world in the ensuing period.

But the dominance of the corporations which their victory in the battle of ideas restored was also a historical process which made the borders of nations more permeable to corporate investment decisions. This period meant that the lobbying and PR industries had to go global to grease the way of the corporations which now straddled the world. This process had to both pursue the sectional interests of corporations as they expanded globally and pursue their class-wide interests. This meant the formation of regional and eventually global business lobby groups which played an integral role in the establishment of the institutions of global governance.

Some defenders of lobbying say that its effects are not as significant as is commonly believed. Sometimes lobbying can affect policy but lobbyists are 'rarely at the centre of decision making' and 'do not really matter' unless the 'context is right'. They seldom influence 'high politics: defence, economics, foreign policy'. Their impact is 'at the margins' on low profile 'technical, non controversial issues'.[11] This kind of nonsense is spouted by lobbyists themselves and by their apologists in academia. They are careful not to downplay lobbying too much lest some client gets the idea that they can dispense with their political bag-carriers' services. In this case the author is a professional lobbyist, who wrote a doctoral thesis on lobbying. In industry seminars he is wont to discuss 'anti-globalisation protestors' as an instance of 'conventional terrorism' like the 'IRA'[12] and believes 'there are many subversive radical networks operating around the world. These webs of campaigners use every tool possible to hurt corporations and their associates with whom they disagree. This form of terrorism is no longer a remote risk.'[13] Amongst his clients at DLA Upstream was the BioIndustry Association, whose members include Huntingdon Life Sciences, the company engaged in breeding animals for experimentation.[14]

On the contrary, lobbying is at the centre of, and can make a significant difference to, decision making. This happens in two ways: first, as is commonly understood, lobbyists attempt to affect particular legislation and can be successful in different ways at this micro-level. But the most important influence lobbyists have is in constructing the political rules of the game under which corporations operate.

One line of defence the industry will use in response to this book is to suggest that the processes we are describing are not really about lobbying at all. We beg to differ. We note that according to *New York Times* journalist Jeffrey Birnbaum 'by 1990... many chief executives argued that government policy was so entwined with the well being of their companies that "lobbyist" had become an unwritten part of almost any CEO's job description'. Edmund Pratt, CEO of Pfizer, notes the transformation during the course of his own career: 'the biggest single change in the management in my forty years in the game has been the revolution of the involvement of the American business people in the government process'.[15] This is the most important way in which corporations and their lobbyists are the real rulers of the world.

Today, all over the world, business lobbyists expend resources and energy ensuring that democratic decision making is business-friendly. Deregulation has been their watchword for the last few decades. In some countries the corporate sponsorship of electoral campaigning ensures a favourable political climate for business, most clearly seen in the US. In most nation states, direct decisions on investment – the classic hidden hand of the market – afford political leverage. But business also depends upon getting its way in the arena of political and economic decision making. They must have the obeisance or at least the tolerance of government at the local, national and global level. To do this requires connections with the political class. Many organisations are created precisely to facilitate such contact. Most of these are not well known amongst the public in the West. They are better known amongst the political elite, since these are the people who are wooed and bought by them.

THE HISTORICAL SHAPING OF TRANSNATIONAL CORPORATE POWER

Elite policy planning groups have a long pedigree. One of the earliest groups – set up in 1919 – was the Royal Institute of International Affairs (RIIA) based in London and often called Chatham House, the name of the building in which the Institute is housed.[16] In the US the Council on Foreign Relations (CFR) — created in 1921 – performs a similar function. Both appear to have emerged from an organisation called the Roundtable set up to pursue a worldwide 'Anglo-Saxon brotherhood' uniting the empire into one state. This project was associated with imperial propagandist Lionel Curtis and other prominent writers, administrators and politicians.[17] Both the

RIIA and the CFR remain key establishment organisations today. For example the CFR is the central upper-class foreign policy think tank in the US. Today the RIIA, rebranded in 2004 as Chatham House, has around 2,000 individual members and more than 250 corporate members.[18]

The organisations set up in the early part of the twentieth century remain important players in national and global decision making. The process of globalisation was put in place by conscious and calculated lobbying and long term policy planning. The Mont Pelerin Society aimed to win the ideological battle and think tanks like the Centre for Policy Studies and the Adam Smith Institute (in the UK) and the Heritage Foundation and the American Enterprise Institute (in the US) aimed to put those ideas into practice. These attempts in the UK (see Chapter 4) and the US (see below) were largely successful at the national level. But this essentially opened up more of a means of implementing new business-friendly structures of global governance which suited transnational capital.

PUTTING THE ARCHITECTURE IN PLACE

As we will see, the architecture for this was put in place by means of these lobby groups. The international groupings emerged gradually over the course of the twentieth century starting in 1920. In general, they developed in line with the three waves of business activism we have noted in relation to both the US and the UK.

A key part of the system of global decision making was put in place by national planning and lobby groups. In the last chapter we saw how the 'plan to end planning' launched by the Mont Pelerin Society and its disciples in the UK like the IEA, the CPS and the ASI, opened the way for the rise of Thatcher and led to concrete reforms which helped the new global system to emerge. Similar processes occurred in the US where the third wave of business activism followed a similar and almost precisely timed course to the UK.

EUROPE: A COMMON MARKET?

As the political, economic and regulatory power of the emerging European Union increased, bodies representing European transnational corporations were founded, and these also coordinated between US and European business. These have been instrumental in putting in place the European dimensions of the global system.

In the UK the predominant view of European institutions offered by the mainstream media is one of a faceless technocracy making incomprehensible and bureaucratic decisions. Sometimes these are seen as direct attempts to undermine British sovereignty and to impose a kind of Euro federal socialist system of overweening regulation. This version of events is widely believed. On the centre left there is a different – though equally misguided – view which sees Europe as a valuable bulwark against either US imperialism or unrestrained US-style capitalism or both.[19]

The reality is very different. In fact the EU has been following the agenda of international institutions and global lobby groups seeking neo-liberal restructuring. As in the UK and US, this had to be put in place by concerted lobbying and co-option of governmental authorities. Among the main bodies driving this agenda have been UNICE (recently renamed Business Europe, the Confederation of European Business), AmCham EU, the Brussels chapter of the American Chamber of Commerce, but most spectacularly the European Round Table of Industrialists (ERT) and the TransAtlantic Business Dialogue (TABD).[20]

The ERT is an elite CEO club. Membership is by invitation only and it is made up of 45 CEOs. It was founded in 1983 and has been an extraordinarily successful lobbyist since. It focuses only on the big picture, particularly the architecture of governance for the EU, including the single currency, enlargement, the strengthening of the EU decision making apparatus and removing national vetoes. The ERT was an early and insistent advocate of the Single European Act in 1986 and was extremely active in the negotiation of the Maastricht treaty, from which it got its desired outcome in the project of the single currency. The ERT policy on competitiveness had 'de facto become the main goal of EU policy' by 1989.[21] In 2000 it was formally codified as such and issued as the declaration of the Lisbon Summit of the member states.

The TABD was set up in 1995 at the joint initiative of the European Commission[22] and the US Department of Commerce, though the ERT was also reported as being behind it. The TABD is made up of some of the biggest EU and US firms. According to Sir Leon Brittan the result of the Chicago conference of the TABD 'was dramatic. European and American business leaders united in demanding more and faster trade liberalisation. And that had an immediate impact.'[23] In the case of the EU it is absolutely clear that the agenda driving trade and competition policy is almost identical to that of the corporations. The influence of the ERT and TABD isn't hidden by policy players: it is openly admitted, even boasted of. The EU is at the heart of the success of business lobbyists aiming to transform the global system in their own interests. For example, the European Commission understands and accepts that international trade rules such as the General Agreement on Trade in Services (GATS) are geared towards serving the interests of transnational corporations. 'The GATS is not just something that exists between Governments. It is first and foremost an instrument for the benefit of business.'[24]

David Hartridge, a WTO official, described clearly how corporate interests dominate GATS. Corporate lobbying was decisive in creating GATS, one of the so-called Marrakesh agreements, concluded at the end of the GATT Uruguay round in 1994.[25] According to Hartridge, former director of the WTO Services Division:

Without the enormous pressure generated by the American financial services sector, particularly companies like American Express and Citicorp, there would have been no services agreement.[26]

VIVA FREE TRADE! THE BIRTH OF NAFTA

Meanwhile on the other side of the Atlantic the North American Free Trade Agreement (NAFTA) was formed in 1994. It was and is an important part of the emerging architecture of the globalised economy and a project of big business and convinced neo-liberals. The story of the creation of NAFTA is a salutary lesson in the power of big business to influence public policy, and its relentless pursuit of cheap labour and lax regulation. Lobbyists and spin doctors were, of course, key players in this drama.

According to some accounts, the idea for NAFTA came to Mexican President Carlos Salinas while attending the World Economic Forum in 1990. Having had his eyes opened to the future of liberalised trade by the globalisers gathered at the Swiss resort of Davos, Salinas couldn't sleep. In his nightgown he visited the room of his Secretary of Commerce and suggested entering a free trade agreement with the US. An approach was made to the American trade negotiator the next day, and the diplomatic ball was quickly rolling for the creation of NAFTA, which would also bring in Canada, to create the world's largest free trading bloc.[27]

Corporations in the US were quick to seize the opportunity that a free trade deal with Mexico offered; principally cheap labour, weak environmental regulation and a host of investment rights and protections that significantly boosted corporate interests. However, the political battle to sell the idea of NAFTA to the American political class and public required a propaganda effort that 'dwarfed' the then recent PR campaign to sell the first Gulf War.[28] A notable element of the spinning of NAFTA was to present it as a trade deal, whereas it was in effect 'an investment agreement designed to protect American corporations in Mexico, lock in the low wage rate, and raise cash for a nervous political oligarchy'.[29]

The lobbying to secure NAFTA intensified after the election of Bill Clinton as president in 1992. The corporations backing NAFTA feared that Clinton was not committed to securing the deal and quickly decided they 'had to change that'. To do so, a select group of some three dozen influencers met in September 1993 under the auspices of the Business Roundtable front group USA*NAFTA, to plan the strategy and campaign to revive NAFTA. This gathering was no ordinary lobbyists' get-together. Rather, it involved

the elite of the influence salesman who stick around the nation's capital year after year, Congress after Congress, administration after administration – a group of people so self-confident and secure in their access to political power that, unlike many other Washington players, they actually strive to keep their names out of the paper... to assemble them in the same room to hear the same message was itself a lobbying coup.[30]

One of the organisers of this meeting described it more straight-forwardly: 'We basically went to [the Business Roundtable] companies and said "Tell your consultants to either show up, or they're screwed". We had literally millions of dollars worth of lobbying talent in a single room... the best of the best... the ones that have the biggest retainers from the biggest companies.'[31] The outcome of this meeting was that these lobbyists committed themselves to using their networks and contacts, built over careers of lobbying, fixing and expensive political donations and fundraising, to spread pro-NAFTA sentiment throughout Washington – to sell NAFTA to the politicians. With Washington's 'life-support system' pushing this message it wasn't long before elite opinion shifted decisively in favour of NAFTA.

There was also the problem of selling NAFTA to the public. USA*NAFTA brought in Lee Iacocca, the former Chief Executive of Chrysler and a popular icon of American business, to sell the message. The media strategy was direct: 'Lee Iacocca offers pro-NAFTA forces an articulate, successful, highly-regarded and well-known leader as spokesperson. Mr. Iacocca's high profile position will enable USA*NAFTA to utilize him extensively and effectively in the "free media."'[32] Iacocca would be used as a celebrity endorser of the NAFTA message in the advertorials and opinion columns produced by PR consultants and then dressed up as independent news and comment. With both the Business Roundtable and the White House promoting Iacocca as a NATFA apostle for the masses, sharing opinion poll data and intelligence, coordinating political strategy and 'the incalculable man-hours at tax-payers' expense devoted by the White House to helping the Business Roundtable with its propaganda', the seamless joining of politics and business in pursuit of neo-liberal policy was complete.[33] As one insider described it: 'you could feel the power of corporate America getting behind this thing... You could feel... the corporate industrial might of this country in terms of its influence. I mean, there wasn't a god-damned editorial page in the country that I remember was against this.'[34] And so, after an intense lobbying and propaganda campaign, NAFTA was signed into law and took effect on 1 January 1994. Since then, it has been credited with undermining democracy by taking decisions on regulatory powers away from elected representatives and giving them to the corporations and their lawyers, failing to deliver jobs and economic growth, increasing income inequality, and facilitating the take-over of food production by agri-business.[35]

GLOBAL ELITE PLANNING

Understanding how global capital exercises power and influence requires an appreciation of the role of transnational business lobbies and policy planning groups. The most significant of these are the International Chamber of Commerce, the Bilderberg Group, the World Economic Forum and the Trilateral Commission. All four are run by and for the biggest transnational corporations and often directly by their CEOs or other board members.

Two of these groups, the Trilateral Commission and the Bilderberg Group, are shrouded in mystery and are a conspiracy theorist's dream. But these are neither fictions nor are they entirely secret.[36] The Bilderberg Group was reported in the *New York Times* as early as 1957 and in 1964 it issued a press statement at the conclusion of its meeting.[37] Both are policy planning, networking and coordinating groups which operate at the transnational level.

INTERNATIONAL CHAMBER OF COMMERCE (1920)

The International Chamber of Commerce (ICC) was formed during the first phase of business political activism in 1920. Although headquartered in Paris, the main impetus for its foundation came from 'the experience of the business men of the United States in building up their great National Chamber of Commerce'.[38] At that time the ICC's membership was made up of national associations of business, rather than direct company membership. The ICC was one of the earliest lobby groups to campaign to harmonise rules for business internationally. Among the 21 resolutions unanimously adopted at the 1921 London congress of the ICC were opposition to 'double taxation' on international trade, 'removal of obstacles to commerce' and cooperation on standardisation, urging the principle of 'free export', moderation in tarriffs and 'international protection of industrial property, including trade marks'. Improvement of transport was urged (including the construction of a 'channel tunnel').[39]

Today the ICC is at the forefront of corporate lobbying against regulation. It is the largest international lobby group representing pure corporate interests – as opposed to being a civil society body or a policy planning forum like the others noted below. It has some 7,000 members from over 130 countries.

The ICC has a record of 'massive lobby offensives' to influence the World Trade Organisation. But ICC starts from a basis of having the 'closest links to the WTO secretariat' and in terms of the interchange of personnel between GATT/WTO, the corporations and the ICC. The Director General of GATT during the Uruguay round which led to the creation of the WTO was Arthur Dunkel, who later became a WTO dispute panellist, a board member at Nestlé and the Chair of the ICC working group on International Trade and Investment, in which role he heads the ICC lobbying of the WTO.[40] These close connections are replicated time and again, as can be seen in the case of one of the most networked members of the elite, Peter Sutherland.

PETER SUTHERLAND: THE LINKER'S LINKER

Peter Sutherland, a portly man in his early sixties (born 1946), doesn't look like much of a mover and shaker on first sight. Yet he is truly one of the global elite. His CV includes many different stints in leading corporate and governmental positions, all taking him closer and closer to the apex of power and influence. Currently Sutherland is the chairman of BP and of Goldman Sachs International (1995 – current). His other corporate positions include board membership at Telefonaktiebolaget LM Ericsson, Investor AB, ABB and the Royal Bank of Scotland (2001–06).

Sutherland's ascent up the corporate ladder began after he abandoned his career in law for the heady mix of big business and high politics. Although he was appointed Attorney General in Ireland by then Taoiseach Garret FitzGerald, he has never actually been elected to any public body or public office. Yet, he is one of the most influential global political figures in the last 30 years. One little known detail of his career is that in 1973 Sutherland stood for election to the Irish parliament (Dáil) in the constituency of Dublin North West for the centre-right Fine Gael. He received 6.24 per cent of the 'popular' vote, and came tenth in a field of ten.[41] The only way was up!

He was appointed Attorney General in Ireland in 1981 and then reappointed in 1982–84, at which point he was the Irish nominee to the European Commission, where he took on various Commission posts including responsibility for competition policy, pushing corporate interests and making him an obvious candidate for work on corporate boards when he left the Commission. In 1988, he was the first EC Commissioner to be awarded the Gold Medal of the European Parliament, and was tipped to succeed Jacques Delors as President of the European Commission. He returned to the commercial world in 1989 as chairman of Allied Irish Bank and the next year was appointed to the board of BP (1990–93). Following this stint in the corporate world he moved on to become the Director General of GATT in July 1993 where he is said to have been 'instrumental in concluding' the Uruguay round helping to open up markets and then doing the same (from 1 January 1995 until the end of April 1995) when he became the founding Director General of the World Trade Organisation, to the advantage of transnational corporations such as... BP. At which point, in 1995, BP reappointed him to the board (becoming chair in 1997) and he became the chairman of Goldman Sachs International.

His current roles mark him out as an extraordinarily influential figure, having key roles in all the major transnational lobby groups. He is on the steering committee of the Bilderberg Group, the European chairman of the Trilateral Commission ('re-elected' in 2003 for a second term), Foundation Board Member of the World

Economic Forum and a member of the European Round Table of Industrialists.

All of these bodies are central to the global power elite, but Sutherland also dips in to the world of the think tank and the lobby group, having roles as President of the Trustees at the Federal Trust, a think tank pushing federalism and market liberalism and positively stuffed with Atlanticist operatives; President of the Advisory Council at the Brussels based and corporate funded European Policy Centre; chair of the board of governors at the European Institute of Public Administration in Maastricht (1991–96). He is also on the board of the intelligence-connected Centre for European Reform (CER), which is a lobby group closely associated with the American Enterprise Institute and particularly the (NATO funded) Atlantic Council of the United Kingdom. The CER is part of the Stockholm Network of neo-liberal think tanks. Sutherland is also well connected in the US elite, a director of the US based Atlanticist think tank, the European Institute (USA) along with a host of other neo-liberal ideologues including former European Commissioners Jacques Delors and Etienne Davignon. He is also on the advisory board of the elite Council on Foreign Relations.

Sutherland is an Honorary President of the European Movement Ireland and in 2005, he was given a role as a Goodwill Ambassador for the United Nations Industrial Development Organisation. A year later he scooped another UN position as the Secretary-General's special representative on migration. One wonders how he manages to fit it all in, but there's more. Sutherland also has the following affiliations: member of the Chief Executive's Council of International Advisers, Hong Kong; and chairman of the Consultative Board of the Director General of the World Trade Organisation.

Sutherland is such an important figure that people appear to be falling over each other to offer him awards. As well as a host of honorary academic degrees and recently being appointed chair of the council of the London School of Economics, he has received the Grand Cross of Civil Merit (Spain 1989), the Grand Cross of King Leopold II (Belgium 1989), the New Zealand Commemorative Medal (1990), Chevalier de la Legion d'Honneur (France 1993), Commandeur du Wissam (Morocco 1994), the Order of Rio Branco (Brazil 1996) and the Grand Cross of the Order of Infante Dom Henrique (Portugal 1998). He also received the David Rockefeller International Leadership Award (1998), and eventually picked up a British gong in 2004.

This remarkable CV testifies to Sutherland's political importance and influence. The connections across the transnational business and political classes are astounding. No public has ever elected Peter Sutherland, yet he has had a far greater political impact in the past two decades than almost all the democratically elected leaders in the world (save perhaps presidents of the United States, and some leaders in the G8 nations).[42]

BILDERBERG (1957)

The Bilderberg Group is one of the most secretive elite policy planning assemblies. It held its founding meeting in 1952 at the Bilderberg Hotel in Oosterbeek in the Netherlands, funded by both the CIA and the Dutch/British corporation Unilever. Bilderberg as a group has a more liberal history, being not simply a lobby group for global capital, but a policy planning and discussion group which also included political elites and even key representatives of organised labour (though union representation has declined in recent years).[43] Nevertheless it has been a venue for the exercise of soft power by most of the largest global corporations including British American Tobacco, BP, Shell, Exxon, IBM, Rio Tinto, General Motors and others.[44]

Bilderberg is neither a prototypical world government nor an incidental discussion forum. Because of its more consensual approach Bilderberg has managed to foster elite consensus. When consensus is reached the participants have 'at their disposal powerful transnational and national instruments for bringing about' their decisions.[45] Indeed their meetings have 'helped to ensure that consensual policies were adopted by the transnational system of the West'. However, in recent years the group's strategy has increasingly aligned with neo-liberal reform agendas.[46]

At the centre of the Bilderberg Group are the key networkers, many of whom are also active in the other global networks discussed here. Etienne Davignon, for example, was on the steering group in 1997. A former European Commission vice-chair, Davignon has also been linked to the Trilateral Commission and through a directorship of Société Générale de Belgique to the ERT. In fact Davignon was present at the inaugural ERT meeting when he was an EU commissioner. Davignon has also been a director of BASF, Fina and Fortis, all politically active TNCs.

A former delegate at Bilderberg conferences notes how these get-togethers relate to the other elite networking venues and events:

Bilderberg is part of a global conversation that takes place each year at a string of conferences, and it does form the backdrop to policies that emerge later. There's the World Economic Forum at Davos in February, the Bilderberg and G8 meetings in April/May, and the IMF/World Bank annual conference in September. A kind of international consensus emerges and is carried over from one meeting to the next... This consensus becomes the background for G8 economic communiques; it becomes what informs the IMF when it imposes an adjustment programme on Indonesia; and it becomes what the president proposes to Congress.[47]

Denis Healey, former deputy leader of the Labour Party, writes in his memoirs how Bilderberg conferences were the most valuable of all the events that rising politicians on the moderate left were invited to (surpassing the CIA funded Congress for Cultural Freedom).[48] The level of debate and the quality of the informal contacts made at Bilberberg were useful throughout a political career. It is a rarity for Bilderbergers to allow themselves to be quoted on the record about the organisation, but Healey noted that:

We make a point of getting along younger politicians who are obviously rising, to bring them together with financiers and industrialists who offer them wise words. It increases the chance of having a sensible global policy.[49]

Another Bilderberg steering committee member revealed that those invited to the conferences are expected to 'sing for their supper'. In 1975 Margaret Thatcher was embarrassed when this was pointed out to her over dinner. The next day 'she suddenly stood up and launched into a three minute Thatcher special... the room was stunned... as a result of that speech David Rockefeller and Henry Kissinger and the other Americans fell in love with her. They brought her over to America, took her around in limousines, and introduced her to everyone.'[50]

   The key difference between Bilderberg and the ICC is in the range of non-business invitees. These are generally globalising bureaucrats, politicians and sometimes those in NGOs and trade unions who can either be relied upon to agree or have potential for co-option into the neo-liberal agenda. No-one imagines that Peter Mandelson is anything other than entirely signed up to the Bilderberg agenda. The presence of others with a past involvement in radical politics is, though, an indication that these are people that the corporations can, literally and metaphorically, do business with. Thus former Green Party activist Jonathon Porritt has attended.

JONATHON PORRITT

Old Etonian Porritt was a Green Party activist, but now he has also been recruited to many of the elite networks which the corporations use to co-opt their critics. Porritt is on the UK government's Sustainable Development Commission and is an adviser to Prince Charles's pet sustainability project, the International Business Leaders Forum. He founded Forum for the Future which is a corporate funded environmental consultancy.[51]

He also has links with the Green Alliance, a business sponsored organisation which presents itself as an NGO in the environmental movement. A recent publication on the PR industry was endorsed by Porritt, and the director of Greenpeace, as well as by BP, the CBI, the ICC and two other elite networkers.[52] These were John Elkington of SustainAbility, a corporate environmental guru, and Will Hutton, an attendee at Bilderberg and Davos, former editor of the *Observer* and now director of the Work Foundation (formerly the Industrial Society).

In 2005 Porritt published *Capitalism: As if the World Matters*.[53] The *Observer* noted his claim that capitalism is 'the only real economic game in town'. The book also attacks the Green Party, of which he was a founding member, accusing them of being 'too narrow, too technical, too anti-business, too depressing, often too dowdy' and of having 'alienated politicians and the public'.[54]

Porritt, in other words, has been incorporated as a useful resource for corporate propaganda.

WORLD ECONOMIC FORUM (1971)

The World Economic Forum (WEF) was set up in 1971 and meets annually at Davos in Switzerland. The Davos event is much less secretive than the Bilderberg meeting and much larger. The WEF announces that it includes '1,000 top business leaders, 250 political leaders, 250 foremost academic experts from every domain and some 250 media leaders come together to shape the global agenda'.[55] The meeting aims to create a 'unique atmosphere' which facilitates 'literally thousands of private discussions'. According to long time Trilateral Commission participant and academic Samuel Huntington, 'Davos people control virtually all international institutions, many of the world's governments and the bulk of the world's economic and military capabilities.'[56]

The WEF claims credit for launching the Uruguay round of GATT which culminated in the creation of the WTO, the most recent institution to join the International Monetary Fund (IMF) and World Bank as the institutions of global economic governance. Since 1999 growing numbers of protestors have turned up only to be repelled by Swiss riot police. In recent years the number of celebrities making an entrance as part of their 'goodwill' missions or to lobby the powerful has increased. In 2006 Davos played host to Angelina Jolie, the film star. Also present was the ubiquitous Bono of U2.

TRILATERAL COMMISSION (1973)

The Trilateral Commission was launched in 1973 by an informal transnational planning body of 'unprecedented standing and organisational and ideological sophistication' by members of the Bilderberg Group, including David Rockefeller and Zbigniew Brzezinski.[57]

A first common task was demarcated, the dismantling of the democratic welfare states, which were judged to enhance the structural power of the working class, and thus to be incompatible with the long term aims of capitalism.[58]

This message has been at the centre of its pronouncements since 1973. In 1999 for example it recommended that: 'Europe must become more competitive by deregulating labour markets and streamlining burdensome welfare systems.'[59] This has been the strategy of the European Commission and the neoliberal governments of Europe since then. Leading on this agenda has been the UK along with Spain (under Aznar) and Italy (under Berlusconi). Latterly, from 2005, German Chancellor Angela Merkel joined the club of enthusiastic liberalisers and deregulators. The EU strategy is expressed in the Lisbon Agenda issued at the conclusion of the EU intergovernmental summit in 2001. The strategic goal set by the Lisbon Summit was for the EU 'to become the most competitive and dynamic knowledge-based economy in the world capable of sustainable economic growth with more and better jobs and greater social cohesion'.[60]

CORPORATIONS ON THE RETREAT: THE SHOCK OF SEATTLE

Transnational corporations have thus been extremely successful in putting into place the new machinery of regulation and government to suit their own interests. But this does not mean they can simply do whatever they want. Nothing illustrates this better than the event which triggered the explosion of the global justice movement into public consciousness in the West: the 'Battle of Seattle'. Along with the defeat of the Multilateral Agreement on Investment – another victory for the movement – Seattle caused panic amongst corporate lobbyists who were unused to being challenged and beaten. After Seattle one of the biggest lobbying and PR firms in the world BKSH (owned by one of the most ethically dubious PR firms Burson-Marsteller, itself in turn owned by conglomerate WPP) produced a hastily put together guide to the 'anti-globalisation' movement. The document was promptly leaked to those it attempted to profile and catalogue.

The spectacle created in Seattle during the WTO Ministerial meeting by a diverse collection of activists may have significant short-term ramifications for the business community. The perceived success of these groups in disrupting Seattle and in contributing to the failure of the WTO meeting will be a dramatic boon to them in several ways. First, their victory and heightened visibility will lead to substantially enhanced fundraising capability. Second, the smell of victory will lead to a deepening of already existing coalitions and will strengthen the recognition that broadening such coalitions to include non-traditional allies exponentially increases effectiveness. Third, the Presidential election campaign and several likely trade votes in Congress this year will give activists golden opportunities to seek wider recognition and gain additional strength. These high profile battles will allow activists to further institutionalize and consolidate their gains, increase coordination, garner greater media attention and expand their targeting of business interests.

    What is less understood – but perhaps more significant – is the potential ability of the emerging coalition of these groups to seriously impact broader, longer-term corporate interests. Seattle was not an anomaly and the consistent anti-corporate message of virtually all the groups who participated there in November is not a temporary phenomenon. Many have traditionally highlighted alleged corporate misconduct in mass mail fund raising campaigns. More recently, some environmental groups have resorted to targeting corporations for contributions in return for suspending their public ire.[61]

One interesting thing about this guide is how ill-informed the lobbyists are about the organisations involved. Incredibly, one of the organisations profiled is the International Congress of Free Trade Unions (ICFTU) headed by Bill Jordan. The ICFTU is a well known Cold War construct set up with the help of the intelligence services to counteract left influence in the trade unions.[62] Bill Jordan is former head of the right wing electricians' union, the AEEU, and has been involved with anti-communist organisations linked to the US Embassy in London, such as the Trade Union Committee for European and Transatlantic Understanding (TUCETU).[63]

Burson-Marsteller might be familiar with the moderate NGOs and even those activist groups which have targeted particular industries or products, but they had absolutely no sense of the breadth and depth of the movement, beyond acknowledging that there were a lot of them.

THE RELIEF OF 9/11

Under challenge from this movement the denizens of PR moved quickly to try to neutralise it. Suddenly PR conferences around the world were stuffed with sessions on how to deal with NGOs. We attended lots of these sessions in San Francisco, Atlanta, London, Brussels, Perth, Cairo and elsewhere in 2000–03. Immediately after 9/11 the response of the business classes was that the movement was finished.

To be fair this analysis did detect a hesitancy on the part of the anti-globalisation movement. Greenpeace suspended its Boycott Esso campaign and instructed its activists to observe a moratorium on attacks on US policy.

But the swift military action against Afghanistan in the absence of any due process for isolating Bin Laden, started to turn the movement around. It was evident that global public opinion was opposed to the attacks on Afghanistan and it was from the seeds of this that the 'alter-globalisation movement' merged with the nascent anti-war movement. The inaugural European Social Forum in Genoa in 2002 called for the worldwide demonstrations against the Iraq war on 15 February 2003 which saw not just the largest demonstrations in British history but also the largest political demonstration in human history.

The new-found confidence of the neo-liberal vulgate was quickly undermined and they went from defeat to defeat – in Iraq, at Cancun, with the 'Non' vote in the Dutch and French referenda on the EU constitution. Nevertheless, they did make some progress in isolating and containing the movement as was seen at the G8 summit in Gleneagles in 2005 or St Petersburg in 2006.

This chapter has shown that lobbying by big business has had staggering effects on putting in place an architecture of global governance which is almost entirely in the interests of the corporations.

Corporate lobbying has been instrumental in the business fight-back from the 1970s onwards and, from the 1980s, crucial in the imposition of the enabling structures of global governance. The examples touched upon in this chapter alone include NAFTA, the Single European Act, European Monetary Union, the conclusion of the GATT Uruguay round and the creation of the WTO, the formation of the GATS and the de facto control of EC competitiveness policy and trade liberalisation. All of this has undermined and more or less abolished the possibility that formal democratic participation can have any significant effect.

The global lobbyists continue to try to impose their vision and progressively to abolish barriers to profit in the form of public health, environmental protection and workers' rights protections. They have not had it all their own way. The 'Battle of Seattle' derailed their efforts and signalled the possibility of resistance. This was followed by fierce campaigning which blocked the Multilateral Agreement on Investment (MAI) and continues in the protracted negotiations for the Doha round of trade talks. It is important to recognise that the campaign to address corporate power must be, and increasingly is, waged at a global level. Therefore, amid the catalogue of corporate victories and the examples of corporate power we have outlined so far, it is worth remembering that the emergence of the global justice movement, encompassing the trade, human rights, anti-war and environmental movements, has been an important development that evidences the strength and durability of the democratic impulse.

7
The Global PR Industry

Defend capitalism or the PR industry dies.
Margaret Thatcher's former press secretary Sir Bernard Ingham[1]

Global capitalism needs global PR. The rise of corporate power and then its spread across the globe was paralleled by, indeed put in place via, the rise of propaganda and the PR industry. As Leslie Sklair has noted, 'global capitalism needs to be politically active to sustain its project'.[2] That political activity includes the myriad endeavours of the PR and lobbying industries. The globalisation of PR is an intrinsic part of the process of corporate globalisation. Global PR and communications firms now operate in every continent defending and extending corporate power. This chapter traces the development of that global industry.

Since the early days of public relations, there have been numerous examples of PR agencies working for international clients. The relationship between Ivy Lee and Nazi Germany is only one among many such contracts. Corporations with international operations have also long used PR around the globe. Sir Edward Edgar was a 'share-booster' and public relations man for Shell in Venezuela as far back as 1919.[3] Since the emergence of the PR industry at the start of the twentieth century the scope and scale of corporate public relations have become increasingly international. There are reasons for this pattern of development which help explain how the world of politics and big business looks today.

The architecture of global governance put in place by big business lobbying both required, and gave a huge boost to, the globalisation of public relations practice and bequeathed a truly global PR industry. The general impression, even amongst informed observers, is that the PR industry is a collection of small to medium sized firms, which is thus not very important economically and perhaps marginal politically. Such a perception would be entirely wrong.

In fact the PR industry is increasingly concentrated and includes not just PR and lobbying firms, but the whole range of communication services including marketing, advertising, events, sponsorship, financial communications, online and increasingly, news and entertainment organisations too. The degree of concentration has been such that most significant PR and lobbying agencies are now actually owned by a very small group of transnational communication conglomerates.

We only have to look at some of the better known examples of PR and lobbying controversies and follow the chain of ownership to recognise the striking concentration in this business. Perhaps the best known spin doctor during the 1980s and 1990s in the UK was Tim Bell. His career in PR began when he helped found Saatchi & Saatchi in 1970, managing to marry self promotion and client promotion. Bell later became a loyal adviser to Margaret Thatcher, playing a key role in the election campaigns for the Tory Party throughout the 1980s and still regularly appearing in the media to defend her legacy.[4] Bell received a knighthood in 1990 and was later made a life peer by Tony Blair. He is the only corporate spin doctor in Britain to have a biography published on his life and high times, and he also set up Chime Communications, which is the holding company for some of the biggest PR firms in the UK (including Bell Pottinger and Good Relations).[5] His biography details less celebrated aspects of Bell's life, including his cocaine habit and his conviction for indecent exposure.[6] Bell's company is linked to the second biggest communication conglomerate in the world, WPP, which owns 21.8 per cent of Chime shares.[7] WPP is run by Sir Martin Sorrell, also a former Saatchi's director.

Hill & Knowlton is one of the most famous, if not infamous, PR firms in the world. It has 71 offices in 40 different countries[8] and has worked for a range of unsavoury clients. One of H&K's most famous accounts was its work for 'Citizens for a Free Kuwait' – which was a front for the Kuwaiti royal family. H&K masterminded the testimony from a 15-year-old star witness 'Nayirah' – her surname was not given – at a hearing of the Congressional Human Rights Caucus in October 1990.[9] Nayirah allegedly witnessed Iraqi soldiers taking 312 babies from incubators and leaving them to die on the floor. It was later revealed that she was the daughter of the Kuwaiti Ambassador to the US and that her story had been a complete fabrication. When H&K were challenged about this story, the leading global communications consultancy became rather uncommunicative: 'The company has nothing to say on this matter.' When asked if such a deception would be considered part of the public relations business they said: 'Please know again that this falls into the realm that the agency has no wish to confirm, deny or comment on.'[10] Hill & Knowlton is also owned by WPP.

Burson-Marsteller is another global PR firm which rivals Hill & Knowlton for scope, income and clients. As outlined in Chapter 2, B-M has worked for a long list of unpleasant regimes and companies needing help with their poor image. Burson-Marsteller, like Hill & Knowlton, is owned by WPP. WPP is a communications behemoth, with over 92,000 staff in more than 2,000 offices across 106 countries.[11] Within the WPP group there are 16 different PR companies.

As the rest of the world watched transfixed as the World Trade Center came crashing down on 11 September 2001, Labour Special Adviser Jo Moore sent her infamous email stating 'it's now a very good day to get out anything we want to bury'. She was later sacked as a result.[12] Less well known is that Moore was a former lobbyist for a London based firm called Westminster Strategy. This company is but one of a group of New Labour oriented lobby shops. Westminster strategy subsequently changed its name to Grayling and is now owned by Huntsworth, the communications conglomerate headed by Peter Gummer, the former Conservative Party Treasurer.

Also in the Huntsworth stable is the firm Citigate Dewe Rogerson. In the 1980s (then known as Dewe Rogerson) this firm, which specialises in financial PR and communicating with analysts and investors in the City, was one of the chief beneficiaries of the wave of privatisations inspired by the Mont Pelerin Society's disciples and put into practice by the Thatcher administration. The expertise developed by those promoting privatisation in the UK would later be exported around the globe. This was made possible because state companies, nationalised industries and public services were opened up to competition as the doctrines of neo-liberalism were enforced through global trade negotiations. Again, the circularity of the process is evident, because those lobbying for and promoting such changes are the very same direct beneficiaries of the policies.

The sequence runs something like this: business demands the rolling back of big government, a reduction in bureaucracy, and for market disciplines across all sectors of society. This is done in the name of modernisation, efficiency and progress, so all can share in the benefits of market capitalism, namely freedom and choice. Lobbyists and PRs help business to make these demands, they craft the messages and target the audiences. Governments have tended to heed such lobbying over the last 20 years, and so states have actively divested many of their key assets. These privatisations have to be sold to investors and the markets. PR steps in to facilitate this process, again, for a fee. Given the expert knowledge developed in this kind of work the PR and public affairs advisers are well positioned to represent these newly privatised companies to their publics (now customers of course, not citizens) and to regulators. They may also be on hand to advise on other matters, such as mergers, acquisitions, refinancing – the kind of lucrative work that would never be available under a public system of ownership. And, happily for UK companies like Dewe Rogerson, they were at the vanguard of this process.[13] The UK led the way on privatisation, but many others have since followed, helped along by the public relations industry that actively promoted these policies in the first place.

Firms like Burson-Marsteller, H&K, Weber Shandwick, Golin Harris, Fleishman-Hillard, Ketchum, Edelman, Ogilvy and MS&L are the global players in the PR industry and we will return to examine them later in this chapter. For now we turn to the process by which PR grew in the UK and spread globally.

THE RISE OF THE BRITISH PR INDUSTRY

The PR industry was not always so important. The decisive shift in British politics (and adopted around the world in the succeeding decades) came as a result of the neo-liberal revolution in US and UK politics. The emergence and growth of public relations in Britain is attributable to a number of factors, not least the end of the post-war consensus based on a compromise between organised labour and capital. This did secure real and significant advances for ordinary working people in the shape of the NHS, the welfare state, universal education, public ownership of key utilities. The consensus allowed some amelioration of inequality in wealth in the UK, but with the rise of the New Right in the 1970s British politics entered an era of more competitive politics, driven by a vision of a smaller state and freer markets. Old corporatist customs and assumptions were displaced by a 'tilt to the market' in government policy.[14] The election of the first Thatcher government in 1979 had profound effects, which were felt keenly in industrial relations. The philosophy of letting the markets free while rolling back the state meant that government would no longer mediate between capital and labour. The result was that 'propaganda would become an essential weapon against industrial muscle'.[15] Communication strategies were adjusted within the nationalised industries as management began to communicate directly with employees rather than allowing the unions to channel information to workers.[16] Michael Edwardes, chief executive and chair of British Leyland, implemented this new style of communication in 1977 in order to drive through major restructuring in the firm, which would result in the loss of nearly half the company's jobs before 1982. His increased use of the media 'proved that the chairman of a state owned industry could use newspapers, radio and television to help secure fundamental change. He showed how management could exploit the news media to the employer's advantage.'[17]

The Thatcherite remaking of British society involved the selling off of national assets. PR played an important role in bringing nationalised industries to market. Inside the major companies to be privatised there was a significant build up of PR capacity to prepare for flotation on the stock market.[18] Allied with this were the promotional efforts of hired consultants like Dewe Rogerson, Lowe Bell, Financial Dynamics and Shandwick. As business boomed there was a clear reshaping of the PR sector in the UK, marked by a succession of mergers and acquisitions, from which emerged a number of large PR agencies able to become players on a global scale.

There has been a continued expansion in PR business over the last 40 years. In 1967 the first edition of PR trade directory Hollis listed 46 PR firms. By 1993 there were 1,300 and one official estimate put the total number of consultancies in 1994 at 2,230.[19] Jeremy Tunstall suggests that in 1963 there were 'perhaps' 3,000 PR people in Britain.[20] By 1986 there were 3,318 people employed in the top 114 PR consultancies alone (i.e. not including PR employees in smaller consultancies, local and central government, in corporations and in trade unions and NGOs). *PR Week*, the trade magazine for the spin industry in the UK, produces an annual ranking of the top 150 PR agencies in Britain. In 1998 this snapshot revealed there were 6,578 employees in these consultancies.[21] By 2005 the *PR Week* survey counted 7,606 people working in the top 150 PR agencies in Britain.[22]

The 1980s appear to have been a key moment for the growth of PR in the UK. Almost half of the members of the Public Relations Consultants Association (PRCA) in 1990 came into existence in the 1980s. Nearly as many PRCA consultancies were formed in the 1980s as in the 1960s and 1970s put together.[23] Consultancy income also increased markedly in this period. Analysis of industry and trade press estimates shows that PR fee income increased rapidly between 1984 and 1987 and further expanded in the 1989–90 period. Fee income rose in real terms by 30 per cent, 35 per cent and 40 per cent in 1984–87 respectively, boosted by the growth in the UK stock market and the increasing volume of government business. Fee income again increased by a further 32 per cent between the years 1989 and 1990. After 1990 the party came to a shuddering halt. The PR industry experienced a sharp decline as the recession (and a lack of government privatisation contracts) took its toll. Between 1990 and 1992 the fee income of the top 150 consultancies was almost halved and staffing levels fell by a fifth. But overall, the available data on the fee income of the biggest consultancies shows that the PR sector expanded eleven-fold in real terms between the end of the 1970s and the end of the 1990s, with fee income of the top 150 just less than £450 million in 1998.[24]

In 2005 the profile of Britain's PR industry is one of continued growth. It is still second only to the US in terms of size, fees and employees. *PR Week* data indicates that fee incomes for commercial PR consultants are still increasing, with the leading 150 agencies now generating a fee income of some £654 million.[25] The vast majority of this work is undertaken on behalf of corporate clients, but commercial consultancy represents perhaps as little as one fifth of the UK market. A survey published by the Chartered Institute of Public Relations (CIPR) in 2005 produced a 'conservative estimate' of some 47,800 people employed in public relations in the UK. Just over 80 per cent of these were identified as working 'in-house' (i.e. working directly for corporations, charities and public bodies) with an even split between those employed in the public and private sectors. Other headline findings of this market research include the estimates that PR now produces a turnover of £6.5 billion, contributing £3.4 billion to the UK's economic activity, and generating £1.1 billion in corporate profits.[26]

THE RISE OF GLOBAL PR

The case of Britain is illuminating because although it is the fifth biggest economy in the world (measured in terms of GDP) after the US, Japan, Germany and China, it has the second biggest PR industry. The PR industry is increasingly global. There are two key dimensions to this: first the expansion, and latterly globalisation, of PR posts in corporations; and secondly the rise of a separate industry offering PR services on a consultancy basis. The first corporations to globalise their activities, whether in terms of sourcing raw materials or in terms of selling products, were the first to globalise their corporate PR. So, for example, PR first came to Singapore in the 1950s while it was still a British colony:

The 1950s... saw a handful of multinational corporations, mainly oil companies, having in-house PR departments... As Singapore prospered into one of the region's key financial centres, it attracted MNCs [multi-national corporations] which in turn, were followed by their international PR consultancies. These foreign consultancies, which included Eric White, Burson-Marsteller, Dentsu, Young and Rubicam, Ogilvy and Mather, Hill & Knowlton etc, came for the purpose of servicing MNC clientele.[27]

The same is true across South-East Asia. 'In Singapore and Malaysia, the greater the level of market development, the more likely it is that government ministries will use private sector advertising and public relations specialists as campaign advisers.'[28] Africa also experienced this pattern of development. Mike Okereke spent many years in Nigeria working for Unilever, which he claims was the first company to employ PR staff in Africa:

UAC of Nigeria PLC, a former Unilever company pioneered the development of Professional Public Relations in Nigeria. The first Public Relations Department in Nigeria was established by UAC in 1947. The company and Shell Petroleum Development Company Ltd appointed the first Public Relations Executive to the Board of their company in the 1960s. Today, membership of the Nigerian Institute of Public Relations has grown to over 4,000.[29]

Nigeria is in fact a key hub for African PR, having by far the largest PR Association on the continent and a long involvement with international PR agencies. During the Biafran crisis in the late 1960s nine separate US and UK PR firms acted for the various participants and their story formed the basis for one of the first book-length studies of PR in Africa. One key lesson that can be drawn from that study is that the use of PR by the various factions probably prolonged the conflict.[30] The success of the Nigerian government in winning over important decision makers in London (and to a lesser extent Washington, which largely took its policy cue from Britain) through the use of PR and lobbying may have helped convince local elites of the efficacy of adopting such communications techniques.

But PR developments are also fundamentally entwined with colonial PR practice. Rosaleen Smyth has shown the important role of propaganda and public relations in colonial practice in Northern Rhodesia (now Zambia).[31] In Malaysia too British officials introduced PR as part of the colonial counter-insurgency campaign of psychological warfare. A detailed study of PR and psychological warfare in British colonial counter-insurgency operations examining Palestine (1944–47), Malaya (1948–60), Kenya (1952–60) and Cyprus (1955–59) found that while there were some differences of approach between Whitehall and the colonial administrators on the ground, public relations and propaganda quickly became central to counter-insurgency efforts:

> Propaganda and psychological warfare were soon regarded as central to defeating insurgents – often without a real understanding of the limitations on what both could achieve. But the colonial governments and the military became increasingly defensive as accusations, in all cases, of brutality on the part of the security forces mounted. In each case, as the Colonial Office's P R Noakes put it, 'an extreme sensitivity to press criticism developed', which produced inappropriate measures to try to curb the unruly local and international press.[32]

The colonial origins of PR left their mark for some considerable period after liberation both in terms of tactics and the organisational importance of PR. But the relationship between specifically British colonialism and PR has an enduring legacy, especially in Africa, where the biggest PR industries and professional associations are to be found in former British colonies (Nigeria, Ghana, Kenya, Uganda, South Africa, Zimbabwe). Aside from Nigeria, where the strength of the PR industry is due mainly to the oil industry, PR in former British colonies is stronger in the public rather than private sectors, bearing the mark of colonial administration.[33] This historical distinction was so marked that the Federation of African Public Relations Associations (FAPRA) attempted to create associations in former French colonies in West Africa (Côte d'Ivoire and Senegal).

> The French speaking African countries have been very slow in embracing professional Public Relations practice. It was for this reason that the Federation of African Public Relations Association decided to hold three of its conferences in Abidjan, Cote d'Ivoire and Dakar in Senegal. At the end of the first conference, FAPRA helped the Public Relations practitioners in Cote d'Ivoire to form a National Association.[34]

These attempts have foundered on a lack of interest and in practice (according to Nigerians active in the Nigerian Association) much of the PR in West Africa is carried out by Nigerian professionals, on behalf of corporations and governments.[35]

PR AND THE SITES OF GLOBAL DECISION MAKING

The global PR industry clusters around the centres of political and economic power. The two most important sites for lobbying power in the world are Washington and Brussels, and both cities are home to concentrated public relations and public affairs businesses. Washington hosts some 34,750 registered lobbyists.[36] In Brussels, according to best estimates (as there is still no official or reliable register of this activity in Europe) there are now some 15,000 lobbyists.[37] Nigeria has the biggest PR industry in Africa largely as a result of the oil industry and PR is expanding in parts of the Middle East, with many consultancies based in the comparatively westernised PR hub of Dubai. PR is more dispersed outwith regional business and political centres, but as a rule wherever there is global capital there is global PR (or its subsidiaries and affiliates). Thus PR centres (mirroring the development of the advertising agencies) include New York, Los Angeles, Chicago, London, Brussels, Tokyo, Hong Kong, and increasingly (since China's accession to the WTO) Beijing.

The example of China

We can look at the process of globalisation by taking the example of the changing configurations of PR in Hong Kong and China. Before its return to China, Hong Kong was the business and PR capital of the region. US PR consultancies opened there quite early on – Hill & Knowlton in 1962 and Burson-Marsteller in 1973. The 1980s witnessed an increase in agency expansion into the Asian markets. Ogilvy & Mather PR opened offices in Kuala Lumpur in 1980, Singapore in 1981, Indonesia in 1985 and Taiwan in 1986. In 1987 the biggest UK PR agency Shandwick (then independent) opened offices in Hong Kong. By the early 1990s according to the CEO of Shandwick Asia Pacific, Alan Mole, Hong Kong was 'increasingly the centre of choice for international PR covering the People's Republic of China, Taiwan, Indonesia, Malaysia, the Philippines, south Korea and in some cases Australia'.[38] The expansion in Hong Kong was fuelled according to observers at the time by 'the establishment and development of stock markets throughout Asia, the privatisation of government run companies, and the increasing number of Asian firms seeking business in international markets'.[39]

The People's Republic of China (like the former Soviet Union and Eastern bloc countries) had very little use for PR under a command economy.[40] PR became important when China started to engage in joint ventures with western enterprises as part of the process of 'opening' China to the world market. According to life-long PR operative Sam Black, 'the concept of public relations first developed in China in the Shenzhen Special Economic Zone through contact with foreign joint venture partners'.[41] Others concur: 'Under the previous planned economy, the field [of PR] was virtually unknown but foreign investment and joint ventures played a key role in advancing the profession.'[42] As early as 1985 companies like Monsanto were investing significant effort in developing markets in China, targeting trade shows in the absence of trade journals and mailing lists. As Monsanto's R.C. Isham noted:

> Just how are you going to promote your industrial products in the Middle Kingdom? You'll probably start with the Chinese trade show and exhibition. It wins almost by default. Approximately 200 trade shows across China are accessible to Western companies. That's incredible when you recall that advertising in all forms was outlawed as a capitalist tool until the late 1970s... Monsanto's experience with Chinese trade shows started with Sinochem '85 [in Shanghai]. The organizers knew how to warm the cockles of many executive hearts. In their promotional brochure, they stated that the Chinese Ministry responsible for chemicals had as its goal to increase the nation's chemical output 500 per cent by the end of this century. A year before that trade show, we committed our company to an 870 square foot area and lined up ten different Monsanto business units to split the costs. To staff the booth, we enlisted 25 Monsanto people from Hong Kong, Singapore, and the U.S. Those who did not speak the official language, Mandarin, were aided by five local translators. Of the 25 Monsanto personnel, 20 routinely travelled throughout China.[43]

He Ming, executive vice-president of the China International Public Relations Association, notes that the early to mid-1980s was a formative period in the emergence of PR in China: 'In November of 1984, Baiyunshan Pharmaceutical Plant of Guang Zhou City set up a PR department which was the first PR department in state-owned enterprises [and]... in 1985, Burson-Marsteller Co. which has a long history and Xinhua News Agency jointly established China Global PR Co. which is the first Chinese PR Co.'[44] After such modest beginnings the Chinese PR sector experienced meteoric growth. A decade later there were an estimated 1,200 PR firms in China, and since 1996 lobbying consultancies (both global and local) have become increasingly important in the Chinese public affairs sector.[45]

Business services such as lobbying, market research, law and media relations have all played their part in pursuit of the interests of multinational corporations in China. Corporate law firms have increased their presence, with over 160 foreign law firms operating in China by 2002, many of which are engaged in policy and regulatory work. A notable feature of the era of centralised economic planning was the development of a corporatist culture of direct relations between government and business (which were of course state owned). This culture persists, placing a premium on direct contact between companies and decision-makers. In this sense PR in China has been described as 'private relations', with many company offices located in Beijing existing simply to facilitate contact between the corporation and its government regulators.[46]

While the political culture in China may be different from established liberal democracies in the West, this hasn't prevented the adaptation of western lobbying techniques and strategies. A key similarity is that government needs business to realise its pro-market policies and ideology. This creates the necessary leverage for lobbying and PR firms. Interestingly, the terms lobbying and interest representation are not used in China, as they 'connote social pressure on and inherent conflicts with the state'.[47] Instead, euphemisms like political 'participation', 'exchanging views' and 'providing ideas' are preferred.

Lobbying, market research and media relations have all played their part in the pursuit of the interests of multinational corporations in China. For example here is a description of the lobbying effort carried out on behalf of western chemical companies to circumvent environmental regulations issued in 1995:

Being engaged to represent one of the major international chemical firms we were commissioned to embark on a study on 'the trends and attitudes of the regulation, the relevant agencies and officials'... Based on the results of the survey, we developed a strategy to convince the relevant officials and departments of adopting internationally accepted practices.[48]

The author of this account, Margaret Ya-fei Yu, lists among her proud accomplishments 'winning the 55 per cent import duty reduction for Mars chocolate and obtaining the approval for the British advertising company Saatchi and Saatchi to set up in China'.[49] The nascent industry has been schooled in western techniques of PR and the information requirements of capitalist market systems. It is clear that the model of PR exported by the multinational corporations and the PR consultants is the US/UK model. After three trips to China in the late 1980s and early 1990s, Sam Black noted 'in general, China has adopted the same definitions and functions of public relations as are currently accepted in the US and Europe'.[50] Since the return of Hong Kong to China the trend seems to have been for regional HQs to begin to be set up in mainland China and for there to be something of an exodus from Hong Kong.

Although the accession of China to the World Trade Organisation may start to change this picture, western PR firms have tended to do most of their work for transnational corporations rather than Chinese firms. When indigenous Chinese corporations have wanted PR advice it has been the multinational PR consultancies (rather than home grown ones) that have dominated the business.[51]

The campaign to admit China to the WTO spawned an unprecedented PR and lobbying campaign in the US.[52] And the headlong rush to exploit cheap labour and the unprotected terms and conditions of employment offered in China was unsurprisingly seen with glee in PR circles. Richard Edelman, CEO of Edelman, the world's largest independent PR group, predicted that China would become the second largest PR market in the world upon accession.[53] Edelman's general manager in China disagreed. Alistair Nichols predicted it would become the biggest. Research by the fledgling China International Public Relations Association apparently showed a growth rate of 50 per cent in the Chinese PR market in 2000.[54] Eleanor Trickett notes that WTO rules will allow direct PR access to Chinese markets:

One market that all eyes are on right now is China. Since its acceptance into the World Trade Organization ... Western agencies have been greedily eyeing the firms there, in preparation for promoting Western brands there, and bringing Chinese brands here. And, as Lou Hoffman, CEO of the Hoffman Agency, points out, 'While it hasn't gotten much notice, the new WTO regulations now allow PR agencies to form what are called Wholly Owned Foreign Enterprises. This is fairly important because previously PR agencies could only form representative offices – which technically can't deliver a service or product – or a joint venture with a local Chinese partner.'[55]

While some observers now claim that the future role of China as a leading economy has been exaggerated, it is also clear that TNCs, and as a result PR consultancies, are making a substantial investment in China.[56] According to *China Daily* in 2001: 'Of the top 20 PR companies in the world, half have entered the Chinese market... Foreign companies with a foothold in the country will continue to expand their presence.'[57] This prediction was borne out by the analysis of Ogilvy PR's managing director in China who claimed in 2006 that 'for global firms with networks [in] Asia, China offices rank as the single biggest growth opportunity'.[58] It is certainly true that the ability of the vast bulk of the Chinese population to become western-style consumers is limited, but even a small percentage of the population would be a significant market. This is a key emerging market segment for PR agencies promoting branded goods in China, like Weber Shandwick's David Lui: 'A lot of the [growth] opportunities are related to this growing middle class, and increasing wealth and spending.'[59] It is also apparent that the Chinese 'market' is desired for its cheap and plentiful supply of labour. PR investment will follow to deal with local regulation and defensive communications. The case of China exemplifies our argument that the rise of PR is closely associated with liberalisation of the economy and the interests of globalising capital.

THE GLOBAL PLAYERS

The biggest PR companies have a global presence. Indeed, their business strategy is predicated on a global network model, being able to deliver seamless cross-cultural communications plans for their largest transnational clients, all around the globe. This requires offices, or at least affiliates, in every continent. Most of the leading PR consultancies today are part of larger advertising and marketing communications groups. Ultimately, many of the leading PR firms are not independent companies at all, but owned by giant communications conglomerates. The biggest of these groups are Omnicom, WPP, Interpublic and Publicis. Observing the leading international advertising agencies in the late 1980s Armand Mattelart's remarks can equally be applied to public relations today:

Whether forefathers of advertising or newcomers, these groups and agencies make up the hard core in the globalisation of the networks. Each, according to its own style – by means of subsidiaries, federation or cross holding – they can be found ultimately in every latitude, regardless of the nature of the political regime or the level of economic development.[60]

In the past quarter century the PR industry has expanded globally in tandem with the global expansion of TNCs. Since the 1990s the marketing industry has witnessed unprecedented concentration and conglomeration, bringing together advertising, marketing, market research, PR, lobbying and a host of other communications services

Table 7.1   The largest global PR firms by revenue, 2001

Ranking	PR firm	Global income US$	Parent company
1	Weber Shandwick Worldwide	426,572,018	Interpublic
2	Fleishman-Hillard Inc.	345,098,241	Omnicom
3	Hill & Knowlton, Inc.	325,119,000	WPP
4	Incepta (Citigate)	266,018,371	(from 2004) Huntsworth
5	Burson-Marsteller	259,112,000	WPP
6	Edelman Public Relations Worldwide	223,708,535	Edelman
7	Ketchum, Inc.	185,221,000	Omnicom
8	Porter Novelli	179,294,000	Omnicom
9	GCI Group/APCO Worldwide	151,081,645	Grey Global Group WPP
10	Ogilvy Public Relations Worldwide	145,949,285	WPP
11	Euro RSCG Corporate Communications	124,158,504	Havas
12	Manning Selvage & Lee Ltd	116,019,465	Publicis Groupe
13	Golin/Harris International	113,247,644	Interpublic
14	Cordiant Communications Group	90,655,000	WPP from 2003
15	Chime Communications	85,482,720	WPP 29%
16	Ruder Finn Group	80,348,000	Independent
17	Brodeur Worldwide	70,001,900	Omnicom
18	Waggener Edstrom	59,890,800	Independent
19	Cohn & Wolfe	57,779,000	WPP
20	Rowland Comms Worldwide	42,666,000	Publicis Groupe
21	Text 100 PR	33,676,739	Next Fifteen Communications Group plc
22	Kreab	29,555,280	Independent
23	Grayling Group	19,514,937	Huntsworth
24	Chandler Chicco Agency	17,903,408	Independent
25	PR21	15,714,232	Edelman

Notes: Global PR agencies are defined as having offices in two or more continents. European income converted at the average rate over 2001: GBP/USD at £=$1.44. Average rate over 2000: GBP/USD at £=$1.51. Company notes: Incepta income incorporates PR-related research, design commissions, events and other communication activities.

Sources: Council of PR Firms (US), PRWeek UK and European Rankings, PRWeek Asia APAC rankings.

in ever fewer and ever bigger communications conglomerates. In 1991 22 of the 25 top PR firms were independent. Ten years later only six of these firms remained independent. Edelman remains by far the biggest of the independent PR firms, with revenues of $324.4 million for 2005, followed by Ruder Finn with $99.3 million.[61] But these independent agencies are dwarfed by the combined business clout of the conglomerates. Take WPP for example. It owns leading PR firms Hill & Knowlton, Burson-Marsteller, Ogilvy PR Worldwide, Cohn & Wolfe, Finsbury and Buchanan. Together these companies generated revenues of $11.4 billion, representing 10 per cent of WPP's business. Likewise Omnicom owns a range of PR agencies, including Ketchum, Fleishman-Hillard, Porter Novelli, Brodeur Worldwide, Clark & Weinstock, Gavin Anderson & Company, and Cone.

The story of the PR industry since the 1990s is one where the 'conglomerates were bent on dominating the US PR counselling industry including taking over the job of reporting fee and income totals of PR firms. They counted paid ads as "PR", thereby skyrocketing revenue totals. No proofs were sought from PR firms.'[62] Enron changed all this. In the wake of the Enron collapse the American political class responded to the perceived failure of corporate governance and accountability by introducing the Sarbanes-Oxley Act. One intention of this legislation was to ensure that investors would not be misled about the financial health and prospects of publicly traded companies. This legislation, when enacted, meant possible jail terms for those responsible for misleading financial reporting. The relentless hyping of the growth and performance of the advertising and PR industry was checked. This has been replaced by a European-style culture of secrecy, according to industry observer Jack O'Dwyer, who suspects that the Sarbanes-Oxley provisions are a convenient excuse for the major communication conglomerates to hide the relatively poor performance of their networks compared to the independents.[63]

Nevertheless, the concentration of marketing communications companies continues. Since 2001 even the conglomerates have been taken over. In 2003 WPP swallowed the ailing Cordiant group, acquired for a mere $17 million (plus assumption of debts). Cordiant had been one of the top ten global agencies in 2001. The group included the well known ad agency Saatchi & Saatchi, where Tim Bell began his career in spin. The Saatchi brothers were so close to the Tories that Maurice Saatchi, ennobled as Lord Saatchi in 1996, held the post of co-chairman of the party from 2003 to 2005.[64] Cordiant also included the leading city PR firm Financial Dynamics, which has since gone independent. Even the independent or privately owned firms like Ruder Finn and Edelman, have expanded through acquisition. Edelman, for example, owns PR21, which was itself in the top 25 global agencies in 2002. In 2005 WPP bought Grey Global,

Table 7.2   PR and lobbying companies of the 'Big Four' communications conglomerates

Omnicom *		WPP	Interpublic	Publicis
Allyn & Company	MediVia	Banner	Bragman Nyman	Capital MS&L
Fleishman-Hillard	Innovative Medical	Corporation	Cafarelli	MS&L
Government	Education	BizEvents	Carmichael Lynch	Rowland
Relations	MedEd Resource	BKSH	Spong	Communications
GPC Public Affairs	Group	Blanc & Otus	DeVries Public	Hass/MS&L
GMMB	Nonprofit	Buchanan	Relations	Publicis Dialog
Mercury Public	Fundraising and	Communications	GolinHarris	Winner &
Affairs	Communications	Bulletin	MWW Group	Associates
Strat@comm	Group	International	Rogers & Cowan	Publicis
VOX Global	Changing Our	Burson-Marsteller	Slay PR	Consultants
Mandate	World	W|R	Weber Shandwick	HEADLINE Public
Blue Current Public	Grizzard	Carl Byoir &	Worldwide	Relations
Relations	Communications	Associates	PMK/HBH	Freud
CPR Worldwide	Group	Chime	The Rhoads Group	Communications
Fleishman-Hillard	Russ Reid Company	Communications	Tierney	(50.1%)
CPR The Remedy	SCA Direct	Plc	Communications	
High Road	TABS Direct	Clarion	The Axis Agency	
Communications	Worldwide	Communications	The Martin Agency	
iStudio	Healthcare	Cohn & Wolfe	Mullen	
Lois Paul &	Communications	CommonHealth	Financial Relations	
Partners	Curtis Jones &	Direct Impact	Board	
Ketchum	Brown Anderson	Finsbury	Rowan & Blewitt	
Concentric	DDB Health &	Food Group	FutureBrand	
Communications	Lifestyle	GCI	Gillespie	
Ketchum	TARGIS	Grey Global Group	KRC Research	
Entertainment	Airon	Hill & Knowlton	Howard Merrell &	
Marketing	Communication	IBI Inc	Partners	
Ketchum Sheppard	Syncronia DDB	IPAN	Cassidy &	
Stromberg	Prins & van Waard	Offspring PR	Associates	
Consulting	Russia	Ogilvy Public		
The Washington	Pressto	Relations		
Group	Fine Healthcare	Worldwide		
Porter Novelli	Elixir	Penn Schoen &		
International	Paling Walters	Berland		
FischerHealth	Athena Medical	PiranhaKid		
Brodeur Worldwide	Public Relations	Communications		
Clark & Weinstock	Pathfinder ICS US	PPR		
Gavin Anderson &		PRISM		
Company		Quinn Gillespie		
Chlopak		Robinson Lerer &		
Leonard, Schechter		Montgomery		
& Associates		Roman Brand		
Cone		Group		
HMC Group		Wexler & Walker		
LLNS (Lyons Lavey		Public Policy		
Nickel Swift)		Associates		
		Y&R Business		
		Communications		

* Diversified Agency Services (DAS) manages Omnicom's holdings in a variety of marketing disciplines, including customer relationship management, public relations and specialty communications. DAS includes more than 160 companies, which operate through a combination of networks and regional organisations.

Source: Compiled from company websites and annual reports.

ranked as the eleventh biggest group by *Advertising Age* in 2004. Grey included the PR division GCI Group as well as the global lobbying firm APCO Worldwide, though APCO completed a management buy out before WPP took control.

Table 7.3   Global communications groups

2005 ranking	2004 ranking	Company	HQ	Revenue 2005	Revenue 2004	+/− (%)
1	1	Omnicom	New York	10,481.1	9,747.2	7.5
2	2	WPP	London	10,032.2	9,645.1	4.0
3	3	Interpublic	New York	6,274.3	6,387.0	−1.8
4	4	Publicis	Paris	5,107.2	4,777.3	6.9
5	5	Dentsu	Tokyo	2,887.8	2,940.6	−1.8
6	6	Havas	Suresnes, France	1,808.0	1,866.0	−3.1
7	7	Aegis	London	1,577.6	1,373.6	14.9
8	8	Hakuhodo DY	Tokyo	1,364.0	1,372.4	−0.6
9	9	Asatsu-DK	Tokyo	444.8	473.3	−6.0
10	11	MDC Partners	Toronto/New York	443.5	316.7	40.0
11	10	Carlson Marketing Group	Minneapolis	370.0	346.9	6.7
12	12	Sapient Corp	Cambridge. Mass.	358.4	281.4	27.3
13	14	Digitas	Boston	340.5	251.6	35.3
14	21	aQuantive	Seattle	258.4	157.9	63.6
15	17	Aspen Marketing Services	Chicago	229.0	180.0	27.2
16	NA	Media Square	London	215.0	NA	NA
17	15	HealthSTAR Communications	Woodbridge N.J	213.0	203.0	4.9
18	16	Cheil Communications	Seoul	210.7	185.9	13.4
19	19	George P Johnson Co.	Auburn Hills Mich	193.0	172.9	11.6
20	25	Epsilon	Wakefield, Mass.	184.4	144.4	27.7
21	32	TBA Global Events	Woodland Hills, Calif.	175.0	110.0	59.1
22	20	Monster Worldwide	New York	168.6	162.2	4.0
23	23	Clemenger Communications	Melbourne	166.0	147.4	12.6
24	22	Doner	Southfield, Mich	164.3	155.7	5.5
25	27	Cossette Communication Group	Quebec City	164.1	140.1	17.1

Notes: Revenue is in millions of US dollars. Revenue supplied by companies.

Source: *Advertising Age*, 1 May 2006.

Another of the big global groups fell to a comparative minnow. Incepta, judged the twelfth biggest communications group by *Advertising Age* in 2004, was acquired by a reverse take-over by Huntsworth, the new venture of Peter Gummer. Gummer – also known by his title, Lord Chadlington – was made a life peer in 1996. He is a well known Tory supporter and brother of Thatcher's former Agriculture Secretary John Gummer, who ironically was responsible for one of the more memorable PR disasters in the last 20 years when he tried to force feed his daughter a burger in order to reassure the public it was safe to eat meat in the wake of the BSE outbreak. When she recoiled (the burger was too hot) the media pack were presented with the kind of gaffe that guarantees all the wrong sorts of headlines.

In the earlier part of his career Peter Gummer built Shandwick into the largest independent PR firm in the world, before selling out to the Interpublic group (it's now known as Weber Shandwick Worldwide). But Gummer has re-entered the PR business and his Huntsworth group now includes PR firms Citigate, Citigate Dewe Rogerson (the agency that specialised in privatisations during the 1980s), Grayling (which includes Westminster Strategy, a lobbying firm associated with New Labour), The Red Consultancy, and Trimedia Harrison Cowley.

In 1991 the worldwide aggregated revenues for the top 25 totalled $1,040,271,054. In 2001 this figure had risen to $3,309,864,350 (unadjusted). The conglomeration and concentration of ownership has been so marked that the biggest conglomerates now control more than half the global advertising, marketing, PR and lobbying market.[65] Since 2001 the tendency toward concentration has continued. According to *Advertising Age*: 'Both the revenues and market caps also show the Big Four clearly bifurcating into the Big Two [Omnicom and WPP] and the Other Two [Publicis and Interpublic].'[66]

The global conglomerates do not go out of their way to enlighten the public about their role or existence. Some are worse than others. According to trade journal *O'Dwyer's* in 2006, John Wren, president and chief executive of Omnicom, had only given three interviews in the previous four years.[67] A communications strategy, based on secrecy and some mystery, has clearly been adopted:

John Wren and Omnicom made spectacles of themselves by holding the Omnicom annual stockholders meeting in a room in its BBDO unit in Atlanta. The attendance of 24 was far below the 160 that smaller ad conglomerate Interpublic faced the week before at a public auditorium in New York. A half dozen irate stockholders raked Interpublic execs over the coals and the *New York Times* devoted 15 inches of type to this shellacking. Omnicom, by fleeing to Atlanta, escaped any notice by the *Times*, *Advertising Age*, *AdWeek* or even the local *Atlanta Journal-Constitution*.

The only reporter present in Atlanta was a freelancer working for the *O'Dwyer's* newsletter, which provides independent coverage on the PR industry (rather than offering uncritical support and the puff pieces that characterise UK publications like *PR Week*):

The freelancer walked into the meeting room without any requests for identification... only when the freelancer asked some questions was identity demanded... The writer held an Omnicom proxy supplied by The O'Dwyer Co. When the freelancer tried to ask additional questions, having received only minimal replies, the freelancer was told that the meeting was over and was escorted out of the room to the elevators. This openly hostile treatment of the press, including the refusal to discuss complicated financial matters, stands on its head every known principle of PR, starting with 'face the bad news and get over it.'[68]

THE GLOBAL PR INDUSTRY AND THE
INNER CIRCLE OF CAPITALIST LOBBY GROUPS

Despite the relative obscurity of the big communication groups, they are well integrated into the planning clubs of the transnational elite, both directly and via their board members. Martin Sorrell, the CEO of WPP, is a neat example. Sorrell is a member of the Trilateral Commission and contributed to its 2001 meeting.[69] WPP is an 'industry partner', a 'meeting partner' and a 'strategic partner' of the World Economic Forum.[70] WPP was also 'commissioned' by the WEF 'to examine ways of finding a new positioning for the continent [of Africa]'.[71] Sorrell is on the advisory council of KPMG, a special adviser to the Board of Loyalty Management UK, a member of the NASDAQ Board and a trustee of the New York corporate lobby group, the Conference Board (referred to in Chapter 3). In 2002 Sorrell was appointed to the CBI International Advisory Board and the Engineering and Technology Board.

Sorrell is close to the Blair administration and has contributed to a number of New Labour policy review bodies. In 1997, he was appointed an Ambassador for British Business by the Foreign and Commonwealth Office and subsequently appointed to the Office's Panel 2000 aimed at overhauling Britain's international propaganda apparatus. In 1999 he was appointed by the Secretary of State for

Education and Employment to serve on the Council for Excellence in Management and Leadership and was knighted in the Millennium New Year Honours list.

In early 2006 it was reported that Tony Blair's eldest son Euan (22) was to 'gain work experience with financial public relations company Finsbury'.[72] Finsbury is owned by WPP. *Private Eye* was not surprised:

Roland Rudd, the Finsbury founder and friend of Peter Mandelson, has been cosying up to 'new' Labour for many years. In 2001 Finsbury's party guests also included the present Culture Secretary Tessa Jowell and Education Minister (and peer) Andrew Adonis, as well as the then Labour party boss, also since ennobled, Lord Triesman. Finsbury previously hired the former private secretary of the Dear Leader's close pal, the Lord Chancellor Lord Falconer. Such contacts and support for Labour events at conference time perhaps helped merit the 2002 contract to advise then Transport Secretary Stephen 'Liar' Byers over the Railtrack collapse. So look out for the pay-off... most likely to come for such a selfless act as explaining to Blair the Younger the dark arts of being paid to lie.[73]

WPP is also active in pushing for European integration. Sorrell was an advisory board member of Britain in Europe funded by Mindshare (a WPP subsidiary), the campaign group created to fight the euro-sceptic lobby in the UK in general, and the much anticipated referendum on the UK's joining the euro in particular. With the French and Dutch 'No' votes on the EU constitution the prospect of a UK referendum disappeared, and so too did Britain in Europe.[74]

WPP is a corporate partner of the Prince of Wales International Business Leaders Forum (IBLF)[75] and a member of Business in the Community,[76] both of which promote concepts of good corporate citizenship, championing social responsibility and sustainability. However, WPP, through its subsidiary companies, is also a key mover behind the Advertising Association in the UK, which has been lobbying government not to introduce regulations restricting the pushing of junk food at children. Hardly socially responsible one might think, but business is business. In terms of sustainability, WPP, and the advertising industry in general, hardly inspire confidence. The trade associations for international advertising produced a report for the World Summit on Sustainable Development in Johannesburg in 2002, which in essence boils down to 'don't blame us for over-consumption'.

There is also a wide misperception that in developed countries, advertising is a root cause of over-consumption... Advertising cannot make people buy things they don't want or need, nor does it change values or create new values.[77]

In a reversal of conventional wisdom, the advertising industry is at pains to pretend it has no social impacts on consumers, though it can affect clients! Consider the following carefully crafted passage:

Advertising agencies represent a link between producers and consumers. They have an influence on the communication strategies of their clients, and their communication skills and creative talents represent an important asset to help detect shifts in consumption patterns and mobilise alternative business opportunities.[78]

This positions the advertising industry as an enabler of sustainability and a force for good. Once business and government decide what to do about sustainability, advertising will help promote sustainability messages (not, of course, that they have any impact on the consumer). A little more reality creeps into the analysis when it is recognised that for very many people around the globe, subsisting on less that $2 a day, 'advertising has no real role to play'.[79] The arguments put forward by the industry, however self-serving, do demonstrate how the communications industry organises politically, and that when its interests are threatened, it can mobilise and respond. As large corporations these conglomerates are directed by people who know how the business of politics works. What else explains the numbers of ex-politicians and officials who sit on the boards of the world's leading TNCs? Businesses, and their political representatives, like the CBI and IoD in the UK, are often found complaining that politicians know nothing about 'the realities' of business. However, many are quick to offer these chronic know-nothings a chance to direct companies when they leave office. Others appear to pass through the revolving door between high politics and peak business often, and with consummate ease.

Board members of WPP fit this profile. Philip Lader, for example, was appointed chairman of WPP in 2001. He was the US Ambassador to the 'Court of St James's' (the UK) from 1997 to 2001. Prior to his ambassadorship and return to the private sector, Lader served as White House Deputy Chief of Staff, Deputy Director of the Office of Management and Budget, and head of US federal government Small Business Administration. Before entering government service, he was executive vice-president of the company managing the late Sir James

Goldsmith's US holdings and president of both a prominent American real estate company and universities in the US and Australia. A lawyer, he is also a senior adviser to Morgan Stanley, as well as on the board of Marathon Oil and AES Corporations. He has strong UK networking links in addition to WPP, being a member of the Council of Lloyd's (Insurance Market), a trustee of the British Museum and on the board of the St Paul's Cathedral Foundation. Lader is also a patron of the Scottish North American Business Council (SNABC), which is chaired by former MI6 agent Andrew Fulton.[80]

An indication that Lader is a significant networker in the inner circles of corporate power is that he is both a director of the RAND Corporation and a member of the Council on Foreign Relations, both of which are immensely influential think tanks at the centre of US foreign policy discussions. Lader is also the founder of Renaissance Weekend, an exclusive retreat popularised by President Bill Clinton. Like other such elite networking opportunities, these are private, invitation-only get-togethers for leaders in business and finance, government, the media, religion, medicine, science, technology and the arts. Conversations are strictly off the record and subject matter ranges widely, tending to focus heavily on policy and business issues. An assortment of the US elite often attends, including various PR and propaganda theorists. The advisory board includes Ann Wexler of lobbying firm Wexler Public Policy (a key player in the campaign to create NAFTA) and Joseph Nye, the academic theorist of 'soft power' or propaganda.[81] Sir Jeremy Greenstock, the former UK ambassador to the UN, David Trimble, the former leader of the Ulster Unionist Party and George Robertson, the former British Defence Minister and head of NATO, are also among the few UK citizens on the advisory board.[82] We should also note, lastly, Lader's roles as patron of the British American Project (BAP), the UK/US elite networking event set up to blunt criticism of the US among the British left. George Robertson, on the advisory board to the Renaissance Weekend, is also an alumnus of BAP.[83]

Lader's most well known contribution to UK public life occurred on 13 September 2001. He was a panellist on the BBC TV programme *Question Time* in the aftermath of the 9/11 attacks in New York and Washington. Both audience members and panellists were critical of US foreign policy during the programme and Lader appeared to find the criticism overwhelming. Some reports said he had 'tears in his eyes'.[84]

'At one point', reported the *Daily Telegraph*, 'Philip Lader, the former American ambassador, who was on the panel, was slow handclapped by a section of the audience. He said with tears in his eyes: "I have to share with you that I find it hurtful that you can suggest that a majority of the world despises the US."' Lader went on:

My parents were immigrants to the US. We have fought as a people and nation for the rule of law and I simply want to say that it saddens me how it is possible on this night, within 48 hours [of the attack], that because of animosity of feeling on political issues we can frankly abstract ourselves from the senseless human victimisation and suffering that has occurred.

Tam Dalyell MP, one of the other panellists on the show, complained when the BBC issued an apology about the programme: 'I know what the feeling may have been, but I think it was representative. It was an audience who were a cross-section of people in London, for God's sake.'[85]

Another advisory board member at the Renaissance Weekend is Esther Dyson, listed on the official website as Editor at Large of CNET. Dyson is also known to Lader by virtue of the fact she too sits on the board of WPP as a non-executive director. The WPP site describes her as an 'acknowledged luminary' in the online/information technology industry and the emerging information technology markets of Central and Eastern Europe.[86] Dyson is the former chair of the Electronic Frontier Foundation, a libertarian campaigning group which at one stage became a pro-corporate lobby group when '90 per cent of the group's funding came from corporations'.[87]

Dyson is also a trustee for the Eurasia Foundation which appears to be a body operating in the former Soviet countries to open up market opportunities for companies like those on whose board Dyson sits. The foundation avers that 'Societies function best when citizens take responsibility for their own civic and economic future. Eurasia Foundation programs promote the skills and vision necessary to bring the greatest social and economic benefits to individuals and their societies.'[88] This does not, however, mean that citizens can and should work together to manage civic and economic matters for the collective good. In fact what the Eurasia Foundation proposes is that there should be no collective management by citizens but that corporations should be allowed to operate without regulation. The Eurasia Foundation grants are aimed at, amongst other things, promoting 'accelerated development and growth of private enterprise'. The foundation is funded by the United States Agency for International Development, the UK Foreign and Commonwealth Office and what the foundation describes as 'indigenous philanthropy'. In practice this means that corporations with mafia connections, such as the Russian oil firm, Yukos, were among the sponsors.[89] Dyson's other activities include positions at the EastWest Institute (along with BP and BAP's Nick Butler) and the Santa Fe Institute. She has been both an adviser to Al Gore as a member of the National Information Infrastructure Advisory Council and to the Republicans through the Progress and Freedom Foundation.[90] She is a member of the Global Business Network, a consulting organisation offering futurology advice and funded by almost 200 of the world's biggest corporations. Dyson also sat on the Markle Foundation's Taskforce on Security in the Information Age. This concluded that:

Information analysis is the brain of homeland security. Used well, it can guide strategic, timely moves throughout our country and around the world. Done poorly, even armies of guards and analysts will be useless... The Federal Government is preparing to spend nearly $40 billion a year to protect the homeland. While this report takes no position on any pending legislation, the White House has developed the important concept of homeland security, the centerpiece of which is the Department of Homeland Security (DHS). But almost no dollars have been directed to creating the capacity for the sharing of information and integrating the way it is analyzed, so that out of information collection comes enhanced knowledge. Neither the White House nor the current appropriations pipeline for the new Department of Homeland Security have yet identified the money to turn information collection into knowledge.[91]

No doubt WPP and the other information management companies involved in the task force would be able to provide some of that expertise – for a price. Other board members at WPP are associated with the Council on Foreign Relations (three of them) and with the following organisations: the Peres Institute for Peace, International Advisory Board of the British American Business Council, the National Academy Foundation, INSEAD's International Council, trustee of the Arab Thought Foundation, Arab Business Council, the Women's Leadership Initiative of the World Economic Forum, board of trustees of the International Center of Photography in New York. What emerges from this sketch of some of the interests of some of the WPP directors is a highly networked, globalised, political board, with personal and professional links across policy making bodies, think tanks, business and civil society in the UK, EU and North America.

By contrast Peter Gummer of Huntsworth is much less active in the key global networking groups. He is in a UK neo-conservative group pressing for closer relations between the US and Europe. The group, the Atlantic Partnership, was set up by then Conservative leader, Michael Howard in 2001. Also involved are Henry Kissinger, former British Prime Minister John Major, James Rubin, the former adviser to Bill Clinton, and John Gilbert, former Labour defence minister, staunch NATO supporter and vice chair of the Trade Union Committee for European and Transatlantic Understanding, an organisation, formerly at least, part-funded by the CIA.[92]

Gummer also has the usual inner circle interest in the arts. He has been chairman of The Royal Opera House, member of the Arts Council of England and a non-executive member of the NHS Policy Board, chairman of the Understanding Industry Trust and a member of the European Union Select Sub Committee B (Energy, Industry and Transport). Gummer was one of the first corporate CEOs to come out in favour of David Cameron as the new Tory leader.[93] But, by comparison, he and the board of Huntsworth are not quite so networked as Sorrell and his crew at WPP.

Also on the board at Huntsworth is Francis Maude MP, the former chair of the Conservative Party, who was chairman of PR firm Incepta when Huntsworth took it over. The rest of the board of Huntsworth have multiple corporate board connections including several who were on the board of Shandwick when Gummer was its CEO. But there are many fewer connections to corporate lobby and political groups, reflecting its much smaller size than WPP. The connections of Gummer and Sorrell are simply a microcosm of the wider links of the PR and communications business. The boards of WPP, Omnicom, Interpublic show strong multiple connections and interlocks with a range of pre-eminent corporate lobby groups. The board of Huntsworth show largely multiple connections to other corporate boards rather than the kind of transnational political activity displayed by the much larger top two. The business and political activities of the board members of the big communication conglomerates show their degree of integration into the inner circle of the global business class. But because of their multiple personalities, via the literally hundreds of companies owned by the major commercial communications conglomerates, a comprehensive picture of all of their political activities is well nigh impossible even in a book like this.

What is abundantly clear from this account of the development of the PR and promotional industries is that they are not simply servants of global capital. They are massive corporations in their own right, and share similar concerns to other big businesses. Moreover, they play a critical role in our society given their unique access to communicative power, both through the very obvious channels of mass advertising, but also through the less well known or understood channels of persuasion that mark the territory of lobbying and public relations. The global PR industry is at the forefront of extending corporate power by engaging in the front-line of the battle for ideas and finding ways to put the interests of the corporation into action.

8
Pulling Labour's Teeth

Benjamin Zephaniah, the radical Black British poet, remembers his experience at the Claremont Hotel well: 'It was in this hotel in California, in Oakland, the Claremont. I remember them all as men in suits or power-dressed women. Oil people, a couple of people from minority groups. I remember loads of trust games. The men were told, "Now take off your tie, and relax, and do some yoga exercises, and go off into a group, and talk about empowerment".'[1]

The Claremont advertised itself as located in Berkeley, although it is technically in Oakland, the working class city which rubs up against Berkeley in the San Francisco Bay area. According to the hotel's own website it 'gained a reputation as a retreat for wealthy San Franciscans'.[2] Its room charges range from $200 to $300 per night and it is situated in 22 acres of grounds. Not really Zephaniah's cup of tea.

He 'started skipping the discussion groups by telling each one that he was going to the other. But after a while he had had enough.' So: 'I escaped. I got out of the hotel. I went down to Berkeley, hung out with some homeless people, went to see a friend of mine.'

Zephaniah is one of the few publicised cases of people for whom the charm of the elite networking group the British American Project failed to work. But the project didn't give up. 'Every year, they kept sending me the report of the last conference. I had a whole shelf of them. Last year, I put them in the bin.'[3]

The British American Project, as it is now known, used to be called the slightly more Orwellian 'British American Project for the Successor Generation'. Each year the project invites 24 American and 24 British delegates to take part in

four days of dinners, parties and discussions (ranging from the nature of the 'special relationship' to security and economic issues). Delegates enjoy comparative luxury (the class of '98 stayed at the $285-a-night Omni Royal Crescent in New Orleans). The aim, to quote the report of the 1985 conference, is 'to create, at a time of growing international strains and stresses, a closer rapport between Britain and the United States among people likely to become influential decision-makers during the next two decades'. Delegates are nominated by existing fellows; once they have come through the process of selection (in the UK, this is based on competitive debating sessions with other nominees), they have their travel and other expenses paid to the more or less exotic locations of the conference. Last year New Orleans, this year... Harrogate.[4]

The power of BAP was trumpeted by its own journal after the 1997 election:

In the summer of 1997, a few weeks after New Labour won power, a striking article about the election appeared in a privately circulated newsletter. Under the cryptic headline Big Swing To BAP, the article began, 'No less than four British-American Project fellows and one advisory board member have been appointed to ministerial posts in the new Labour government.' A list of the names of these five people and of other New Labour appointees who were members of BAP followed: 'Mo Mowlam ... Chris Smith ... Peter Mandelson ... Baroness Symons ... George Robertson ... Jonathan Powell ... Geoff Mulgan ... Matthew Taylor ...' The article ended with a self-congratulatory flourish and the names of two more notable BAP members: 'James Naughtie and Jeremy Paxman gave them all a hard time on BBC radio and television. Other fellows, too numerous to list, popped up throughout the national media commenting, criticising and celebrating.'[5]

The BAP was a key means for detaching a section of the Labour Party from social democracy. 'The project was first suggested in 1982 by Nick Butler, a Labour Party insider of the old right and a research fellow at the Royal Institute of International Affairs (Chatham House).'[6] Butler had been a long time member of the Fabian Society, an economist at BP and an adviser to Neil Kinnock. He is now group vice-president of Strategy and Policy Development at BP. As well as founding BAP Butler has also been instrumental in setting up a series of right wing think tanks such as Centre for European Reform and the EastWest Institute. In 2000 he created what he described as 'an exact clone' of BAP in the US–Japan Leadership Program and he is a member of the World Economic Forum, the Executive of Chatham House and the Council on Foreign Relations in the US. 'Along with many others in the US and Britain who viewed the special relationship favourably, he had become concerned about the growing tide of anti-American sentiment, particularly within his own party. This was the time of Greenham Common, CND and the battles over US deployment of cruise missiles in Europe. Vietnam and Watergate were fresh in everyone's memory.'[7]

Butler's response was to propose a series of conferences, similar in format to the annual get-together of the Anglo-German elite at Konigswinter, developing personal relationships between the participants and broadening understanding. This rapidly gained backing from Chatham House, then from other establishment bodies, such as the Royal United Services Institute and the US embassy in London. But at this stage there seemed little prospect of funding.[8]

But after the initial worries the funding seems to have flowed in. By 2004/05 the project was declaring support from a blue chip sponsorship list including American Airlines, Boeing, United Parcel Service, BP, Centrica, Foreign and Commonwealth Office, US Embassy (London), JPMorgan, BAe Systems and Vodafone amongst others.

Support in kind has come from the BBC, Traidcraft (the fair trade company), media institutions such as *Time* magazine and the *Chicago Tribune*, as well as right wing institutes such as the International Institute for Strategic Studies, recently exposed as using disinformation to push for an attack on Iran.[9]

Today the BAP is run by a collection of corporate leaders and pro-corporate and pro-US politicians. Patrons include the former CEO of BP Lord Browne, the former Secretary General of NATO and former UK Defence Secretary, George Robertson together with the former US Ambassador to the UK Philip Lader. Continuing the theme, Michael Maclay is on the UK advisory board of BAP and has been on the board of the corporate intelligence firm Hakluyt which was set up by former MI6 officers and was exposed for spying on Greenpeace and the Body Shop using an undercover operative.[10] The US advisory board included Paul Wolfowitz, one of the chief architects of the attack on Iraq in 2003.

The project proved enormously successful at detaching key elements of the Labour Party from their scepticism about big business. 'European notions such as socialism, the welfare state and high levels of government spending were judged, in the slightly sweeping way of clever young thinkers, to be in difficulties. American notions such as less regulated capitalism, a smaller enabling state and a world kept safe by the Pentagon came to be regarded as sensible, inevitable', writes *Guardian* journalist Andy Beckett.[11]

Perhaps the best illustration of the effect of this on those who did not – like Benjamin Zephaniah – rebel against the BAP experience is the conclusion of Trevor Phillips, currently the chair of the Commission for Racial Equality.[12] Strongly identified with New Labour he has advocated more 'choice' in the NHS, otherwise known as privatisation.[13] Phillips' own account is that 'five years before I joined BAP, I thought wealth creation and progressive politics were completely incompatible... BAP was one of the things that made me think that was absurd'.[14]

The BAP agenda is plain, and it is clear that it has played an important role in socialising a generation of Labour politicians towards an uncritical or at least less critical perspective on the US and on global capital. BAP is food and drink to conspiracy theorists, but it is incorrect to see BAP as having supernatural powers of persuasion. In fact as Lord Lipsey, Labour peer, BAP member and think tanker (chair of the pro-market Social Market Foundation) puts it: 'BAP was one of a number of streams that came together in New Labour'.[15] Together the streams created a torrent that successfully swept away Labour's threat to money and power.

THE THREAT OF THE LEFT: TARGETING THE LABOUR PARTY

But back in the early 1980s the Labour left and the trade union movement still remained a potential threat. In the US the left had long since been bought off and organised Labour rendered safe.[16] But in the UK the business lobbyists and their allies in the worlds of intelligence, government and the military foresaw a longer term struggle against the Labour Party.

One aim was the transformation of British society so that business would be free to do what it wanted. Government would simply be a mechanism for allocation of resources to business. Even at this stage few of them saw that government might become like a business.

A second aim, on which US based business and intelligence circles were especially keen, was to draw the sting of socialism in the Labour Party so that it was no threat to business interests. Both of these aims were largely accomplished in a remarkable period of political turmoil between 1979 and 1997.

To neuter the Labour Party was arguably a world historical task undertaken not simply by business, but also in alliance with government and intelligence agencies in the US and UK. A whole network of Atlanticist foundations, think tanks and front groups was at work in the trade unions, the media and academia to turn the left leaning elite towards the US and away from social democracy, suspicion of big business and opposition to US foreign policy.

Today many critics of the New Labour project imagine that the party was corrupted by big business and pro-US forces in the 1980s.

There is certainly some truth to this as we will see below. But it is also clear that the proudest achievements of the Labour Party in the Attlee administration which won a landslide victory in 1945 – the NHS, nationalisation, comprehensive education – were under attack from within the Government and the Civil Service as early as 1945.

From the election in 1945 British foreign policy was supposed to follow a middle way, to be a 'third force' in world politics. The Foreign Secretary Ernest Bevin, a right winger, had urged during the war that 'diplomacy should be expanded from relations between governments and elites to relations between peoples' and on appointment to the Foreign Office had apparently believed 'that publicity could be used overseas as a suitable tool for the projection of British social democracy'.[17] This was in keeping with the philosophy of the 'third force' as an alternative to communism and unrestrained capitalism. But the Foreign Office had other ideas and from at least 1946 was urging the establishment of an anti-communist propaganda operation. Bevin authorised one in Iran in the same year, but it was pressure from the US which was decisive in turning the policy from a middle way to the American way.

The US was holding some important political aces in the form of the Marshall plan. In Washington, the British Embassy was informed 'that Britain's socialism could stand in the way of the loan... Congress was greatly concerned to establish that US dollars weren't going to be used to bolster up a red dictatorship or, equally perverse, to subsidise welfare measures.' In the informal surroundings of Bohemian Grove, the British Consul General Frank Evans reported that he 'could not but be depressed by the violent dislike and distrust manifest by these men towards the British experiment in social democracy'.[18]

As a result Ernest Bevin arranged that leading left wingers would be kept out of the US or stopped from meeting the President. The chair of Labour's powerful National Executive Committee (NEC) Harold Laski, the renowned socialist intellectual, formerly at the London School of Economics, was allowed to visit America but British Information Services in the US were 'instructed to keep quiet about his visit and deny any knowledge of it'.[19] When asked they would refuse 'to give out information on his itinerary'.[20] This all suited a Foreign Office that was in any case unimpressed by Labour's reforms. One witness to this was a former assistant of Prime Minister Clement Attlee, Grant Mackenzie, who had been posted to direct the British Information Office in Washington. He noted that in US publicity work on the Labour Government there had been 'an air of embarrassment and apology, as if something has happened that was "not done". The word "socialist" has been banned, and repeated efforts made to explain away the socialist decisions of the government.'[21]

The Foreign Office were not interested in 'relations between peoples' and had been urging since 1943 that propaganda should 'concentrate less' on the British way of life and more on 'immediate British interests'. These included pre-eminently focusing on allying Britain with the US.[22] 'The most productive measure, suggested by the embassy's surveys of [US] public opinion in the summer of 1947, would be to launch a campaign expressing the Attlee government's abhorrence of Soviet communism.'[23] In policy terms it also meant abandoning any further reforms such as nationalisation. The US Ambassador said as much in July 1947. 'It would help the US obtain from congress the help which the United Kingdom required if it were made clear that there would be no further nationalisation of great industries in this country.' In June the next year the Foreign Office recommended that the nationalisation of iron and steel should be postponed if not abandoned for the sake of 'Anglo-American relations'.[24]

The Labour right succumbed to the pressure from the US and the Foreign Office. The planned nationalisations were postponed and this period witnessed the creation of a covert anti-communist propaganda department within the Foreign Office called the Information Research Department (IRD), which worked closely with the Economic League and Aims of Industry.

But IRD was not created with the knowing support of the Labour Cabinet. The author of the paper which went to the cabinet – Christoper Mayhew – was a Labour right winger and cold warrior. He dissembled to the cabinet about the purpose and function of the IRD by claiming that it was to be a 'Third Force' campaign, understood as policy intended by the left to be independent of both the US and the USSR. According to Mayhew himself:

I thought it was necessary to present the whole campaign in a positive way, in a way which Dick Crossman and Michael Foot would find it hard to oppose. And they were calling for a Third Force... so I recommended in the original paper I put to Bevin that we call it a Third Force propaganda campaign.[25]

As Mayhew noted, 'the turning point' was the speech of George Marshall the US Secretary of State in June 1947. From 'the middle of 1947 onwards, decisions were taken towards uniting the free world, at the expense of widening the gap with the Communist world...

our immediate objective changed, from "one world" to "one free world"'.[26]

The Atlanticist tendency within Labour was not new. But the split in the party in the late 1970s which culminated in the creation of the Social Democratic Party (SDP) was encouraged and exacerbated by US linked organisations often connected with the CIA. The US funded social democrats because this was a means of ensuring that European governments 'continued to allow American capital into their economies with a minimum of restrictions'.[27] But, for some sections of the movement for the restoration of corporate power, the Labour Party was not social democratic. It was in the grip of the far left and indeed was said to be 'thoroughly penetrated'[28] by the KGB, by activists like Brian Crozier, drawing on the views of the conspirators in the Wilson plot (Chapter 5). Crozier 'had long nursed the idea' that the problem of a 'subversive opposition' which 'might come back to power could only lie in the creation of a non-subversive alternative party of government'.[29]

The interest of the CIA and of corporate funded think tanks and right wing US foundations in an alternative to Labour was clear. But the history books neglect to mention much in the way of trans-Atlantic connections of the Gang of Four and their co-conspirators. They often miss out the well known links of Shirley Williams with the right wing Ditchley Foundation,[30] or those of Robert Maclennan, a founder of the party, with the Atlantic Council, the pro-NATO policy group. Indeed all four leaders of the SDP had been 'career long' members of the American tendency in Labour. When the SDP merged with the liberals to form the Social and Liberal Democrats 'one of the authors of the proposed joint policy statement was seconded to the job by his employer [CSIS] a propagandising Washington foreign policy think-tank much used by successive American administrations in pursuit of its foreign policy goals'.[31]

More important are the connections of two of the other founders, Stephen Haseler, an academic at the City of London Polytechnic, who along with fellow lecturer Douglas Eden (a US national) formed the Social Democratic Alliance and issued 'a string of alarmist reports about the inroads being made into the Labour Party by the left'.[32] Haseler had written a book condemning *The Death of British Democracy*. The SDA attracted the attention and the financial help 'on a small scale' of Brian Crozier, the spook and corporate activist. As Crozier himself notes, the 'true story of its prehistory has not... been told'.[33] Crozier admits that he already knew both Haseler and Eden, the latter from early meetings of the extreme National Association for Freedom. The three met at Crozier's office in the Institute for the Study of Conflict – hardly an auspicious meeting place for members of the Labour Party.[34] Haseler later worked for the right wing, corporate funded Heritage Foundation and used Heritage money to set up the Institute for European Defence and Strategic Studies, intended to challenge CND in the 1980s.[35]

Once the SDP was formed, several right wing Labour MPs who had decided to join the SDP voted for Michael Foot in the leadership contest with the right winger Denis Healey. Their votes ensured Foot's victory and were intended as the death knell for the Labour Party. 'It was very important', one of them wrote, that they 'destroyed' the Labour Party.[36] The creation of the SDP not only split the anti-Tory vote at the 1983 election, but also contributed to the defeat of the Labour left in elections to local councils across the UK in the mid 1980s.

Even after this, and the defeat of the miners in 1984–85, the Atlanticists feared that their job was not done. Crozier's view was that the SDP project had been confounded by Roy Jenkins' 'unwillingness' to 'use the party for the purpose for which it had been created' and play the role in history allotted to him by the machinations of Crozier, Eden and Haseler. Instead of attempting to 'split the Labour Party' he tried to attract Tory votes.

And so the problem of Labour remained on the agenda. Or rather the problem of popular democracy.

CHANGING LABOUR

The British American Project started two years after the 1983 election, by which time the left had been able to make significant advances inside the party. Between 1983 and 1991 the counter attack to wrest control of Labour by the pro-US factions and the right of the party was in full swing, resulting in a leadership determined to abandon Labour's previous policies and adapt to Thatcherism. It was in this key period that Labour leaders started to position themselves as the alternative party of big business. But before that could happen the Tories needed to destroy the other key obstacle in their way: the power of the trade unions. What happened in Britain in 1984/85 bears comparison with the fate that befell the US unions in the period between 1936 and 1948, both in the sense that the conflict was real and intense and had only one victor and in the sense that propaganda and opinion management were central.

THE 1984/85 MINERS' STRIKE

The 1984/5 miners' strike was a year long confrontation between the Thatcher government and the business classes and organised labour. It resulted in the smashing of the labour movement and was a key milestone in the destruction of countervailing forces to the interests of the market. *Guardian* journalist Seumas Milne, who wrote the best book about the assault on the miners, *The Enemy Within*,[37] notes that 'it pitted the country's most powerful and politicised group of workers against a Tory administration bent on class revenge, and prepared to lay waste to our industrial heartlands and energy sector in the process, regardless of cost'.[38] Class revenge for past defeats, certainly, but also a forward looking strategy for imposing market mechanisms everywhere. The conduct of the strike learned from strike-breaking tactics in the US described in previous chapters. The first and most obvious parallel with the US approach to strike-breaking was the appointment of Ian MacGregor as boss of the Coal Board. MacGregor was known for his uncompromising union-busting tactics in the US. When head of mining company Amax, MacGregor had been the only one of nine major mining corporations to refuse to sign a deal allowing miners to move between employers without losing benefits. 'Amax clearly had no intention of conceding union recognition', and in a classic move pursued strike-breaking and union-busting by using communications. 'It wrote to the strikers threatening those who did not want to return to work with dismissal. It sent advice to them on how they could resign from the union and strike-break without penalty.' Whenever Amax faced objections, 'it resorted to either legal or public relations solutions. It never met the objectors to hammer out a compromise.'[39]

In Britain the aim of the dominant element of the Thatcher government was the 'decisive defeat' of the National Union of Mineworkers, in the words of the Chancellor of the Exchequer at the time, Nigel Lawson. Lawson was, of course, formerly the right wing journalist who had written a report for the Institute for the Study of Conflict. He and the others around Thatcher were highly class conscious and saw the dispute as a means to break union power. MacGregor was their ideal vehicle. Within a month of the strike starting it was realised that the public relations apparatus of the

Coal Board was not singing from the same aggressive hymn sheet and so they had to be downgraded and some of them eventually replaced by PR advisers who were more obviously class conscious. In his autobiography, *The Enemies Within*, MacGregor recalled that he took to Tim Bell, the PR operative who had sold the Tories in 1979 and 1983, because he could fight the propaganda battle with no holds barred. This was not a matter of a 'dispute settled in the classic way', but was an 'offensive in PR terms too'.[40] MacGregor went on: 'This had all the makings of a gloves-off job and I wanted a man who could handle the rough and tumble.'[41] The strike, as Bell put it privately, 'destroyed the NUM as a political force and was also a necessary step to preserve the monetocracy and meritocracy of Thatcherism'.[42] Bell was appointed MacGregor's personal PR adviser in May 1984, and performed a central role, not least in liaising with the 'The Lady' as they called Thatcher – keeping her informed and passing on her latest views.

From very early on the idea that the strike should not be settled but that the miners should be humiliated and forced back to work was central to the strategy of the cabal around MacGregor and Thatcher. Joining Bell as the organiser of many of the direct actions against the miners' union was David Hart, a far right businessman who was also an unofficial adviser to Thatcher. Hart was introduced to MacGregor through his brother (Tim Hart had worked with MacGregor at Lehman Brothers) and Ralph Harris, the founder of the Institute of Economic Affairs.[43] This again shows the links between the free market think tanks and the more 'direct action' end of corporate activism.

Hart too was of the view that 'you're fighting a political war. You're fighting for the freedom of the individual against the tyranny of the collective. It seems to me that there is only one viable strategy and that is outright victory.' Hart's strategy bore no small resemblance to the Mohawk Valley formula of the 1930s. 'MacGregor's new adviser argued that the way to break the strike was to launch an offensive on three fronts: first, a massive propaganda campaign to encourage miners to return to work; second, organise and finance working miners to catalyse this process; and third, wear down the NUM by legal action, using the government's new employment laws.'[44] Hart described his strategy as 'The Gulliver plan', because the union would be 'held down by dozens of tiny ropes'.[45]

Early in the strike Hart arranged for himself to be accredited as a *Times* feature writer and toured the mining areas looking for disaffected miners. He set about organising a network of disaffected and strikebreaking miners. Overcoming with cash and force of personality the suspicion that not surprisingly greeted his efforts, this bizarre Biggles-like figure travelled more than 35,000 miles in three months crisscrossing the coalfields, holding secret meetings in pubs and hotels. Hart encouraged a spirit of clandestinity. He adopted the alias David Lawrence... Hart put together around twenty five cells of dissident miners to rally the back-to-work movement under the auspices of the National Working Miners Committee. Hart originally financed the committee himself.[46]

Hart also arranged for money to be channelled into the fight from pro-business and anti-communist sources to support the numerous legal challenges. Tim Bell queried the possibility of this strategy: 'Legal action is costly', the working miners 'won't be able to pay', he said. Hart replied: 'Oh, I'll raise the money. There's plenty of people who want to help with the struggle.'[47]

Help came too from the forces of the state, particularly the Special Branch and intelligence services with whom Hart had close contacts. The use of informers and spies was a feature of the strike, with MI5 and the Special Branch exceptionally active in surveillance and in running agents inside the trade union movement and amongst industrial correspondents. In addition, it now appears that there was a fourth element to Hart's strategy which was 'to monitor the intentions of the NUM'. This was achieved, wrote Brian Crozier, 'through indirect but reliable access to two members of the executive' of the NUM.[48]

The propaganda campaign was directed by Bell. As Nick Jones writes:

Bell's great strength was that he could provide a direct link with the editors and executives of those newspapers which were urging the Prime Minister to stand firm and defeat Scargill. Once the dispute developed into an all-out confrontation between the mine workers and the state, many of the labour and industrial correspondents such as myself found it increasingly difficult to obtain inside information about the initiatives being taken behind the scenes by the management and the government. Because we were regarded as being too close to the NUM and the rest of the trade union movement, we were effectively being bypassed by MacGregor's advisers.[49]

The campaign was a success. As Nick Jones concluded 20 years later:

I recognise that the balance of the coverage tipped firmly in the management's favour once it became clear there was no longer any chance of a negotiated settlement. For the final six months of the strike, television and radio reporters became, in effect, the cheerleaders for the return to work. What had happened was that Margaret Thatcher had succeeded in setting the agenda: the outcome was going to be determined by the National Coal Board's success in persuading miners to abandon the strike and return to their pits... Each weekend as the strike wore on, the newspapers were full of stories warning the miners they were fighting a lost cause; this was backed up by new offers of increased redundancy money for those willing to return. The aim was to put pressure on the men's wives to persuade their husbands to give up the struggle.[50]

The conclusion we can draw from this is that the fight against the miners did have propaganda at the centre of it but it also required direct action to break the strike (including national mobilisation of the police and creation of the working miners organisations). Furthermore, it is clear that the propaganda campaign was not separable from the direct action and that indeed the propaganda itself had a coercive intent in undermining the morale of the strikers and their determination to carry on.

As a result, the power of the unions was for most purposes smashed for a generation. All that was left was to turn the Labour Party towards business.

SMITH AND THE DRIFT TO BUSINESS

The most intensive period of reform inside the Labour Party came between the aftermath of the 1987 election defeat and the 1992 election. John Smith was installed as Shadow Chancellor with Gordon Brown as his deputy. Smith's biographer refers to his appointment following 'a covert operation by the solidarity network' (an important anti-Bennite faction of the party).[51] The same source reveals that earlier in Smith's career a 'group of sympathetic industrialists had been so impressed by Smith that they clubbed together to pay for an extra researcher'.

On his appointment an 'Economic Secretariat' was created around Smith which also drew on the advice of a group of City economists including Gavyn Davies from Goldman Sachs. Davies went on to play a central role in New Labour as an adviser to Brown and friend of Blair and Mandelson. Before the 1997 election Davies and his wife Sue Nye (who runs Gordon Brown's private office) were involved in organising expensive dinners for City bosses as part of the Labour Party's bid to win them over. Davies recommended the partial privatisation of the BBC in the funding review he chaired in 1999.

The next year he was appointed vice-chair and in 2001 chairman of the BBC. He fell victim to the Hutton Inquiry in 2004 and resigned from the Corporation.[52]

The other main route into Labour for business was through the Labour Finance and Industry Group (LFIG), set up in 1972 but more or less moribund during Michael Foot's leadership of the party. It was resurrected by Kinnock and reached its peak under Smith. The LFIG 'undertook much of the preparatory research behind Labour's adoption of the Private Finance Initiative and claims authorship of "much of the work which went into developing systems for using private sector funding to deliver public sector capital projects and service provision"'.[53] LFIG was also a way to channel corporate money into favoured parts of the Labour Party via the mechanism of the 'blind trust'. As Tim Pendry, former deputy chair of the group, has explained:

I resigned from the Labour Party in 2000 after nearly a decade of trying to halt, Canute-like, centralisation of power and lack of accountability. Even before Tony Blair became leader, wealthy individuals were competing with one another for the attention of the rising stars. There was an informal political club of supporters, with its roots in the Wilson–Callaghan era, that has never entirely been understood outside the circle of immediate donors and their political beneficiaries.[54]

In Pendry's view:

There is nothing wrong with encouraging private interests to fund a party of the centre-left if both sides engage with their eyes open. But we have to ask a number of questions. Why have both sides been so desperate for so long not to have it revealed that they are engaged with one another? Why were prominent business figures as early as the mid-1990s operating opaquely to fund the private offices of rising politicians, internal party campaigns and individual bids for power? Who were they? What were their interconnections? What did they get in return? Did any of them have overseas connections? Who is now investigating this matter of central public interest?[55]

The answer to Pendry's last question is of course 'no-one'.[56] One of the first beneficiaries of the LFIG initiative was John Smith who was the main beneficiary of the Industrial Research Trust, established in April 1993.

The review of policy set in train after 1987 led to the Labour Party adopting the key policies that made business amenable to supporting them. In particular by 1988 Kinnock, Smith and Brown, had concluded that Labour should 'embrace UK membership of the then EEC and that it should advocate British membership of the European Exchange Rate Mechanism (ERM) as the first step towards an eventual single European Currency'. According to Robin Ramsay, 'the Labour leadership did not decide to advocate ERM membership for economic reasons, but because it was perceived by them to be a way of demonstrating to the City that they were trustworthy... By 1988 most of Labour's leaders had concluded that the City of London was too powerful to challenge.'[57]

By November 1989 the new orthodoxy was being spelt out to the Shadow Cabinet. And the mission to explain their new policies to the City was outlined. 'This would mean... meeting industrial and financial leaders to establish trust before election day.'[58] This mission became known as the 'prawn cocktail offensive'. As Ramsay observes, calling it an offensive was mere spin: 'It would have been more accurately named the prawn cocktail surrender'.[59] But the surrender – an essentially negative and defensive response to corporate power – released all sorts of other possibilities, not least of which was the headlong embrace of business as a positive force for good. From that moment the capture of the Labour Party by the corporations was under way.

In the same year as the Shadow Cabinet was briefed on Labour's changed orientation its economic spokesperson, John Smith, was able to do some explaining to the global elite who gathered at La Toja, Spain, for the annual Bilderberg Group meeting. Smith had joined the Steering Committee of Bilderberg in 1989 and remained on it until 1992. Bilderberg is one of the key global policy planning groups representing corporate interests, and as we have noted in Chapter 6, it is very keen to inculcate up-and-coming politicians before they achieve power. Gordon Brown, one of the key architects of New Labour, attended the 1991 meeting with Smith. Tony Blair attended the 1993 meeting when he was Shadow Home Secretary.

Smith's sudden demise in 1994 cleared the way for Tony Blair to become Labour leader and for the project of turning Labour into a party of business to accelerate. It should not be imagined, however, that this process was not already fairly advanced with the preparatory work done by Kinnock and the decisive shift made by Smith. Blair and Brown were to transform Labour from an apparently grudging acceptance that the market could not be bucked to an enthusiastic advocate of neo-liberalism.

9
Blair and the Business Lobby

New Labour is intensely relaxed about people getting filthy rich.
Peter Mandelson, 1998

THE 'PRAWN COCKTAIL OFFENSIVE'

Labour's courting of business encompassed much more than simply quieting market nerves about the possibility of Labour returning to government. It involved the spread of free market ideology throughout the party. This happened in several ways. First there was the prawn cocktail offensive to carry the message to the most important audience: the City. Second, there was the process of acclimatising ambitious young careerists in the party to the idea that the market could not and should not be trifled with. The British American Project was one avenue for that. Third, was the process by which lobbying and PR oriented to the new Labour machine. Fourth, was the operation of spreading this wisdom across the party and in public debate, which was done by the creation of a range of new think tanks and policy groups.

Labour's schmoozing of the City was the product of four successive election defeats, desperation and the attempts of corporations and US interests to undermine the confidence of the left and turn those who could be turned. Neal Lawson, a former adviser to Gordon Brown, said in 2001 that 'Labour got to the stage in the early 1990s where we'd give up virtually anything to get elected, and that was right to do so'.[1] The other three parts of the process were also driven by the increasing involvement of the business in the party.

Convincing the City was just the start. Then Labour had to convince big business to support it financially, otherwise they would remain dependent for funding on the trade unions. After Blair became leader the Labour Finance and Industry Group was supplemented by the groups around Michael Levy who took charge of fundraising. Blair had been introduced to Levy at the Israeli Embassy following a trip to Israel funded by the Labour Friends of Israel, the Zionist lobby group which Blair had joined on becoming an MP.[2] Levy and Blair became friends and tennis partners. The tennis was put to good effect in Levy's fundraising efforts for the party:

Lord Levy is famously a very good host... He will invite people to his home and maybe invite them to play tennis on his private tennis court and say, 'Well, Tony might just turn up'. Tony does turn up, they play a round of tennis, Tony leaves. Twenty minutes later, he will be sweet-talking them into making a donation, and many people are only too happy to cough up.[3]

Levy reportedly raised over £10 million for the party. Alongside this were the efforts to raise funds more widely with Labour supporting celebrities and business people, notably the famous dinners run by Julia Hobsbawm (a BAP alumnus) and Sarah Macaulay (later married to Gordon Brown). Hobsbawm joined the fledgling Labour Party high value donor unit in 1991 and managed the party's 1000 club for donors of £1,000 and up. When she launched Hobsbawm Macaulay Communications (HMC) in 1993 the newly formed agency ran gala dinners and other fundraising activities. This was one of the earliest links between the Labour Party and the PR and lobbying world. HMC also took on the Labour Industry Forum, a breakaway from the Labour Finance and Industry Groups associated with businessman Gerald Frankel and then Shadow Minister for Trade and Industry, Jack Cunningham. Cunningham was on the far right of the party and had a long history of working with business. In 1991 Cunningham disclosed in the Register of Members' Interests that he was an adviser to Albright & Wilson, Leather Chemicals and Dow Ltd, the latter being the company responsible for the Bhopal disaster in 1984.[4] But the Industry Forum did not easily attract the support of those CEOs it targeted. As Tom Pendry recalls:

I attended as guest a meeting for Jack Cunningham with a room full of Directors of Public Affairs. I suspect that Cunningham's team wanted the organ grinders of the FTSE-100 but got their PR monkeys instead. This was a sign that New Labour still did not understand how the system worked; big business was going to stay aloof until it was clear that Labour would win. Even then it would delegate all but the most important contacts to their lobbyists; but the road to Drapergate and to avowedly New Labour lobby firms was beginning to be laid.[5]

Nevertheless, by 1995 the group announced that over 100 large companies had joined including Thorn EMI, Glaxo Wellcome, 3i, National Westminster Bank, and Nissan.[6] HMC lubricated the intermingling of Labour and business interests and provided a model for involvement of PR and lobbying firms. But HMC also acted for

New Labour think tanks such as Demos and the IPPR which formed a second and important strand of the integration with big business.

LOBBYING AND THE RISE OF 'SLEAZE'

The 'cash-for-questions' scandal was a key ingredient of the decline and fall of the Tories. The climate of 'Tory sleaze' rocked a party already divided over its orientation to Europe. This is often portrayed as an opposition between diehard Tory little Englanders and a more liberal internationalism of the Tory left. But playing underneath this was the opposition between nationally based business (largely manufacturing and SMEs) and globalising transnational corporations who were in favour of the euro, Maastricht and of the whole European project to liberalise markets and integrate economies into the global market. Here was another critical factor behind big business beginning to favour Labour. The third reason for the decline of the Tories was that they lost their reputation (largely won by virtue of spin and doing what business wanted) for safe economic management. Perceptions of economic incompetence play very badly with the electorate and this was not entirely unconnected with losing the confidence of big business.

The face of Tory sleaze and the cash-for-questions debacle is that of Neil Hamilton, now a B-list 'celebrity' who is hired out along with his wife Christine by after-dinner speaking agencies. The agencies report that Christine costs £4,000 a go plus expenses and accommodation and that Neil is thrown in for nothing as part of the package.[7] But it should be remembered that Hamilton was only one link in a chain of corruption stretching from Parliament and Whitehall to the lobbying industry and through to the corporations. The cynicism and the corruption were not just a question of the foibles of a few dodgy Tory MPs or even a couple of iffy lobbying firms. They were the logical consequence of the shift to the market accomplished so effectively by Thatcher in the 1980s unleashing energies – most obviously the 'big bang' in the City in 1986 – that would later overwhelm both her and the Conservative Party.

The lobbying industry grew exponentially in the 1980s in the same way and broadly for the same reasons that the PR industry expanded. The earliest books on PR and lobbying in the UK – even up to Mark Hollingsworth's 1991 *MPs for Hire* – record the pre-history of lobbying by reference to a handful of colourful figures and an 'old boy' network running through London club-land. Invariably they mention

Commander Powell, as the grandfather of the industry and founder of one of the UK's earliest lobbying firms Watney & Powell.[8]

But in the 1980s the industry expanded rapidly as the opportunities to influence government policy mushroomed. This was not just a question of a more business-friendly government but of a series of measures designed to give business a much freer hand – to free the market, by contracting out, privatisation, and the wholesale attack on trade unions and the public sector. So corporations employed lobbyists to push for contracting out or later privatisation: the lobbyists were then able to exploit the business opportunities of working for the contract winner or privatised industry when the lobbying was successful.

PRIVATISATION IN THE 1980s

The move towards the privatisation of national assets and the deregulation of service provision in state institutions was not sparked by a simple decision at the centre of government. Privatisation of the utilities was not mentioned in the 1979 Conservative manifesto[9] and was not really an issue in the 1983 election campaign.[10] Deregulation was the objective of key currents in the Conservative Party and also of certain business interests who were in a position to take advantage of it. The lobbying campaign for deregulation of NHS services was by all accounts extremely effective and had already started by the 1978 Conservative Party conference. Industry trade associations met with the Minister of Health in October 1979, five months after the Conservatives' election victory. Here we can pick up the story of a young Westminster City Councillor, who followed a now traditional route through the revolving door of power, moving between local politics, think tanks and PR and ending up as a Minister in charge of part of the deregulated industry he helped to create. This was Michael Forsyth, author of two key pamphlets for the Adam Smith Institute mentioned earlier (Chapter 5).

The latter of the two, *Reservicing Health* (1982),[11] 'considerably strengthened' the contracting-out campaign just as the former, *Reservicing Britain* (1980),[12] had 'strengthened' government commitment to competitive tendering in local authorities.[13]

In 1981 Forsyth set up his PR firm, Michael Forsyth Associates. Among their clients were firms and trade associations from the catering, cleaning and textile maintenance industries which stood to gain from contracting out, such as the Association of British

Launderers.[14] Others hired backbench Tory MPs or employed civil servants formerly in charge of monitoring contracting out.[15] For example, the Contract Cleaning and Maintenance Association hired John Gorst MP, director of PR firm John Gorst Associates, and both they and Johnson the Cleaners employed leading PR firm Good Relations, which in turn retained Tory MPs Michael Mates and Sir Anthony Grant. Sketchley, an office cleaning company, meanwhile, retained Biss Lancaster who hired Neville Trotter MP as a consultant.[16] After Forsyth's election to Westminster in 1983 he became a parliamentary consultant to one of his PR firm's clients, the contractors Pritchard Services. The success of the lobbying campaign was as Ascher notes in 'telling the government something it wanted to hear',[17] but the impact of the lobbying according to one of the contractors 'far exceeded our wildest expectations'.[18]

A *Financial Times* poll in 1985 found that 41 per cent of 180 major British corporations surveyed were using political consultants, paying them an average of £28,000 per annum. Over a quarter (28 per cent) of the 180 corporations used PR companies for government relations work, paying an average fee of £33,000.[19] 'A decade of deregulation and privatisation', wrote Mark Hollingsworth in 1991, 'has been as prosperous for lobbyists and MPs as it has been for merchant bankers and contract seeking companies. Back benchers and former ministers have run willingly into the arms of the brokers and consultants despite the conflicts of interest.'[20] In January 1991, 35 MPs were paid advisers or directors to lobbying or consultancy firms.[21] The shift to the market under the Conservatives created added potential for conflict of interest because the more the market became involved in politics the more the potential for institutional corruption increased. MPs were not required to declare their clients in the Register of Members' Interests. 'Consequently, an MP can act for any organisation or company and merely disclose the innocuous-sounding lobbying or family firm. For example, George Gardiner, Conservative MP for Reigate, was employed by T.A. Cutbill and Partners between 1985 and 1987. But his constituents remained unaware that this was a public-relations outfit whose clients included the Wines and Spirits Association and the brewers Whitbread Ltd.'[22] Timothy Brinton, consultant to Communications Strategy Ltd from 1982 until 1987, told Mark Hollingsworth:

I am available to Communications Strategy for help and advice, but I am not prepared to enter into correspondence as to which clients may be involved, or indeed what consultancy fees may be paid. Parliament makes no requirement that I should do so and I would regard this as a private matter between myself and Communications Strategy.[23]

It was the mid 1980s before many of the big transnational corporations began to hire lobbyists systematically. It was in this climate that Ian Greer Associates worked its charms with the Minister for Corporate Affairs – Neil Hamilton – and the MP Tim Smith. Smith is not remembered now because he admitted doing what he was accused of and resigned. Hamilton tried to brazen it out and became a symbol of Tory corruption.[24] Greer – 'the embodiment of the Westminster hustler' – adopted the practice of paying MPs to work for him and in particular of 'making secret payments' to MPs who introduced clients to him.[25] This was the practice which the *Guardian* exposed in the cash-for-questions affair, when it revealed that Smith and Hamilton had been taking secret cash payments in return for asking questions in the house.

The Conservative Party had been in power for so long that some of them believed they were invulnerable. Neil Hamilton in particular had been exposed as a far right politician, and for his involvement in an incident involving an alleged Hitler salute outside the Reichstag in Berlin, in the 1986 Panorama programme *Maggie's Militant Tendency*. Hamilton contested this account in court claiming that he had no clear memory of any salute. The BBC had been so cowed by the Tories that the management were ordered by the governors to give in without a fight and apologise. After the case against him collapsed, Hamilton 'displayed one of his now infamous lapses in "candour"'. Writing for the *Sunday Times* 'he admitted he did give a little salute with two fingers to his nose to give the impression of a toothbrush moustache. "Somebody on the trip clearly did not share our sense of humour," he wrote.'[26] Hamilton must have thought he could do whatever he liked.[27]

In the 1980s and early 1990s the lobbying game was an almost entirely Conservative affair. There were examples of Labour MPs with their fingers in the lobbying till, but they were few and far between.[28] The realignment of the Labour Party was to change all that. Lobbyists are interested in one thing: getting their way. If they can do so by managing a Labour Party made safe for capital then they will. The change from Tory to Labour was not a change from corrupt to clean politics. It was a handover of power from one party of business to another. It should not have surprised us that the Labour Party would thereafter come to be involved in the same kinds of corruption as the Tories. They were operating the same kinds of policies in the same interests and the institutional corruption of the Tory years was only exacerbated by New Labour.

THE LOBBYISTS GET THE SCENT

In 1995 the *New Statesman* listed 16 Labour activists working for lobbying companies. By 1997–2001 the recruitment of Labour activists and advisers by lobbying firms and the recruitment by Labour of former lobbyists had exploded. A list of only the most obvious is in Table 9.1. Of the first wave of 79 special advisers appointed by the

Table 9.1   Labour Party activists associated with lobbying firms

Ex-Labour activists and advisers	Lobbying firm
Derek Draper	GPC Market Access (now Fleishman Hillard)
Mike Craven	
Anna Healy	
Joy Johnson	
Ben Lucas	LLM Communications
Neal Lawson	
Jon Mendelsohn	
Colin Byrne	Shandwick
David Hill	Bell Pottinger Good Relations
Cathy McGlynn	
Howard Dawber	
Karl Milner	GJW Government Relations
Roger Sharp	
Roger Liddle	Prima Europe
Mike Lee	Westminster Strategy
Jo Moore	
Michael Burrell	
Tom Engel	
Nick Pecorelli	Politics International
Tim Allan	BSkyB then Portland PR
Mark Adams	Foresight Communications
Sarah Pearce	
Jack McConnell	Beattie Media
Kevin Reid	
Mike Watson	PS Communications
Henry McLeish	Halogen PR
Nicki Lewis	Dewe Rogerson, then AS Biss
Alan Donnelly	Sovereign Strategy
Baroness Billingham former MEP	

Sources: www.spinprofiles.org; D. Osler, *Labour Party plc*, Edinburgh: Mainstream, 2002.

Blair government in 1997, 13 went on to join lobbying or PR firms (or do PR or lobbying for corporations) and a further seven to corporate funded think tanks.[29]

The impact of New Labour's landslide election victory on the UK lobbying industry was immediate. Overnight, the stock of advisers to New Labour's front bench rocketed among commercial lobbying firms whose growth and success had been inextricably linked with successive Conservative administrations.[30] Special advisers and party advisers-turned-lobbyists quickly became embroiled in controversy regarding their ability to gain access to ministers on behalf of commercial interests.

CASH FOR ACCESS

The cash-for-access scandal of July 1998 was the result of a 'sting' operation by the *Observer* newspaper. Posing as a US business representative, journalist Greg Palast secured offers of access to cabinet ministers from Derek Draper and Roger Liddle. Both Draper and Liddle had previously been partners in the lobbying firm Prima Europe. At the time, Draper was working as a lobbyist for GPC Market Access (which had taken over Prima Europe) while Liddle was employed as a special adviser in the Number 10 policy unit. Draper resigned from GPC, although Liddle remained in post. Within a few weeks, the government had announced the tightening of rules governing the conduct of special advisers and civil servants.[31] But the assumption of the rule changes was that Draper was a 'rogue elephant' rather than the much more uncomfortable truth that a system of institutionalised corruption had neatly transferred itself from the Tories to Labour.[32]

Palast supplied evidence to the Committee on Standards and Privileges, insisting 'Members of the Government passed sensitive, confidential information to key lobbyists and did so systematically [and that] members of the Government have established a system of privileged access for industry clients of connected lobbyists'.[33] He was politely ignored.

The re-orientation of the lobbying firms towards Labour was of course in part because New Labour was pretty sure to win the 1997 election. But in previous election contests in 1945, 1964 or 1974 for example, there was not a rush for lobbying firms to recruit Labour activists. It could only happen once two changes had occurred – first a decisive shift in governance towards the market which had given a huge boost to the PR and lobbying industries, and second, a decisive shift by Labour towards becoming a party of business.

By the 2001 election Labour's campaign was being run by lobbyists. While it is usual for lobbyists to work on secondment for the campaigns of all the main political parties, the role of lobbyists in the New Labour campaign was unmissable: 'The People's party is now the Lobbyists' party', writes Mark Hollingsworth.

At 7.30am most days during the [2001] election campaign Colin Byrne, chief executive of the public relations consultancy Weber Shandwick Worldwide, has

---

Turning up the stones

A snap-shot of the remaking of Labour under Blair was revealed in the BBC documentary *Living With the Enemy*[34] which brought together New Labour lobbyist Derek Draper (former aide to Peter Mandelson) and Paul Dainton, an Old Labour trade unionist from Wakefield. The film, shot just days before Draper became embroiled in the cash-for-access scandal, vividly captures the hubris and swagger of New Labour's inner circle. The programme had some telling moments, such as Draper driving through Whitehall in his convertible Mercedes as he hails Peter Kilfoyle in the traffic, who shouts 'very impressive, Derek' before accelerating away. Then they encounter a couple of corporate lobbyists outside the Commons: 'Now hello you two, how are you? Patrick Law[35] ...We're making a television programme.' At this point the other lobbyist, who has just come into frame, recoils sharply – perhaps the instinctive reaction of lobbyists to publicity? 'I don't want to be in it', comes the reply 'People might say I'm close to you Derek.' 'Exactly', Draper jokes as he tells the camera: 'They're two of my clients from British Gas. Obviously they've been off lobbying themselves today. They don't need me really.'

Old Labourite Dainton clearly agrees. He is aghast at Draper's charge-out rate of £250 per hour, and is left unmoved by the efforts of Draper and his mentor, Peter Mandelson, to convince him the Millennium Dome is a good use of tax-payers' money. In a monologue to camera Dainton prophetically exclaims: 'These spin doctors... are a bunch of con-men. They're a bunch of lobbyists of the worst ilk of the old Tory regime. I haven't seen a redeeming feature amongst anybody... People are using their positions for their own financial gain.' The favours-for-favours culture among special advisers is caught as Draper does some 'pro-bono' work for Dainton's local community campaign against a landfill dump. He phones a friend in John Prescott's office to inquire why a petition from the campaign has been ignored... and ends up agreeing to buy a report on business and politics that the special adviser has written for the Cranfield Management Centre for £145!

The disdain for Old Labour is palpable throughout the film. Draper refers to Paul behind his back as 'Yosser', a limp reference to the Alan Bleasdale character from *Boys from the Blackstuff* (1980), whose catchphrase was 'gissa job!' In Draper's private members club, Soho House on Old Compton Street, one of his circle can't bear to listen to Paul's political views any longer and whispers into Derek's ear, 'How many young, forward-looking, interesting, intelligent people would vote for that moaning git over there?'

a meeting with Clive Hollick, chief executive of United News and Media plc, at Labour's headquarters at Millbank. Hollick heads the party's business relations unit and Byrne has been working closely with him – 'in a personal capacity and outside of working hours', as he puts it – to persuade the corporate sector to support Labour.[36]

The huge increase in interaction between lobbyists and PR consultancies and the Labour Party signals a major shift from a professed identification with representing voters to representing special interests, almost exclusively business interests. This is reflected in the closer relationship between Labour MPs and business. In 1991 a total of 17 labour MPs were either directors or advisers of private corporations.[37] In 2005 more than 40 had directorships or were paid by corporations as advisers or received donations from them.[38] (See Appendix for details.)

Among the high rollers was David Blunkett who made between £145,000 and £150,000 on top of his MP's salary that year. Among his activities were fees for two speeches at events organised by PR firm Weber Shandwick; a fee for facilitating discussion on business links with tertiary education organised by BT; and an after-dinner speech for Portland PR for which Blunkett was paid more than £5,000. Alan Milburn also spoke at a Portland PR event and Stephen Byers spoke for a fee at an Adam Smith Institute event, on investment in the Ukraine; Brian Donohoe received a donation from Scottish PR firm Media House run by the former editor of the Scottish edition of the *Sun*; Doug Henderdon was paid for his advice to McDonald's. Jimmy Hood, George Howarth, Eric Illsey, Mark Tami and Joan Walley acted as consultants for Scottish Coal, William Hill, the Caravan Club, Guild of British Travel Agents and the Lighting Industry Federation respectively.

Among the MPs who took corporate funded trips were:

- Frank Field, who declared a trip to Australia funded by the market fundamentalist Centre for Independent Studies.[39]
- Kevan Jones, who travelled to Washington DC to meet congressional and business interests and British diplomats, to discuss the UK/US defence trade. His flights and accommodation were paid for by the UK Defence Forum. The forum is a secretive organisation which does not reveal its funding sources but does note that membership is open 'to UK companies with UK

employees supplying equipment or services to the UK defence industry'.[40]

- Linda Gilroy, whose 2004 trip to Kazakhstan was paid for by the Consolidated Construction International Company and British Gas.
- Phil Hope who received corporate hospitality from Provident Financial
- Tom Levitt, whose centre-court tickets for Wimbledon in 2005 were donated by Nestlé plc.
- Frank Roy, whose week-long trip to South Africa in 2005 was also generously supported by Nestlé.

This list does not include those MPs who have previously declared directorships or payments such as James Purnell who has previously declared working for a PR company employed by BSkyB (to which we will return below); nor the MPs who travel to events paid for by the corporations such as Mark Fisher's trip to the British-Spanish Tertulias which is the Anglo-Spanish version of the British American Project. Substantial numbers of Labour MPs do still get sponsorship from the trades unions and are markedly less likely than the Conservatives to have extensive corporate directorships, but the involvement of the corporations in putting help in the way of Labour MPs is hard to miss.

THE THINK TANK EXPLOSION

Another of the streams that ran through New Labour was the creation of a rash of 'left leaning' think tanks. The first was the Institute for Public Policy Research (IPPR) set up to assist Kinnock in reforming the Labour Party in 1988. The SDP got in on the act the year after with the formation of the Social Market Foundation, which after the split in the SDP moved in an increasingly Thatcherite direction.[41] Meanwhile many of the key activists of the SDP found themselves returning to the fold of the Labour Party under Blair. Or rather joining a party which had become what the SDP had intended to be – market friendly and pro-US. Amongst those returning was Roger Liddle, one of the conspirators who left the party to join the SDP and later, after a spell in lobbying in which he made a fortune, worked at the Downing Street policy unit in 1998 before joining Peter Mandelson in Brussels in 2005.

Other think tanks followed including Peter Mandelson's corporate-funded brainchild, The Policy Network, and most importantly Demos and the Foreign Policy Centre. All of these were means for big business to channel funds to 'left leaning' think tanks as part of the reorientation towards Labour. The IPPR was set up by Clive Hollick, the long-time business backer of Labour with a £1 million donation. John Eatwell, a former Kinnock adviser, was also involved. Both now sit in the House of Lords. The IPPR was established so that 'its fellows might study how the then modish phrase "market socialism" could be put into practice'.[42] It assumed an important role in the Kinnock policy review after the 1987 defeat, hosting two secret meetings organised by those who wanted to turn the party towards business (including Peter Mandelson, Patricia Hewitt and Charles Clarke).[43]

James Cornford, its first director, was succeeded by Gerry Holtham, 'who reputedly took a £250,000 pay cut to move from the City to the institute's offices in Covent Garden. The IPPR became even more business-friendly. One complacent report claimed that the NHS did not need greater resources.' The election of Labour saw IPPR people move into government. Patricia Hewitt and Baroness (Tessa) Blackstone became ministers; Cornford became a Special Adviser in 1997 and one of his successors, the Blair and Mandelson protégé Matthew Taylor, went on to become the head of Blair's policy unit.[44]

Of the new think tanks, Demos, set up in 1993, was integral to the realignment of Labour as a pro-market party. Among the tributaries for this initiative was the trajectory of *Marxism Today*, technically the 'theoretical journal' of the Communist Party of Great Britain, but which performed the role of coalescing those within the party who agreed with the founders of New Labour that the left had to abandon its key policies. Of course they put it in slightly fancier language, but the import was the same. Under editor Martin Jacques, *Marxism Today* started questioning left principles and opened up the journal to the right, including free marketeers who had helped deliver Thatcherism through the influential right-wing think tanks.

The 'Euro-communist' faction around *Marxism Today* thought Thatcherism had succeeded because it had a project. It was determined to roll back the advances of 'socialism'. With its project came a 'narrative' which had won consent – or had constructed a 'hegemony' which was bought into by key sections of the working class.

This kind of analysis was most strongly connected with the pre-eminent theorist of the faction, Stuart Hall. With Jacques he produced the key book of the period in 1983. Credited with inventing the phrase 'Thatcherism' the book of the same name pushed the line that to combat Thatcher, the left also need a project and a narrative to go with it.[45] This project had to take as its starting point that the working class had deserted Labour for a new-found consumerist politics. The new left project would have to abandon old left certainties and embrace the market. This was the kind of current which found much favour with the emerging reformers in the Labour Party. As Decca Aitkenhead has written, *Marxism Today*

Fetishised and feted the core essentials of Thatcherism – individualism, the market, private ownership, consumer culture. As the issues progressed, the magazine moved on from flirtation with Thatcherism to a preparation of the ground for Blairism. Almost every fundamental of New Labour can be found in the pages of *Marxism Today's* back issues. Rights and responsibilities, community and citizenship, love of modernisation, they were all dressed up rather unconvincingly as a 'progressive' take on Marxism.[46]

The project would also need to be sold and this required a narrative. Yet again the ideologues of the Communist Party (CP) were able to offer something to the reformers in Labour who were busy in this period under Mandelson, Philip Gould and Byrne trying to find new ways to sell the Labour Party. The post-modern notion of narrative, which essentially required that Labour tell its own story, was useful in this endeavour. The beauty of the concept, derived from Left Bank theorising and largely introduced into English speaking academia and the left intelligentsia by Stuart Hall, was that it abandoned any notion of the reality of class divisions (or anything else) in favour of a conception that there were only contending stories.

This was taken up with enthusiasm in New Labour. Peter Oborne tells us that the first reference he has been able to find of this usage of the word 'narrative' in New Labour circles was by Geoff Mulgan in 1994.[47] Mulgan, a former writer for *Marxism Today*, became the first head of Demos. Demos was set up out of the ashes of *Marxism Today*, by the journal's editor Martin Jacques, and Stuart Hall was appointed as one of its advisers. In a long process of meetings in London in the early 1990s they drew together people from across the political spectrum including some on the left in the Labour Party, but crucially also people from advertising, marketing, PR and business. According to Jacques: 'I saw what Labour Party sectarianism could be like, and realised I had to get rid of all the undergrowth that had accumulated.' 'We had stupid disagreements about whom to invite', said Jacques: 'We're not having them, they're on the wrong wing of the Labour Party.' Bob Tyrrell, managing director of the Henley Centre, who became an adviser to Demos, agreed: 'It was also still too left-wing. It's important that Demos should be seen as neither left nor right, nor too traditionally political, with people drawn from all walks of life.' 'I knew from the outset', said Jacques, 'that Geoff [Mulgan] had to be the director, that he was the one person who could give it the necessary intellectual drive.' In one of his most telling remarks, Jacques said of Mulgan: 'he's not encumbered by ideology from the past'.[48]

Demos found the £100,000 core funding needed to launch from business. Core sponsors, who, 'like think-tank sponsors generally, tend to remain anonymous, include two manufacturing companies, a big retailer, an advertising company, a media organisation, a service company, and a trade union'.[49]

Demos performed several key functions for business. First it was a means of donating to the Labour Party without having to give the money directly. As Geoff Mulgan has noted, 'Big business has come to see funding for think tanks as a more acceptable way to establish links with political parties than direct funding.'[50] Second it was a way of giving cover to corporate demands – the third party trick in action. It was also a way of moving the party towards business by virtue of an educational process facilitating indirect opportunities to meet with influential Labour people in seemingly neutral surroundings. Lastly it was a means to link together the 'New Labour' ideologues even more firmly with free market think tanks.

What could be better than involving ex-communists, who had already shown their openness to the views of the new right? Along with Leadbetter and Mulgan and other ex-associates of the Communist Party such as Stuart Hall, were Sir Douglas Hague (Institute of Economic Affairs and Centre for Policy Studies), Graham Mather (Institute of Economic Affairs), Arthur Seldon (Institute of Economic Affairs, Mont Pelerin Society), David Marquand (ex SDP, Renewal, co-editor of a book with Seldon), Martin Taylor (Barclays Bank, Bilderberg Group, IPPR), Bob Tyrrell (Centre for Policy Studies, Henley Centre – owned by WPP) and Dennis Stevenson (Pearson, SRU). Some on the right were evidently a little sceptical of getting into bed with recently reformed communists. Arthur Seldon is also on the Advisory Council of the Libertarian Alliance. Its journal *Free Life* described Demos as part of a cavalry of Trojan horses within the citadel of leftism. The intellectual agenda is served up in a left wing manner, laced with left wing cliches and verbal gestures, but underneath all that the agenda is very nearly identical to that of the Thatcherites.[51]

Together with fellow *Marxism Today* regulars, Demos became a key ideologue for New Labour. Charles Leadbetter wrote a manifesto for the new 'weightless' economy and also joined Demos as a research associate. 'I live on my wits', he wrote, as if that was or could be a universal condition.[52] Blair anointed his book, *Living on Thin Air*, by describing Leadbetter as 'an extraordinarily interesting thinker'. In it he shows the distance that Labour had travelled from a seeming grudging acceptance of the market to becoming its advocate. Lauding Paul Drayson and his company, PowderJect, for creating a product (the needle-less injection) out of 'knowledge' as opposed to manufacturing, Leadbetter tells us that 'it is only by treating people like Drayson... as heroes for creating wealth from knowledge that Britain will develop a fully fledged entrepreneurial culture'.[53] Drayson, a Tory supporter[54] and the former head of the Bioindustry Association, gave £100,000 to the Labour Party while the Ministry of Defence (MoD) was considering his tender for smallpox vaccines. In what has been called a 'cash-for-contracts' scandal, the government awarded Drayson's company, PowderJect, the smallpox vaccine contract without any competition. The contract was worth £32 million and Drayson is thought to have made around £20 million for PowderJect from this deal.

It later emerged that Drayson had been in a group of businessmen who had breakfasted with the Prime Minister in Downing Street at about the time MoD experts were meeting to decide what type of smallpox vaccine to buy. When the vaccine deal came to be finalised, officials discovered that Drayson had already made an exclusive deal with the manufacturer of the Lister smallpox vaccine, thus cornering the market in the vaccine the MoD had decided to buy.

Drayson has also been a biotechnology lobbyist via his role as head of the BioIndustry Association and his support for pro-biotech propaganda organisations. Drayson's company, while he still headed it, was a financial supporter of the pro-GM Science Media Centre (SMC) – a pet project of Lord Sainsbury's. PowderJect's support for the SMC dried up following Drayson's departure. Drayson has also served on a working party of the controversial pro-GM lobby-group Sense About Science.[55] He was given a peerage by Blair in highly controversial circumstances in 2004 and within weeks wrote another cheque to Labour for £500,000.[56] In 2005 Blair appointed Drayson a minister at the MoD.[57]

This is the new politics of the weightless economy: Not very enticing and not very different to the relations between business and government found in the Victorian era.

DENNIS THE MENACE

An influential role in the process of the take-over of the Labour Party by big business seems to have been played by a key conduit with a very low profile. We had not noticed Dennis Stevenson for most of the period of researching this book. If someone had mentioned Lord Stevenson of Coddenham, we would have been none the wiser, until we came across the research of Billy Clark.[58] This cast a light on a power broker who is central to the New Labour–business nexus, but who has an incredibly low public profile for someone with so many fingers in so many pies.

Stevenson was one of the early funders and advisers to Demos. He sat on their advisory council for over ten years until 2004. Stevenson has had a varied and colourful career. He was a member of the Labour Party in the 1960s, and was appointed by Prime Minister Ted Heath to negotiate with the Japanese banks on the government's behalf at the tender age of 26. He founded a consultancy in the early 1970s called SRU with the 'Sloane Ranger' marketing guru Peter York (real name Peter Wallis). He has been on a dizzying number of corporate boards including Consignia, BSkyB, Lazard Bros, Manpower Inc., Thames TV, Tyne Tees, J. Rothschild, St James Place Capital and many others. He was board member (from 1986) then chair of the board of Pearson (owner of the *Financial Times* and *The Economist*) from 1997 to 2005 and of Halifax from 1999 and the merged Halifax Bank of Scotland from 2001.

Stevenson joined the board of Pearson and almost immediately became chairman, recruiting Marjorie Scardino of the Atlantic Council of the United States, the NATO funded think tank and lobby group. Stevenson says that on taking over 'we stopped all party political donations, including a substantial one to the Labour Party'.[59] At the time Pearson said it would 'instead make donations to policy institutes across the political spectrum'.[60] In other words – across the pro-market political spectrum, Demos included.[61]

For a time (from 1997) Stevenson was an unpaid special adviser to Blair in Downing Street. Other official jobs include an appointment to the cultural propaganda outfit the British Council and in 2000 chairing the newly created House of Lords Appointments Commission to appoint the new 'people's peers' which he notably failed to do. Stevenson caused some controversy when noting that hairdressers, for example, would be unlikely to be appointed: 'You haven't got your hairdresser in this list. But, if you go back to our criteria, one of them is that the human being will be comfortable operating in the House of Lords.'[62] Instead the list of people's peers included Sir John Browne, then CEO of BP, amongst other members of the already existing political elite.

Stevenson's connections with New Labour are deep, being close to most of the key movers. He says he first met Geoff Mulgan

when I was giving a talk to the Council on Foreign Relations in New York. They're very high-powered, I'm very busy, and I wanted some help. Somebody pointed me in Geoff's direction – he was still working for Gordon Brown then, as his researcher – and he was wholly wonderful, incredibly widely read... and he came up with new thoughts, interesting angles.[63]

Stevenson recruited Mandelson for SRU in 1990 before he was an MP and after his time as Labour Party Communications Director. He describes Mandelson 'as a close friend, but it has nothing to do with politics'.[64] His connections with Mandelson reportedly go back to the 1970s 'when both were involved in youth movements', reports the *Sunday Times*. At the time, Mandelson was deeply involved with the British Youth Council (BYC) and was elected chairman in 1977, the year it disaffiliated as the British chapter of the World Association of Youth, a CIA funded front group. The BYC was also funded by the Foreign Office to pursue British state interests.

SRU acted 'as problem-solver for companies including ICI, Unilever, Marks & Spencer, BAT, Clarks Shoes, Allied Dunbar, Thorn EMI, WH Smith and Ladbroke. In 1988, Marks & Spencer gave £25,000 to the British United Industrialists group (which donated most of its money to the Conservative Party). BAT gave £4,000 to the Centre for Policy Studies, the think-tank founded by Margaret Thatcher, and £2,500 to the right-wing Aims of Industry.'[65] In other words Mandelson was arguably – by this stage – working for the other side.

Stevenson was an under-recognised gateway for big business into Labour, saying in 1998 that: 'I have known Tony Blair for about 10 years, both socially and through work, and he has always wanted to make Labour into an alternative party of business. There were some big businessmen who were always pro-Labour: Lord Hollick and Chris Haskins for instance. Blair wanted to meet the others, so I organised evenings where he could meet friends of mine, people running FTSE companies.'[66]

Stevenson's dinner guests included Bob Ayling of British Airways, Mike Blackburn of Halifax, Niall Fitzgerald of Unilever, and many others. 'As a result,' he says, 'they were more inclined to do things for the government – just as they would have done for the Tories.' 'Blair has involved businessmen to a huge extent', says Stevenson. 'In fact, he has almost delegated power to them. I think there is a legitimate question about the extent to which that is actually right.'[67] A legitimate question indeed, but not one about which Stevenson appears overly concerned. As he notes: 'I am not in the category of people who think profits are a bad thing. If you set up a company and employ people and create wealth, you are doing a lot of good – as much as a social worker.'[68]

Stevenson has a shareholding in the New Labour-connected PR firm Lexington Communications. He also has a shareholding in the PR group Huntsworth run by Tory peer Peter Gummer (Lord Chadlington). Stevenson is also chancellor of the University of the Arts and a former director of the Tate Gallery.

The distinction between the think tanks and their sponsors is minimal, but in the recent past there has been a greater recognition of this in public debate. The think tanks are now recognised simply as lobbying fronts for its sponsors. 'You won't hear ideas being discussed very much in think-tank offices: organising the next event, publishing the next policy paper and chasing funding must come before changing the world', says Rob Blackhurst, formerly spin doctor for the Foreign Policy Centre. 'To survive, most have to turn themselves into unofficial lobbyists. Corporate sponsors pay (the going rate is about £4,000) to have their chairman or chief executive at the same event as a cabinet minister – sometimes so that he has the chance for a discreet whisper, sometimes to borrow a bit of respectability.'[69] A Demos report in 2002 was mocked by the *Guardian* for simply reproducing what its sponsor telecoms company C&W wanted. The headline: 'Break up BT, says Demos. Its sponsor? C&W.'[70]

THE REVOLVING DOOR

The consequence of all the overlapping relationships is the formation of a new ruling nexus between New Labour, lobbying and PR firms, think tanks and corporations. It is identifiably distinct from the old Tory ruling elite, but there are connections to an extent unimaginable in the 1980s. The nexus involves a revolving door between government, lobbying, think tanks and industry through which special advisers, ministers and other Labour Party workers move with apparent ease. Ministers such as Derry Irvine have become consultants (to Hutchison Whampoa Limited (HWL) better known in the UK as mobile phone operator, '3'). Former leader of the Lords Baroness Jay is a '"consultant" to PFI firm Amey and also has a seat on the BT board'. Ex-culture secretary Chris Smith 'has literally become a Mickey Mouse politician: he is a paid adviser to the Disney Corporation'. Frank Field, 'now supplements his MP's salary with a seat on the board of private health insurer Medicash'. Peter Mandelson worked 'for the advertising firm Clemmow Hornby Inge'. Ex-Labour general secretary Tom Sawyer 'sits on the boards of Reed Health and the Britannia Building Society'. David Clark, former defence minister and former Labour whip Lord Hoyle 'are now taking the arms industry's shilling: Clark sits on the board of French weapons firm Thales; while Hoyle now works for the arms trade lobbyist Whitehall Advisers'.[71]

The links between business lobbyists and Labour officials, ministers and MPs are now so intricate that very often individuals have multiple simultaneous roles. We can illustrate this nexus further by examining a couple of examples.

First, take Tim Allan who was deputy to Alastair Campbell in the Downing Street press office and subsequently took a six figure salary at BSkyB as a corporate spin doctor in 1998. Later Allan set up Portland PR, working for – amongst others – BSkyB and Asda (Wal-Mart). Allan took his Westminster connections with him to Sky and kept them going at Portland. One of his connections was his friend from the Royal Grammar School in Guildford, Surrey, James Purnell, who was his best man and with whom he worked in Tony Blair's Office up until 1992. After the election that year Purnell went to work for a consultancy and ended up at the IPPR think tank, rejoining Allan in 1997 as a special adviser at Number 10 after a spell at the BBC. When Allan left to join BSkyB, Purnell stayed until 2001 'doing the groundwork' for the Communication Act 2003 and coming up with the name and idea for Ofcom, with the result that the media system became more commercialised and BSkyB, amongst others, would be able to exploit the opening more easily. In 2001 Purnell became an MP, following which he hooked up with his old pal Tim Allan again, who by this time had set up Portland PR and was working for his ex-employers BSkyB.[72] Purnell declares in the House of Commons Register of Interests, 'Speech writing consultancy work in April and June 2003 for Sky, commissioned by Portland'. Purnell is also associated with Labour Friends of Israel (as its chair in 2002) and is on the advisory board of the Social Market Foundation.[73] After the 2005 election Purnell was promoted by Blair to Minister for Broadcasting at the Department for Culture, Media and Sport. One wonders how Purnell's relationship with commercial broadcasters, and his work for Sky in particular, might colour his views on public service broadcasting.

Meanwhile Allan's Portland PR also worked for Asda earning £50,000 as part of a campaign to de-recognise the GMB union at some Asda stores. An employment tribunal in Newcastle upon Tyne in January 2006 uncovered the fact that Allan had been involved in union-busting. 'A leaked email between Marie Gill Asda's head of industrial relations (distribution) and Mr Allan on December 24 2004, entitled "Washington – Modern Alternative", reveals that he fully endorsed Asda's plans to sack workers refusing to accept a 10 per cent [pay] rise in return for quitting GMB.'[74]

Asda was forced to pay £850,000 to employees at its Washington distribution depot in Tyne and Wear for 'unlawfully offering financial inducements to vote away union negotiating powers'. The tribunal found Portland's leaflets for Asda 'very hostile to trade unions'.[75] The acting GMB general secretary Paul Kenny noted:

The tribunal nailed Portland and this email nails Allan as a union buster. That somebody who worked for a Labour Government should be collaborating with the human resource director of Wal-Mart/Asda to sack GMB members, solely for the reason they refused to give up their union memberships, is absurd, bizarre and disgraceful. We are sending the tribunal finding to all Labour MPs and asking them to have nothing further to do with this sell-out merchant.[76]

Another example of the nexus in action is lobbying firm Sovereign Strategy, an object lesson in institutional corruption. The consultancy was set up in 2000 by Alan Donnelly, the former Labour MEP. With little trace of irony Donnelly notes that

I'd always wanted to set up my own company, that was another big motivation to leave politics, and eventually I decided to bite the bullet and set up Sovereign Strategy. I'd been on the receiving end of lobbying for 11 years, I'd seen the good approaches and the bad ones, and over time I'd developed my own ideas about how I'd do it.[77]

Donnelly, who used to work for the GMB union, signed up a raft of former MPs, MEPs and ministers including Baroness Billingham, Carol Tongue (both former Labour MEPs) and Lady Olga Maitland, the far right Conservative who set up the pro-nuclear lobby group 'Families for Defence' which was set up to undermine CND and promote NATO. Amongst its biggest names are Jack Cunningham, the notoriously pro-nuclear ex-MP for Copeland, and former defence minister Lewis Moonie, who signed up before he stepped down as an MP in April 2005.[78] Sovereign's work on Formula One racing has attracted attention. The sports minister Richard Caborn has 'been fantastically supportive of the project. He spent a lot of time brokering agreements between different people', says Donnelly. Caborn himself was a key guest at a 'high level dinner' organised by Sovereign at Durham Cricket Club on 28 January 2005 – a fact not mentioned in the MPs' Register of Interests or disclosed as a 'meeting' with Sovereign under the Freedom of Information Act.[79]

On nuclear issues Sovereign works for Fluor, the US multinational which is one of the world's biggest nuclear firms. The *Sunday Times* exposed Donnelly's role in funding the renovation of the constituency office of David Miliband, the environment secretary. The paper revealed 'that Sovereign Strategy paid £2,000 for building works at a terraced house in South Shields, Tyneside, which serves as headquarters of the local Labour party and contains Miliband's constituency office'.[80]

Senior Fluor executives and government ministers, including Blair, have attended events organised by Sovereign Strategy. The lobbying firm's marketing material boasts that it provides 'guidance on legislation issues in the field of environmental performance.' Donnelly also founded and helps to run the Transatlantic Nuclear Energy Forum (Tanef), an organisation that aims to foster 'strong relationships' between nuclear power companies and governments.

Jack Cunningham chairs the forum. The payment for the renovations was reportedly 'declared to the Electoral Commission', which oversees donations and election expenses, though Miliband failed to declare it in the Commons' Register of Members' Interests which is expected of MPs receiving financial help in their constituencies. This case is compounded by the fact that Donnelly is simultaneously the chair of Miliband's constituency party and that Sovereign have contributed around £80,000 to the Labour Party. In such circumstances the line between lobbyist and lobbied has broken down.

Sovereign's habit of paying serving members of the Houses of Parliament is noteworthy – something which is against the rather feeble self-regulatory code drawn up by the Association of Professional Political Consultants (APPC), the lobbyists' lobby group. Sovereign has refused to join the APPC.[81] It has also snapped up former ministers, putting further pressure on the already inadequate rules. In 2005 it employed former ministers Lewis Moonie and Alan Milburn. Both 'were fast-tracked by a government appointments watchdog to take up work with a Labour donating lobbying company which ignores a voluntary code of conduct not to pay or employ politicians'.[82] Moonie became an associate director and consultant for Sovereign Strategy in December 2004, having stood down as defence minister in July 2003. Milburn took a paid post to run a seminar for Sovereign Strategy in March 2004, having stood down as health secretary in June 2003. Moonie told the *Guardian* that 'My job will be to teach clients how to lobby government, not to lobby government for clients.'[83] Thus are the rules subverted. Moonie will be able to give advice on how to lobby and who to lobby as if this is somehow different from lobbying 'proper'. Portland PR has also been involved in paying sitting MPs – notably James Purnell in 2003. Portland too is not a member of the APPC, which again suggests the inadequacy of a system of voluntary rules dreamed up by the industry as a means of looking clean and avoiding statutory regulation.

Both of these examples show the web of connections between New Labour and the corporations primarily mediated via lobbying, and PR consultancies and think tanks. It is practically meaningless to ask whether the connections make any difference to the decisions on corporate interests made by government. More and more there simply isn't any difference between the corporations and the government. They are part of the same network of vested interests, believing in the same ideologies about the need to release markets. It is not that the business lobbyists are successful in their lobbying efforts to influence government. They have – for many intents and purposes – *become* the government.

10
Cameron and the Neo-cons

By the end of the Blair era the distinction between Labour and Conservative had all but dissolved. More important were the emerging divisions between the neo-conservatives (in both parties) and the rest. The rest includes those who variously: are attached to the previous pragmatic liberal approach to *realpolitik*, are in favour of a power bloc leadership role for the European Union, and those who favour transnational corporate power. These latter positions are not always separable from each other and indeed all these positions are best thought of as elite opinion constituencies, as opposed to any being recuperable for progressive politics. The British neo-cons' defining orientation is as partner to US imperial power. Both Blair and Brown are fully signed up to this agenda.

Perhaps the place to start with Cameron is to challenge those accounts which see him as any of the following:

- A mild mannered reformer who wants to move the Conservatives in a more liberal direction, removing the stain of their reputation as the 'nasty party'.
- A left wing liberal who is determined to sell out all the Conservative Party's traditional principles and supporters (especially those most associated with the aristocracy). His policy pronouncements on the environment and his 'hug a hoodie' speech being obvious examples.
- A vacuous professional politician whose only aim is to get into power, leading him to ape the spin and presentational tactics and policies of New Labour. This view sometimes also includes disparaging comments about Cameron being a 'toff', having gone to school at Eton.

All of these perceptions have their own conditions of existence and in many respects reflect the interests of various constituencies of opinion in Britain. But they are also responses to a spin campaign launched by Cameron and his followers to present a nice cuddly image. This will certainly turn off some elements of the Conservative Party, but it is designed to convince key sections of the Labour vote to return to the Conservatives. The vacuous appearance is just that: appearance, carefully crafted by a team of spin doctors and ideologues.

Behind this campaign is of course a spin doctor. Steve Hilton first met Cameron when they both worked at Conservative Central Office. Later he became an advertising executive at Saatchi & Saatchi, before leaving to set up his own PR consultancy, Good Business. He was the person who masterminded the 'demon eyes' campaign in the 1997 election smearing the Labour Party. He was described by *PR Week* as the 'intellectual driving force' behind many of Cameron's statements. Hilton, it stated, 'is the influence behind the new Conservative leader's position that businesses have responsibilities as well as being a vehicle for wealth creation'.[1]

'More than any other person, apart from Mr Cameron', reported *The Times*, 'the former marketing man is the mastermind behind the party's strategy for changing its image, moving to the political centre ground, and then getting into government. His influence can be seen in the trip to the Norwegian iceberg and the embracing of Nelson Mandela, the new oak-tree logo, Cameron's webcasting and public cycling, and the party's embracing of social justice.'[2]

Hilton's 'seminal' contribution to rethinking Tory philosophy on the market economy hinges on getting businesses, governments and charities to really engage in corporate social responsibility (CSR), and the exhortation for businesses to go one step further and get involved in corporate social leadership, meaning companies adopting a dual purpose: social and commercial. The following ideas and insights give a flavour of what the new, Tory-lite agenda might be. This begins on familiar ground with the warning that governments should not try to do any more than they already do. They can however begin to rethink their role and ought to look for more partnerships with the private sector.

As a practical suggestion – and we have to assume this is to be taken seriously – it is recommended that governments wishing to change various social behaviours might simply put single line advertisements on a website: 'Help stop smoking', 'Join the fight against obesity', 'Stamp out reoffending'. Corporations could check these out, and where they match their commercial strategy, they could decide to help. Imagine the marketing talents of British American Tobacco dedicated to extinguishing cigarettes, or McDonald's depicting the health dangers of burgers, fries and shakes, or the Group4/Reliance partnership to Make Prisons History! No need for cumbersome contracts. Social change will be effected by the magical power of the corporate brand, and this can work at all levels, with all sorts of companies. In time Hilton thinks society might get around to working out some rules to ensure this doesn't turn into a form of corporate lobbying. To incentivise more of this activity the creation of a Nobel Prize for social entrepreneurs is mooted.[3]

So much for the spin. What of the real policies and ideologies behind the New Tories? Well, the most obvious element of this in terms of our interests in spin and propaganda is the close connections with corporate and neo-con linked think tanks and with the corporations themselves. There are several aspects to this which show, first, the contemporary links with the PR and propaganda business; second, the continuities with earlier periods of corporate activism (including generational, familial and organisational links); third, the interlocking links with Conservative, Atlanticist and neo-conservative think tanks; and lastly, the political pedigree and views of the circle around Cameron.

We can start with the links to the PR and lobbying industry. Cameron himself is a former corporate communications executive for Carlton TV in the 1990s, working with Michael Green to drive forward the break-up of public service broadcasting.[4] Green later described him as 'Board material'.[5]

Cameron's circle has other connections to the PR and lobbying business. The most obvious of these is via his new spin adviser Steve Hilton, mentioned above.

Other PR industry backers include Peter Gummer, the CEO of Huntsworth, one of the biggest PR firms in the world. Gummer, who prefers to go by the title Peter Chadlington (after his Lordship title), also financially supported Cameron's leadership bid. Former chair of the Party, Francis Maude, is associated with Cameron. Along with being an MP, Maude finds time (as of 2007) to sit on the board of the following companies:

- Benfield Group Ltd, from 2 May 2002 (non-executive deputy chairman from March 2003); reinsurance brokerage.
- Benfield Limited (non-executive) from 4 November 2004, wholly-owned subsidiary of Benfield Group Ltd.
- Prestbury Holdings PLC (chairman) from 1 August 2002; non-investment financial services.
- Jubilee Investment Trust PLC (non-executive chairman) from October 2002; an investment trust.

- Globalink International Ltd (non-executive chairman from January 2004); provider of telecommunications services.
- Mediasurface (non-executive director from 26 August 2004); a web management software provider.
- The Mission Marketing Group (non-executive chairman from 1 February 2006).
- UTEK Corporation Inc. (non-executive, from June 2006); a technology transfer company based in the US.

These are only the ones that he has to declare in the Register of Members' Interests, because he is paid for them. Other sources confirm that he is also a director of Conservatives for Change and a former director of the Policy Exchange (both think tanks).[6] Until 2006 Maude also sat on the board of communications and PR firm Huntsworth and was formerly chairman of PR and communications conglomerate Incepta, prior to its merger with Huntsworth. From 1992 to 1999, he was a non-executive director of Asda Group and from 1997 to 1999, of Gartmore Shared Equity Trust. From 1992 to 1993, he was director of Salomon Brothers and a managing director of Morgan Stanley & Co. Limited from 1993 to 1997.

There are other Tories with PR industry backgrounds who are or have been close to Cameron and his advisers. These include Graham Brady MP, Shadow Minister for Europe (former lobbyist at Waterfront Partnership; previously worked for Shandwick), Mark Francois MP, Shadow Paymaster General (former lobbyist for Market Access International and then his own business, Francois Associates), and Charles Hendry MP, Shadow Minister for Transport and Industry (former PR consultant with Burson-Marsteller and Ogilvy & Mather PR).[7]

Cameron is also surrounded by aides and advisers with strong links to a wide range of market fundamentalist, Atlanticist and neo-con think tanks and lobby groups. Among Cameron's closest aides are Michael Gove, Ed Vaizey and George Osborne, all three of whom were, like Cameron himself, in their thirties when their new leader won the top job in the party. Gove was formerly a deputy editor of *The Times*, and is still a columnist there. Osborne, another former public school boy and heir to the Osborne & Little wallpaper fortune, says 'he has been a Conservative all of his life. He describes one of his earliest jobs in politics, as official Conservative Party observer at Labour's annual conference, as the worst he has had.'[8]

Vaizey is a key figure in Cameron's circle. He is a former lobbyist and part owner of Consolidated Communications. Vaizey disposed of his shares in Consolidated in 2005,[9] having left the consultancy in May 2004 to become chief speech writer for Michael Howard, then Conservative Party leader.

Vaizey's father was a long-time Labour Party official who publicly backed Margaret Thatcher in 1980. Another of Cameron's key lieutenants is Oliver Letwin, who like Cameron is an Old Etonian. Letwin's parents – Shirley and William Letwin – were both economists and members of the Mont Pelerin Society.

The following organisations show the close connections between Cameron's supporters and wider right wing forces.

Henry Jackson Society Project for Democratic Geopolitics

Both Gove and Vaizey (along with other Cameron allies like David Willetts) are signatories to the statement of principles of a British neo-conservative organisation, the Henry Jackson Society Project for Democratic Geopolitics, which was launched in Peterhouse College, Cambridge, in 2005.[10]

Henry Jackson was a Democrat member of the US Congress for over 40 years until his death in 1983. He opposed détente with the Soviet Union, and is the ideological forebear of modern neo-conservatism. Richard Perle and Paul Wolfowitz worked for him in the 1970s, and went on to work for Ronald Reagan.[11]

'International patrons' of the Society include leading American neo-conservatives, such as Robert Kagan, William Kristol, editor of the *Weekly Standard*, Joshua Muravchik of the American Enterprise Institute, and Michael McFaul of the Hoover Institution. Also signed up are Richard Perle of the Bush administration, James Woolsey, former director of the CIA, and perhaps most significantly Irwin Stelzer, who is Rupert Murdoch's representative in the UK and introduced Blair to Murdoch. The Society

campaigns for a 'forward strategy' to spread 'liberal democracy across the world' through 'the full spectrum of "carrot" capacities, be they diplomatic, economic, cultural or political, but also, when necessary, those "sticks" of the military domain'. Calling for the 'maintenance of a strong military with a global expeditionary reach', the society bemoans the fact that 'too few of our leaders in Britain and Europe are ready to play a role in the world that matches our strengths and responsibilities'.[12]

This is a vehicle for spreading the influence of the neo-cons in British politics and defending the role of the British state as partner for US imperial strategy.

Policy Exchange

In 2003 Gove, along with Nicholas Boles, another Jackson signatory and Francis Maude, founded a new conservative think tank, the Policy Exchange, said to be Cameron's 'favourite' think tank.[13]

Its key areas of interest, according to Boles, 'will be economic competitiveness, security and terrorism, childcare, the environment and public service reform'. It is funded by a 'business forum', which costs £5,000 to £10,000 to join. BP, SAB Miller, BSkyB and Bupa are among the members. Naturally enough the lines between think tank and lobbying shop are a little blurred and Boles is on record as saying that this causes him some disquiet. 'Corporates want intelligence about the policy directions and instincts of how a Cameron-led government would think', he notes. 'We're nervous of the perception that corporates are sponsoring research because that undermines our credibility.'[14] In effect the think tanks are another vehicle for lobbying activity.

C-Change

C-Change (or Conservatives for Change) is another in the cluster of think tanks pushing for a Conservative renewal. It shares both an office and some key advisers with the Policy Exchange. Francis Maude is the chair and others close to Cameron include Ed Vaizey, David Willetts and Theresa Villiers (promoted by Cameron to the Shadow Cabinet after just seven months in Parliament). Also of note is Archie Norman, formerly an MP (until 2005) and the boss of Asda (1991–2000) as well as helping to found the Policy Exchange. According to its own website, C-Change works

to modernise the Conservative Party and to ensure that it reflects the realities and complexities of contemporary Britain. Through a programme of constructive activity C Change seeks to play a full part in the process of Conservative recovery.[15]

C-Change used to be run by Conservative activist Dougie Smith who caused mild excitement in the press when it was revealed that he also ran 'Fever Parties'.[16] According to the Fever Parties website, these are 'select swinging parties for young and attractive couples in London and occasionally Manchester and abroad'.[17] Smith left C-Change to become Cameron's principal speechwriter.[18]

Politeia

Politeia was established in November 1995 under the patronage of the Marquess of Salisbury. Another Old Etonian, the Marquess, in the endearing fashion of the British upper classes, also has a real name, Robert Gascoyne-Cecil. He is, however, better known by his 'courtesy title', Viscount Cranborne, which he uses in the House of Lords. Gascoyne-Cecil comes from a long line of landowners and right wing activists and was close to John Major, acting as Leader of the House of Lords for much of the 1990s.

Among the MPs on Politeia's advisory council who are close to Cameron are Oliver Letwin, Francis Maude and David Willetts. Politeia focuses on the role of the state and asks how it can be minimised. One of its five 'aims', which indicates its approach, is 'How far should it [the state] seek to follow, in its social policies, the economic liberalism which proved so successful in the 1980s?'[19] Unsurprisingly the answer – at minimum – is 'quite a lot'.

Open Europe

The European issue has been a defining fault-line for Conservatives for a generation. A less well known think tank, but arguably a very significant organisation connected to Cameron's advisers is Open Europe. This think tank focuses on the European Union and is unusual in that it is directly supported by business leaders. 'Open Europe believes', says their website, 'that the EU must now embrace radical reform based on economic liberalisation.'[20] What this appears to mean is integrating all EU countries further and faster into the global economy but with a distinct eurosceptic tinge. The Marquess of Salisbury is on the board of this organisation too. Amongst its supporters are John Sainsbury (Lord Sainsbury of Preston Candover), who donated to Cameron's leadership campaign along with fellow donor Peter Gummer.[21]

The Stockholm Network

Open Europe, like both Politeia and the Policy Exchange, is a member of the Stockholm Network of free market think tanks whose membership also includes the stalwarts of the free market right from the early stages of the neo-liberal revolution such as the Institute of Economic Affairs, the Adam Smith Institute, the Centre for Policy Studies and the Social Affairs Unit (of a total of 19 UK member organisations).[22]

The Stockholm Network is the 'main liaison channel' for free market European think tanks. It was founded in September 1997 and claims to bring together over 120 think tanks from across Europe.[23] The member groups are primarily dogmatic free-marketeers who want to introduce minimalist 'flat taxes' (thus ending redistribution via taxation), terminate social protection systems and privatise healthcare. They attack socially or environmentally progressive legislation, which is in place or under discussion, and that places restrictions on market activity. For example, these think tanks consistently cast doubt on the seriousness of climate change, oppose environmental regulations and promote free-market pseudo-solutions to virtually every problem.[24]

The Stockholm Network links also to the network of right wing think tanks in the US. It has close links with the Heritage Foundation, which 'frequently' sends staff to Europe and has 'worked closely with five like-minded European think tanks to produce and launch a European edition of their Index of Economic Freedom', which ranks countries according to market friendly criteria like tax reduction and deregulation.[25]

The think tanks depend on corporate funding and in some instances are even set up at the instigation of the corporations. Pfizer is one company which has engaged in this kind of activity.

Michael W. Hodin, the company's Vice President Corporate Affairs Europe, played an active role in creating both the Stockholm Network and the Centre for the New Europe. At a February 2003 Stockholm Network seminar on 'How to grow a think tank', Catherine Windels, Director of Policy Communications at Pfizer, spoke on the theme 'What do business sponsors look for from think tanks?' Windels is also a board member of the Centre for a New Europe.[26]

There are two other recently formed organisations with which Cameron's close supporters are linked. They share important common characteristics in that both are Atlanticist, free market organisations.

The Atlantic Partnership

The Atlantic Partnership is an elite policy planning group set up to foster closer relations between the US and Europe, though its main impetus in Europe seems to have come from pro-US forces in the UK including those with close links to NATO and other Atlanticist groups. According to its own account:

Atlantic Partnership is a bipartisan initiative that aims to foster debate about the relationship between America and Europe while promoting the benefits of a strong and stable Atlantic community of nations.[27]

Founded by Conservative Party leader Michael Howard in 2001, AP 'seeks to influence the transatlantic debate through sought-after breakfast meetings, occasional conferences and the media activities of our impressive stable of chairmen, vice-chairmen, patrons and panelists'. Peter Gummer and Michael Howard are on its executive.

Amongst its directors is one of Cameron's close aides, Catherine Fall, who previously ran Michael Howard's Business Liaison Unit and who

met Mr Cameron at Oxford and worked with Mr Osborne in the research department. An identical twin, she is beautiful and enigmatic, preferring to keep out of the limelight. The daughter of a former ambassador, she concentrates on making sure Mr Cameron is always well briefed and on time and ensures he keeps in touch with MPs, donors and dignitaries. She developed her skills working in Michael Howard's office and as director of the think tank The Atlantic Partnership.[28]

Atlantic Bridge

The Atlantic Bridge is yet another conservative Atlanticist group which aims to 'establish, and then develop rapidly, a strong, well-positioned, network of like-minded conservatives in politics, business, journalism and academe on both sides of the Atlantic'. The aim is to build 'on the common thinking which underpins the natural trans-Atlantic alliance between the UK and the USA'.[29] In essence the Bridge is an elite conservative dining and networking club-cum-think tank.

Amongst its funders is the pharmaceutical giant Pfizer and the project is run by Liam Fox MP. The researcher on the project was Gabrielle Bertin – former equity trader at BNP Paribas who went on to become an adviser to David Cameron. US involvement comes in the form of Clark S. Judge, managing director of PR firm the White House Writers Group, and Grace-Marie Turner of the Galen Institute, a US free market think tank dedicated to privatising health care.

The connections to the free market and pro-US networks are many and varied and the views adopted and policies promoted are distinctively free market fundamentalist, coupled with Euroscepticism and a neo-conservative devotion to US imperial interests. The extent of the admiration for the neo-conservatives is clear in the public statements of Cameron's aides. In an article in February 2004, George Osborne confessed to being a 'fan' of George Bush:

I'm a signed-up, card-carrying Bush fan. I have been ever since I met him when he was governor of Texas... He found an answer to this question: what is the Right for in the age of Clinton–Blair?[30]

Former Conservative MP Matthew Parris writes:

Listen to this: 'England is going back to sleep. And little wonder when we're told every day by sages in our national media that the War on Terror is misconceived, that the terrorist threat is exaggerated, that what we've done in the last three years has only made matters worse, and that the Iraq war was a ghastly mistake that is best forgotten... There are few voices to be heard putting the other view: that the terrorists pose a fundamental threat to our way of life, that fight them we must, that Iraq was part of that fight and that we are winning.'

'This is taken', Parris continues, 'from an article that appeared in *The Spectator* only 22 months ago [March 2004]. Its author did not realise that within little more than a year he and his friend David Cameron would be the two most powerful figures in the Conservative Party. Or that in time they would be odds-on to form the next government.' As Parris concludes, 'The thought, sentiment and fervour behind his article are of a clever, thoughtful neoconservative: more Wolfowitz than Bush, more egg-head than jar-head, but neo-con nonetheless.'[31]

Like Osborne, Cameron aide Michael Gove is a fan of Bush and an enthusiast for Operation Iraqi Freedom. 'If you had to identify what you might call Michael's abiding passion in politics', argues Matthew Parris, 'you would find it in a consistent, intelligent rage against what he would see as the unwitting appeasement of wicked and violent men by flabby, woolly-minded liberals. Now in Parliament, he is part of the small group of Tories, somewhat mis-named the Notting Hill Set, in control of the higher brain functions of that great and ancient political beast, the Conservative Party.'[32]

To what extent Cameron shares these views is a little difficult to determine given the carefully manicured nature of most of his public pronouncements. But we can tell something about his views from his career trajectory, starting with his job as a spin doctor for Michael Green's Carlton Communications.

Cameron's reputation for honesty and trustworthiness as a spin doctor was, however, not high. Jeff Randall, the journalist who was appointed to the BBC to turn its coverage decisively in a pro-business direction, said he would not trust Mr Cameron 'with my daughter's pocket money'.[33]

'To describe Cameron's approach to corporate PR as unhelpful and evasive overstates by a widish margin the clarity and plain-speaking that he brought to the job of being Michael Green's mouthpiece', wrote the ex-BBC business editor. 'In my experience, Cameron never gave a straight answer when dissemblance was a plausible alternative, which probably makes him perfectly suited for the role he now seeks: the next Tony Blair', Randall wrote.[34] *Sun* business editor Ian King, recalling the same era, described Mr Cameron as a 'poisonous, slippery individual'.[35]

Cameron even attracted attention in the press for rubbishing a story in the *Sunday Express*: 'we reported on September 19 that subscriber numbers would be at least 400,000 and possibly much higher. That story inspired Carlton's spin doctor David Cameron to call City analysts in an effort to rubbish the story. Carlton likes to "manage" expectations and was miffed by the accuracy of our story. City analysts may now be a little miffed with Mr Cameron and his Monday morning briefing three weeks ago.'[36]

After working at Carlton, Cameron's political ambitions took him back to the Tory Party. He progressed through the ranks and had direct connections to the Tory regime of 1979–97. Cameron was part of John Major's 'breakfast club' which advised Major in 'pre-dawn meetings on confronting Labour in parliament. Cameron pumped Major with slick arguments against the minimum wage, compassionately claiming that rises for the low paid would leave them unemployed'.[37]

Cameron then became special adviser to Tory chancellor Norman Lamont. 'In his memoirs, Lamont recalls that he was "a brilliant Old Etonian with a taste for the good life". Cameron stood by Lamont when the chancellor said mass unemployment was a "price worth paying", and when he wasted billions failing to prop up the pound on "Black Wednesday".'[38]

He had a sudden loss of compassion, however, when Lamont resigned, after which he got a new job as special adviser to Michael Howard. A hurt Lamont recalls his first, awkward, post-resignation Tory cocktail party. 'The next person I saw was David Cameron, my former special adviser at the Treasury. He cut me dead.'[39]

Does any of this start to sound familiar? What we see with Cameron is to a large degree a mirror image of New Labour. Each 'side' has its own networks and connections with think tanks and lobbyists, and through them with corporations. Expressing a preference for

New Labour or the Tories is something like saying you prefer Shell to Exxon. Either way, the corporations retain their privileged access and influence. The politicians are simply their different flavoured agents. But one of the consequences of the closeness of these policy networks is that they overlap. There are Labour signatories to the Henry Jackson Project, and Labour-supporting businesspeople interlock with Conservative networks too. Take the example of Robin Renwick (Lord Renwick of Clifton) who sits on the Labour benches in the House of Lords. He has connections with the RAND Corporation, with the spy company Hakluyt and with the elite networking Ditchley Foundation. He also links to a host of corporations on whose board he sits or has sat (including British Airways, the nuclear firm Fluor, brewers SAB Miller and mining firm BHP Billiton).[40] He is also patron of Atlantic Partnership and is part of Open Europe.

The corporations don't much mind which side they network with, preferring as the *Financial Times* puts it, in relation to BP, to 'play both sides'.[41] Thus the Labour member and founder of the British American Project, Nick Butler, works at BP with the right wing Richard Ritchie, BP's chief UK lobbyist. Ritchie was a former aide to Enoch Powell and also sits on the board of the Centre for Policy Studies. Cameron's circle are on the guest list for their functions. In the past BP, for example, has sponsored David Willetts to attend the Franco-British Colloque (the French equivalent of the British American Project); in 2006 George Osborne was invited as a speaker.[42]

We have focused on Cameron as an instance of an important tendency in contemporary British party politics. From this portrait it is clear that those in power or likely to assume power in Britain are in the grip of business ideologues, in the grip more precisely of the professional idea warriors, the think-tankerati, the spinners, the lobbyists. It has been central to our argument in this book that such people, such professions were invented to try to ensure that democracy could not work. The campaign to undermine democracy has made extraordinary advances, as we have tried to sketch in previous chapters. It is now in many ways symbolised by the meteoritic rise from relative obscurity of Cameron: the man who could become the next Prime Minister is in temperament, philosophy and practice a professional public relations operative.

11
Corporate Propaganda and Power: The Manufacture of Compliance?

We use the term 'the cutting edge' in the title of this book to suggest that corporate propaganda and political action are at the forefront of making the world safe for capitalism. If you think this is pretty self-evident, so much the better. But there are strong currents of opinion in public, political and academic debate that contest this. We suggest that propaganda and PR do matter, that they facilitate the exercise of considerable power and that they need much closer attention than they are usually given. The lack of scrutiny is itself partly a question of the success of propaganda. Critics may bemoan the decline of democracy, the rise of the pseudo-politics of spin, but are reluctant to use the term 'propaganda' or see more than the communicative surface features. Citizens in effect comply with how things are rather than consenting to them. By contrast we see propaganda as organising conduct and social relations. Not simply an issue of ideas and consent, more a question of compliance.

There are some on the left – believe it or not – who seem to think that the hidden hand of the market carries all before it, or that it is the economy which is the driver of mere ideas. We, on the other hand, think that it is social and economic interests which are embodied in the institutions created and operated by real humans which provide the link between the economic and the ideological. Ideas are produced and fight their fight only in the context of the material circumstances in which all – economy, polity, ideology – operate. This also means that ideas in conflict are never divorced from interests and that ideas can have consequences, in that they organise, legitimate and make possible certain decisions and actions. Ideas have efficacy, but not on their own, not in a vacuum, not outside the context of the interests which create them. On the other hand interests need ideas to survive and prosper. They are bound up together.

So it is just as wrong to imagine that the market runs the game by itself as it is to assume, as some have, that ideas can float free; that discourse can be elevated to the principal subject of study or debate, that there is no reality or at least that the only reality is the one 'appropriated through discourse'.[1]

So, we have included 'the cutting edge' in the title of this book because we strongly believe ideas matter. But, they don't advance a cause unless and until they form part of a wider struggle. This is the lesson of Thatcherism and of neo-liberalism. This was eminently clear in the development of the movement to build a 'neo-liberal thought collective'.[2]

THE BATTLE OF IDEAS

The neo-liberals understood the necessity of winning the battle of ideas but it was the Adam Smith Institute and associated groups which understood the vital importance of putting ideas into practice. The early ideologues around the Mont Pelerin Society had been more focused on ideas alone. They agreed, paradoxically, with their adversary J. M. Keynes who, in his great work *The General Theory*, noted that:

The ideas of economists and political philosophers, both when they are right and when they are wrong, are more powerful than is commonly understood. Indeed, the world is ruled by little else. Practical men, who believe themselves to be quite exempt from any intellectual influences, are usually the slaves of some defunct economist. Madmen in authority, who hear voices in the air, are distilling their frenzy from some academic scribbler of a few years back. I am sure that the power of vested interests is vastly exaggerated compared with the gradual encroachment of ideas.[3]

This passage was specifically singled out by Hayek for praise in his opening address to the first Mont Pelerin meeting in 1947 and was the only passage from Keynes' work which was 'prominently displayed' in the offices of the Institute of Economic Affairs. But in order to put their ideas into practice, the later neo-liberals – such as those at the Adam Smith Institute – were clear that ideas alone were not enough. In 1988 Madsen Pirie of the ASI wrote:

The successes achieved by the new-style politics allowed for the rise of the attractive but erroneous view that the work of lonely scholars, their acolytes and their advocates had finally paid off. And brought results in its train. That these results had not come in the earlier administrations which attempted them was put down to a wrong climate or wrong personnel. In fact, it was wrong policies. It was the policy engineers, coming in the wake of the pure scientists of politics and economic theory, who made the machines which made events. The ideas had been sufficient to win the intellectual battle, but this was not enough. Men and women with spanners in their hands and grease on their fingers had first to devise the ways in which the ideas of pure theory could be turned into technical devices to alter reality. The idea at the core of micropolitics is that creative ingenuity is needed to apply to the practical world of interest group politics the concepts of free market theory.[4]

On this point Pirie was much closer to the practical ideas of Karl Marx and Friedrich Engels, who famously wrote in the *German Ideology* that:

We do not set out from what men say, imagine, conceive, nor from men as narrated, thought of, imagined, conceived, in order to arrive at men in the flesh. We set out from real active men, and on the basis of their real life-process we demonstrate the development of the ideological reflexes and echoes of this life process. The phantoms formed in the human brain are also, necessarily, sublimates of their material life process, which is empirically verifiable and bound to material premises. Morality, religion, metaphysics, all the rest of ideology and their corresponding forms of consciousness thus no longer retain the semblance of independence. They have no history, no development; but men, developing their material production and their material intercourse, alter, along with this their real existence, their thinking and the products of their thinking. Life is not determined by consciousness, but consciousness by life.[5]

Perhaps surprisingly, Pirie and the ASI seemed to share with classical Marxism the understanding that it is ideas in practical struggle that change things rather than ideas in the abstract. Certainly it was at the core of their mission to take forward the ideas outlined by the Mont Pelerin Society and its various off-shoots and put them into practice. The role of the think tanks was clearly crucial in advancing so far along this road. In our view the promotion of neo-liberal ideas were inseparable from the attempts to put them into practice.

For example, in an otherwise interesting account of the development of neo-liberal think tanks by Radhika Desai, the identification of think tanks with the realm of ideas is overpowering: 'a crucial factor in the successes of Thatcherism was that these ideas formed part of a coherent outlook on society. This could pose as an explanatory framework, an alternative governing ideology, a vision and help Thatcherism retain the intellectual offensive.'[6] It was not its alleged 'coherence' that allowed Thatcherism to establish itself, but the concrete decisions that were legitimised and taken. Desai goes on to acknowledge the 'critical function' in the think tanks of 'working out aspects of this ideology into feasible plans and blueprints, ready for implementation'.[7] We agree that this was a crucial strategic function but it is not just a matter of 'thought' and 'ideas' but of putting them into practice – not simply a discursive process. The think tanks remained, as Desai rightly points out, 'proselytizers, not originators'. The point here is that this is not simply a question of ideological struggle, but of concrete political struggle in which ideas and ideologies play a crucial role. The production of blueprints and plans is a material process in which ideology plays a part: specifically it plays a part in providing a rationale for proposed changes, in masking the interests at work, in finding ways to present reform as more palatable in order that the real interests lying behind it – freeing the market, transferring resources from the poor to the rich – can be hidden. Ideology, in other words, plays a critical role, but it is a mistake to see the battle of ideas as entirely taken up with ideology or as not being itself a predominantly material process.

Throughout this book we have tried to show how ideas are produced as part of the struggle over which way a society should go. There is no easy separation between ideas conceived in the abstract and practice on the ground, but in any case, ideas are produced as part of a material process – the 'cramped' office of the IEA in the 1950s needed an influx of money from a wealthy battery chicken farmer before the space could expand and staff go forth and multiply. The 'battle of ideas' is also a material process in which there is the production of forms of ideas (books, newspapers, mass communications, email) as well as their distribution and exchange. All of these can have effects in terms specifically of outcomes and decisions. When the Centre for Policy Studies targeted the take-over of the Conservative Party it did not intend to get Margaret Thatcher elected, but that outcome was certainly a victory for them. Was this a victory in the battle for ideas? Yes, in the sense that they waged a struggle which was partly ideological, but not in the sense that is often imagined, that the winning of hearts and minds was the limit of their ambitions.

Perhaps one way to put this is to cite Thomas Friedman's 1998 *New York Times* magazine article on projecting American power:

For globalization to work, America can't be afraid to act like the almighty superpower that it is. The hidden hand of the market will never work without a hidden fist. McDonald's cannot flourish without McDonnell Douglas, the designer of the F-15, and the hidden fist that keeps the world safe for Silicon Valley's technology is called the U.S. Army, Air Force, Navy and Marine Corps.[8]

This quote is usually used to show the importance of the link between imperial power and corporate power, but it can also be noted that Microsoft and McDonald's and Macintosh and News Corporation are needed by the US Army. Without them there would be less to defend and fewer resources to pay for the military or to provide services for them (whether by direct contracting or in propaganda and ideology). On the other hand neither the military nor the corporations – even the most despoiling and polluting industries (Exxon, BP, BHP, Rio Tinto, etc.) – can survive without the think tanks, front groups, lobbyists and PR people. Equally, the communicative and public relations strategies of the corporations – be it McDonald's or McDonnell Douglas – could not operate without their economic and political activities. For global corporate power to work, Silicon Valley would have no conditions of existence without WPP, British Aerospace could not fly without Burson-Marsteller. The velvet glove that keeps the fist veiled is called public relations, lobbying and propaganda.

IDEAS AND ACTION

A result of the separation of ideas and action is that some writers underestimate the effects and power of ideas (and of propaganda and PR). Some historians conclude that it is an advance for us to be 'persuaded' rather than beaten around the head by the corporations. Put that way there can be little argument or little doubt that the 'effects' of persuasion are less than many have feared. That, as some have argued, they mainly affected only the elite.

But one mistake here is to assume that what is being fought is simply a battle for opinion rather than a battle for morale, advantage, freedom of action and concrete outcomes. A battle by the corporations, in other words, for compliance. It does not matter to them if they win the battle of public opinion (in the sense of people being persuaded of their case). What matters is that they get their own way and this is crucially why the battle fought in PR and propaganda is a battle for compliance and not a battle for opinion. Or at least not only a battle for opinion, where opinion is conceived as something separate from and alien to the breaking of heads, the instilling of fear and the use of blackmail.

A further problem is that the search for 'persuasive power' ends up by deferring questions of outcomes to the black box of some other discipline. So Tedlow argues, for example, that 'the results of the campaigns which have been recounted dispel the fear that public relations men can turn public opinion off and on "like a faucet"'.[9] But only if one considers 'public opinion' to mean the opinions of the public and not the aggregate of what is possible in society or the limits of the elite consensus. The two are not necessarily – indeed not usually – the same.

There is some acknowledgement of this when Tedlow argues that the PR campaigns he studied, created the 'appearance of public support if not the reality'.[10] This has the effect of giving the corporations 'licence to take certain actions'. This is precisely what is at stake and the consequence is that corporate power can increase even against the grain of public opinion since 'public opinion' has been either, manufactured and faked, ignored or won over. A further consequence is that the notion that democratic decision making can survive in such circumstances is untenable. In other words we are pushed towards the conclusion even by the findings of apologists for PR that the rise of corporate propaganda is a means for subverting democracy rather than a symbol of its health.

It is only by having such a narrow version of what the struggle is over (ideas in the abstract) and a simple model of how ideas work (a sort of liberal functionalism that assumes that public opinion influences policy making), that writers on the history of PR can undertake book length studies of a subject which they latterly conclude is not very interesting or effective. Karen Miller concludes that Hill & Knowlton's campaigns 'mostly' affected its 'own clients and people who already thought like they did'.[11] On the contrary: to the extent that they were successful, they influenced the course of history and the decisions taken about the direction in which society goes. In other words the horizon of historical social change is back on the agenda for studies of propaganda and communications. What we are discussing here is nothing less than the manufacture of compliance to vested interests and not simply a question of persuasion or even of consent.

PERSUASION AND COERCION

In mainstream writing about propaganda and about think tanks and the role of persuasion and ideas in history, there is a rather unthinking and easy contrast drawn between coercion and consent. We have tried to show that this contrast is not so clear-cut. In particular we think that the shift from coercion to consent with the rise of democracy is not nearly as absolute as many writers have thought. Consent is ringed and guarded by coercion and the threat of coercion. This is most obviously the case in strike-breaking and other areas of open conflict between corporate power and democracy. But it is also clear in routine propaganda battles where there is no actual use of force and when it is not even threatened. The use of media campaigns against the latest threat to corporate interests is a case in point and the strategic rituals of coverage of the global justice movement show the same traditional resort to warnings and threats.

We have also tried to show that communication itself can be coercive, as in the case of deception, misinformation and strategic use of information – techniques all well developed by the PR industry. Douglas Rushkoff, once a prophet of the democratising potential of the internet, refers to the contemporary use of consumer marketing as coercive:

Coercion is much more debilitating than persuasion or even influence. Persuasion is simply an attempt to steer someone's thinking by using logic. Influence is the act of applying readily discernible pressure: I want you to do this; I have power over you, so do it. Coercion seeks to stymie our rational processes in order to make us act against – or, at the very least, without – our better judgement. Once immersed in a coercive system, we act without conscious control.[12]

For Rushkoff, this point applies to marketing as well as to advertising and PR and newer techniques like 'viral marketing' in particular. Blurring the line between coercion and persuasion also implies reconsidering how we think of popular concepts like 'hegemony'. Hegemony is too often used as a synonym for consent.[13] This is said to be the distinctive meaning developed by Italian socialist Antonio Gramsci even in sophisticated accounts by contemporary authors.[14] It is as if in situations of formal democracy, the coercion of authoritarian regimes somehow disappears. This book is testimony that this is false. On the contrary, democracy brings more threats to the powerful and thus they invest more in techniques for managing it. But it is clear that, for Gramsci, hegemony meant a variety of things from popular assent to the status quo, through corruption, to its original meaning of leadership with all the attendant coercive apparatus which that implies.

Colin Leys tries a middle way between the reductionism of Bob Jessop and his colleagues and the ideologism of writers such as Stuart

Hall.[15] Leys writes that it is not necessary for an ideology to be 'loved' to be hegemonic. It is 'merely necessary that it have no serious rival'.[16] This seems to us correct. But we would go further, asserting that it is not necessary for the ideology even to be respected for it to be able to 'rule'. What we have attempted to show throughout this book is that power can be organised in a formally democratic system which can bypass popular opinion. Leadership here refers not to leadership of the popular classes but leadership of the elite. Hegemony in other words may simply refer to the possibilities of ruling class unity.

There is an historical dimension to this which has been at the centre of our argument. Under social democratic conditions it makes relatively more sense to talk of consent. Under neo-liberalism, this is progressively less compelling. The transformation we have documented in this book has enabled the corporations to wrest power from democratic control and increasingly the only constituency they need to satisfy are closely related fractions of their own side – in politics, the media and civil society.

FOR THE STUDY OF COMMUNICATION AND POWER

There are now a range of academic disciplines which have been indelibly marked by – indeed produced by – the interests and actions of the propagandists. The field of Public Relations research, the discipline of marketing, some aspects of Human Resource Management and Management and Business Studies more generally all bear the mark of propaganda victories by their systematic refusal to face their origins in propaganda. Nor have sociology, psychology and political science dealt with their demons over this.

It is an incredible victory for great power that there is no institute for the study of propaganda (in its real meaning) anywhere in the world. Those that remain studying propaganda do so almost entirely from within the authorised framework that this happens largely in war.

Let us be clear about this. We *do* mean that most academics have been 'persuaded' and have come to see things in terms conducive to great power. But as we have tried to emphasise in the rest of this book, one of the most important aspects of propaganda is that it organises conduct even in the absence of fully informed consent. It secures compliance.

In 1976, following the debacle of Vietnam and Watergate, Alex Carey wrote in favour of 'the difficult road back to truth and an honouring of the democratic rights of citizens – a road that cannot be totally traversed until the subject of propaganda and its control in American society – almost entirely neglected for forty years by political scientists – is afforded an urgent priority'.[17] More than 30 years later the road has been considerably lengthened and the role of propaganda has strengthened markedly in Britain, the EU, in most other western nations and – a new departure – at the global level. This book has been an attempt to document that process of the strengthening and widening of the power of propaganda, but the subject remains almost entirely neglected. We agree with Carey about the need for a raised level of academic and public debate on these issues and we would add that the problems faced at the time of Watergate and Vietnam have only intensified. The global crisis of democracy, (accompanied by the newly emerged crisis of unaccountable global governance), the crisis of environmental sustainability and the crisis of ever increasing class polarisation all are under-girded by the subordination of communication to great power.

The debate on propaganda has more or less disappeared, but it reappears in different guises. It does this because the issue which it raises cannot be suppressed. It re-emerges because of the material (meaning also communicative) conditions which underlie the structural conflict between great power and the rest of us. The debate is ongoing in campaigns around secrecy and freedom of information, in campaigns to make corporations accountable and to disclose lobbying and other influence operations of the corporations. And it is ongoing throughout the world in campaigns to resist the market and protect or extend democracy. We agree with the business operatives, PR people, lobbyists, neo-liberals and neo-conservatives that we have quoted in this book when they have discussed the organic nature of communicative and campaigning strategy. It is necessary to operate on all fronts across the range of society; from academic discussion to popular debate. But we disagree with the techniques used and the philosophy underlying what they do.

Communication cannot be studied in the abstract as something which is separate from action, which describes the world and which may or may not influence it. Communication is part of the social world and is integrally part of strategies of domination and resistance. There is no divorced, clean, clear, liberal world in which 'debate' and 'persuasion' take place outside the context of power and action. Communication presupposes the world and takes place in it. It is no more 'ineffective' that any other human action. It is – to be sure – implicated in differential forms and 'faces' of power.[18]

But it would be wrong to identify communication as being wholly on the 'persuasive' side of the coercion and consent dichotomy. Communication can both coerce and constrain, as we have sought to show in this book.

Our view on this is certainly a minority one in media studies as it is in sociology and psychology and political science. But it is not a lonely position since it connects very strongly with the renewed analysis and action outside academia to which this period in history is playing host.

The great movements of our time against war and for global democracy are very much concerned with communication and power and we think the time is more auspicious for a return to these questions than it was in 1976 when Alex Carey wrote about them. Within three years the neo-liberals won tremendous victories in both the UK and US, ushering in the transformation of those societies and the global spread of the neo-liberal virus. But now neo-liberalism is under threat.

In conclusion, we agree with Hayek that the battle of ideas is an important element of the struggle to turn human societies this way or that. And we agree with Madsen Pirie that ideas need to be put into action. We do not, however, agree that the aim of such a struggle should be to refurbish class power and widen inequality by undermining democracy. Nor do we think that the battle of ideas is important to the extent that it can be won by means of manipulation, deception and misinformation on the one hand and policy planning, sabotage and subversion on the other. The battle of ideas is important precisely because of the necessity for that approach to communication and power to be swept away and the possibility of democratic dialogue, deliberation and decision making established.

Does this mean a counter-hegemony? No doubt, but it is clear that this is not just a question of finding the right ideas, but of constructing an alternative worldview as part of a concrete coalition of interests; a counter-hegemony which is not afraid to act. For Gramsci this was a matter of the optimism of the will, meaning – lest we need to spell it out – communicative action in the world as opposed to the endless elaboration of concepts. For all the pessimism of the intellect revealed in this book, writing it has been borne out of a relentless optimism of the will. Now more than ever, such optimism is justified and needed.

Appendix:
Labour MPs' Business Interests, 2007

Labour Party MPs	Remunerated directorships	Remunerated employment	Corporate donations	Registrable shareholdings
Banks, Gordon	Cartmore Building Supply Co Ltd, Fife; builders' merchant.			
Barron, Kevin	J T Investments Ltd; property and investment company (no salary currently being paid).			J T Investments Ltd.
Betts, Clive		Fees for lectures given for Neil Stewart Associates. (Up to £5,000)		
Blunkett, David	HADAW Productions and Investments Ltd, through which I have a contract with Bloomsbury for the rights to my forthcoming journals. Signature payment due (£95,001–£100,000).	Adviser to Indepen Consulting Limited, giving seminars on relationship between government and business (late January–5 May 2005). (£15,001–£20,000) Adviser to ORT (Organisation for Research and Technology). (February–5 May 2005). (£15,001–£20,000) 11 March 2005, fee for speech at communications seminar organised by Weber Shandwick. (£2,000) (Up to £5,000) (Registered 1 November 2005) 16 March 2005, fee for speech at event organised by Weber Shandwick. (£2,000) (Up to £5,000) (Registered 1 November 2005) 5 April 2005, fee for facilitation discussion on business links with tertiary education organised by BT. (£5,001–£10,000) (Registered 1 November 2005) March 2006, fee for after dinner speech for Portland PR. (£5,001–£10,000) (Registered 4 April 2006)		

Labour Party MPs	Remunerated directorships	Remunerated employment	Corporate donations	Registrable shareholdings
Byers, Stephen		Consultant in relation to the non-UK commercial activities of Consolidated Contractors International Co., an international construction company founded in Lebanon with its head office now in Athens. Chairman of the Board of YES (the Yalta European Strategy); a policy network established to promote ideas, debate and Ukraine's membership of the European Union. Fee for speech to the Ukrainian Investment Summit on 23 May 2006 organised by Adam Smith Conferences. (Up to £5,000) (Registered 24 May 2006)		
Cook, Frank		Parliamentary adviser, with particular emphasis on environmental issues, to DSM Demolition Ltd and its associated companies. (£5,001–£10,000)		
Cooper, Yvette			I receive support from a former constituent, David Newton of Newton-Smith Associates, who is creating and will service a website for me free of charge.	
Donohoe, Brian			My election fighting fund has received registrable donations from Media House, Glasgow. (Registered 24 February 2005)	
Field, Frank			Trip to Australia to participate in conferences on welfare reform organised by the Centre for Independent Studies, who paid for four nights of accommodation, my return flight to Sydney and a return flight between Sydney and Cairns.	
Follett, Barbara Gardiner, Barry		Communications consultant to Ken Follett. Sponsorship of my Constituency Reports by the Asian Marketing Group.		
Henderson, Doug	Ergonomy Ltd; marketing company.	Member of the Advisory Board of McDonald's Restaurants Ltd.		

Hewitt, Patricia

27 November 2004, my husband, son and I attended the England Australia rugby match at Twickenham as guests of John Windeler, Chairman of the Alliance and Leicester plc. *(Registered 4 January 2005)*

Stemcor Holdings Ltd; international steel trading.

Hodge, Margaret

Hood, Jimmy

Parliamentary Consultant to Scottish Coal. *(£5,001–£10,000)*

Howarth, George

Parliamentary adviser to the William Hill Organisation. *(£25,001–£30,000)*

Hoyle, Lindsay

Screen Arts Ltd; screen printing.

Illsley, Eric

Parliamentary adviser to the Caravan Club. *(£5,001–£10,000)* Member of Academic Board of Cambridge Online Learning.

Ingram, Adam

My election fighting fund has received registrable donations from: Lynnet Leisure, Glasgow
City Refrigeration, Glasgow
Cleartech Water Solutions Ltd, Hamilton
24–28 July 2005, to Washington DC, to meet congressional and business interests and British diplomats, to discuss UK/US defence trade, especially current technology transfer issues and UK/US defence policy. My flights and accommodation were paid for by the UK Defence Forum. *(Registered 19 August 2005)*

Jones, Kevan

22–24 August 2005, to Norway, on defence issues. Flights to Norway and accommodation paid for by Scandef. UK flights paid for by Northern Defence Industries. *(Registered 6 October 2005)*

Labour Party MPs	Remunerated directorships	Remunerated employment	Corporate donations	Registrable shareholdings
Lammy, David			I received support from Lord Sainsbury of Turville towards the cost of employing a social policy research assistant. *(Registered 11 October 2005)* I received support from Lord Alli towards the cost of employing a social policy research assistant. *(Registered 11 October 2005)*	
Laxton, Bob			Contribution towards my constituency office operations from Bowmer & Kirkland Ltd, company office, Belper, Derbyshire.	
Lewis, Ivan				Broome & Wellington
Malik, Shahid				Penmarric plc. Bestways PLC Forbes Campbell
McAvoy, Tommy	County Pub Company Limited, trading as The County Inn Public House.			International County Pub Company Ltd.
Meacher, Michael				Planet Organic (organic food retailing).
Milburn, Alan		Fee for speech on 14 September 2005 at a dinner organised by Portland.		
Palmer, Nick				Millholt Investments Ltd.
Plaskitt, James			Calor Gas funded the production and distribution of my 2004 official Christmas card. *(Registered 20 December 2004)*	
Rammell, Bill	Randalls of Uxbridge Ltd.	Sponsorship as a Member of Parliament by Uxbridge Portcullis Club (private business club)		Randalls of Uxbridge Ltd. Aquila Termeszetvedelmi Es Idegenforgalmi KFT (Aquila Nature Conservation and Tourist Ltd); Hungarian eco-tourism company.

Reed, Andy	From 16 June 2004 I have the services of a researcher who is employed by Business in Sport and Leisure (BISL) to work for me in my capacity as Chair of the Sports Caucus, a small group of MPs with a common interest in sport. Through BISL he is paid for his work on the Caucus by Sport England, UK Sport, the Local Government Association and the Fitness Industry Association, each of whom pay in excess of £1,000.	
Robertson, John	22–29 August 2005, to Canada as member of the All-Party Parliamentary Group for Nuclear Energy UK delegation. Travel and accommodation paid for by Atomic Energy of Canada Limited (AECL). *(Registered 7 September 2005)*	
Robinson, Geoffrey	New Statesman Limited.	TransTec PLC; specialised engineers (in liquidation). New Statesman Ltd. United Wholesale Scotland Limited;
Sarwar, Mohammad		
Sheerman, Barry	Networking for Industry, a not for profit company promoting UK competitiveness and parliamentary communication with industry. Urban Mines Ltd; a not for profit charity promoting sustainable use of resources.	Member of Environmental Scrutiny Board of Onyx UK Ltd; environmental waste management company
Simon, Sion	7–8 July 2005, to Portugal, to support the launch of new Jaguar XJ Diesel, which is made in Erdington. Flight and overnight accommodation provided by Jaguar.	

Labour Party MPs	Remunerated directorships	Remunerated employment	Corporate donations	Registrable shareholdings
Smith, John			9–13 August 2004, to Washington DC with parliamentary delegation. Travel and accommodation paid for by the UK Defence Forum. *(Registered 30 November 2004)*	
Stewart, Ian			6–10 February 2005, to Washington with the All-Party Parliamentary Internet Group. The cost of the flights, accommodation and transport were met by Microsoft, MessageLabs and Interregnum plc. *(Registered 1 March 2005)*	
Tami, Mark		Fee from the Guild of British Travel Agents for provision of information on parliamentary and European parliamentary processes and legislation, which I give to charity. *(Up to £5,000)*		
Walley, Joan		The Lighting Industry Federation pay part of the salary of a researcher in my office who provides support to the All-Party Parliamentary Lighting Group of which I am Joint Chair.		
Williams, Betty			20–26 September 2004, to Western Canada with the All-Party Parliamentary Rail Group, organised by the Rail Freight Group. Travel, including travel within Canada, and accommodation paid for by the Rail Freight Group. *(Registered 12 October 2005)*	
Woodward, Shaun			Funding for a campaign assistant in St Helens constituency provided by Mr E W Davidson, chairman of property development company.	J. Sainsbury PLC.
Wyatt, Derek	Cottage Industry Productions Limited; specialising in television production and consultancy.		7–10 February 2005, to USA, for meeting with Internet Caucus and other IT bodies on Capitol Hill. Air fares and hotel costs met by Message Labs and Microsoft. *(Registered 17 May 2005)*	Cottage Industry Productions Limited.

Notes

CHAPTER 1   THE CUTTING EDGE OF CORPORATE POWER

1. John Hill, *The Making of a Public Relations Man*, Chicago, IL: NTC Business Books, 1992 (originally published 1963), p. 161.
2. Richard Kisch, *The Private Life of Public Relations*, London: MacGibbon and Kee, 1964; J. L'Etang and M. Pieczka (eds), *Public Relations: Critical Debates and Contemporary Practice*, New Jersey: Lawrence Erlbaum Associates, 2006; Kevin Moloney, *Rethinking Public Relations: The Spin and the Substance*, London: Routledge, 2006; Scott Cutlip, *The Unseen Power: Public Relations. A History*, Hillsdale, NJ: Lawrence Erlbaum Associates, 1994.
3. William Dinan and David Miller (eds), *Thinker, Faker, Spinner, Spy: Corporate PR and the Assault on Democracy*, London: Pluto Press, 2007, chapter 1.
4. Kurt Vonnegut, *Player Piano*, London: Macmillan, 1953, p. 84.
5. Ibid., p. 206.
6. Edward Bernays interviewed on Adam Curtis, 'Happiness Machines', *The Century of the Self*, Part 1, BBC2, 29 April 2002. http://www.bbc.co.uk/bbcfour/documentaries/features/century_of_the_self_episode_1.shtml.
7. See Claus Offe, *Disorganised Capitalism: Contemporary Transformations in Work and Politics* (edited by John Keane), Cambridge: Polity Press, 1985; Claus Offe, *Contradiction of the Welfare State* (edited by John Keane), London: Hutchinson & Co., 1984.
8. See for example the reviews of the business–politics nexus in Neil J. Mitchell, *The Generous Corporation: A Political Analysis of Economic Power*, New Haven, CT: Yale University Press, 1989, and *The Conspicuous Corporation: Business, Public Policy and Representative Democracy*, Ann Arbor, MI: University of Michigan Press, 1997.
9. C. Wright Mills, *The Power Elite*, New York: Oxford University Press, 1956.

CHAPTER 2   PUBLIC RELATIONS: THE ZELIG COMPLEX

1. *Zelig* (1983), http://www.geocities.com/SunsetStrip/Club/9542/zelig.html.
2. Francis Harris and Bruce Johnston, 'Dramatic End for the PR Chief who Lobbied for Tyrants', *Daily Telegraph*, 4 May 2005. http://www.telegraph.co.uk/news/main.jhtml?xml=/news/2005/05/04/wklob04.xml&sSheet=/news/2005/05/04/ixworld.html.
3. Adam Bernstein, 'Tyrants' Lobbyist, Flamboyant to the End', *Washington Post*, 3 May 2005, p. A01. http://www.washingtonpost.com/wp-dyn/content/article/2005/05/02/AR2005050201380_pf.html.

4. Ibid.
5. Ibid.
6. Ibid.
7. Ibid.
8. In George Creel, 'Poisoners of Public Opinion: Part 1', *Harper's Magazine*, 7 November 1914, p. 436, cited in Stuart Ewen, *PR! A Social History of Spin*, New York: Basic Books, 1996, p. 79.
9. Ivy Lee, 'Publicity' address before American Electric Railway Association, 10 October 1916, Atlantic City, cited in Ewen, 1996, p. 81.
10. Larry Tye, *The Father of Spin: Edward L. Bernays and the Birth of Public Relations*, New York: Crown Publishers, pp. 28–31.
11. Ewen, p. 8.
12. Scott Cutlip, *The Unseen Power: Public Relations. A History*, Hillsdale, NJ: Lawrence Erlbaum Associates, 1994, p. 114.
13. Bernays interview featured on Adam Curtis, 'Happiness Machines', *The Century of the Self*, Part 1, BBC2, 29 April 2002. http://www.bbc.co.uk/bbcfour/documentaries/features/century_of_the_self_episode_1.shtml
14. David Miller, 'British Propaganda in Ireland and Its Significance Today', *Spinwatch*, 24 March 2006, http://www.spinwatch.org/content/view/227/8/.
15. Jonathan A. Epstein, *German and English Propaganda in World War I*, paper given to the New York Military Affairs Symposium on 1 December 2000, City University of New York, Graduate Center/NYMAS. http://libraryautomation.com/nymas/propagandapaper.html.
16. See Brian Murphy, *The Origins and Organisation of British Propaganda in Ireland 1920*, Glasgow: Spinwatch and London: Aubane Historical Society, 2006. Available from http://www.spinwatch.org.
17. Mariel Grant, *Propaganda and the Role of the State in Inter-War Britain*, Oxford: Oxford University Press, 1994, pp. 125–6.
18. Murphy, pp. 28–9.
19. Murphy, p. 29.
20. Alan Clarke, 'The Life and Times of Sir Basil Clarke, PR Pioneer', *Public Relations*, Vol. 22, Part 2, 1969, pp. 8–13.
21. Ibid., pp. 8, 10, 13.
22. Keith Middlemass, *Politics in Industrial Society: The Experience of the British System Since 1911*, London: Andre Deutsch, 1979, pp. 353–4.
23. H.B.C. Pollard, *The Secret Societies of Ireland: Their Rise and Progress*, London: Philip Allan, 1922, cited in Murphy, 2006.
24. Graham Turner and John Pearson, *The Persuasion Industry*, London: Eyre and Spottiswoode, 1966, p. 177.
25. See Chapter 1.
26. Tye, p. 111.
27. Edward Bernays, *The Biography of an Idea: Memoirs of Public Relations Counsel Edward L. Bernays*, New York: Simon and Schuster, 1965 (originally published 1955), p. 652.
28. Tye, p. 111.
29. Ray Eldon Hiebert, *Courtier to the Crowd: The Story of Ivy Lee and the Development of Public Relations*, Ames, IA: Iowa State University Press, 1966, p. 386.

30. Ibid., p. 288.
31. Cutlip, p. 149.
32. Hiebert, p. 288.
33. Irwin Ross, *The Image Merchants: The Fabulous World of Public Relations*, New York: Doubleday, 1959, p. 32.
34. The FPA and CFR being the premier elite foreign policy groupings. Ross, pp. 32–3.
35. Ross, p. 289.
36. Ross, p. 290.
37. Ross, p. 290.
38. Hiebert, p. 291.
39. *The Nation*, 29 November 1933, cited in Cutlip, p. 548.
40. Cutlip, p. 549.
41. Cutlip, p. 148; Hiebert, p. 288.
42. Cited in Ross, p. 119.
43. Richard Tedlow, *Keeping the Corporate Image: Public Relations and Business, 1900–1950*, Greenwich, CT: JAI Press, 1979, p. 96.
44. 'Daniel J. Edelman, founder & chairman, Daniel J. Edelman, Inc.', The James C. Bowling Executive-In-Residence Lecture Series, University of Kentucky, Community Programmes, 2003. http://www.uky.edu/CIS/JAT/bowling.html.
45. Ibid.
46. Harold Burson, *Public Relations and the Human Experience*. Remarks by Harold Burson, Founding Chairman, Burson-Marsteller, New York, Leeds Metropolitan University, 29 September 2001. http://www.burson-marsteller.com/pages/insights/pubs/articles/as-09–29–2001.
47. Marion Nestle, *Food Politics*, Berkeley: University of California Press, 2002, pp. 107–8.
48. Tye, pp. 160–78.
49. David McKean, *Peddling Influence: Thomas 'Tommy the Cork' Corcoran and the Birth of Modern Lobbying*, New Hampshire: Steer Fort Press, 2004, pp. 214–15.
50. Tye, p. 177.
51. McKean, p. 225.
52. Tye, p. 177.
53. Susan Trento, *The Power House: Robert Keith Gray and the Selling of Access and Influence in Washington*, New York: St Martin's Press, 1992, p. 94. It should be noted that Burson-Marsteller also enjoyed a close relationship with the CIA. In 1983 CIA director William Casey recommended the creation of the Office of Public Diplomacy in the White House upon advice from senior figures in the US public relations industry, including B-M executives. See John Stauber and Sheldon Rampton, *Toxic Sludge is Good for You: Lies, Damn Lies and the Public Relations Industry*, Monroe, ME: Common Courage, 1995, pp. 162–6.
54. Trento, p. 268.
55. M. Davis, *Interpreters for Nigeria: The Third World and International Public Relations*, Chicago: University of Illinois Press, 1977, pp. 159–62.
56. See Andy Rowell, *Green Backlash*, London: Routledge, 1996, pp. 116–17.

57. P. Brogan, *The Torturers' Lobby: How Human Rights Abusing Nations are Represented in Washington*, Washington, DC: Center for Public Integrity, 1992.

58. For further details see Spinprofiles: http://www.spinprofiles.org/index.php/Burson-Marsteller.

59. Rowell, pp. 119–20; Sharon Beder, *Global Spin: The Corporate Assault on Environmentalism*, Devon: Green Books, 1997.

60. See, Todd Hunt and James Grunig, *Public Relations Techniques*, Fort Worth: Harcourt Brace, 1984, pp. 8–10; Larissa A. Grunig, 'Public Relations', in Michael B. Salwen and Don W. Stacks (eds), *An Integrated Approach to Communication Theory and Research*, Mahwah, NJ: Lawrence Erlbaum Associates, 1996, pp. 464–5.

61. Donn James Tilson and Emmanuel C. Alozie (eds), *Toward the Common Good: Perspectives in International Public Relations*, Boston: Allyn and Bacon, 2004.

62. Comments by James Grunig at 'A Complicated, Antagonistic and Symbiotic Affair: Journalism, Public Relations and their Struggle for Public Attention', The Swiss School of Journalism, Lucerne, Switzerland, 18 March 2006.

63. Ross, pp. 87, 93.

64. Noel Griese, *Arthur W. Page: Publisher, Public Relations Practitioner, Patriot*, Tucker, GA: Anvil Publishers, 2001, p. 304.

65. Ibid., p. 360.

66. David Miller, 'Nuclear View: Spin Doctor Defends Lying', *Spinwatch*, 28 March 2006, http://www.spinwatch.org/content/view/230/8/.

67. Ibid.

68. 'The Truth Hurts', *PR Week*, 2 March 2007, p. 22.

69. Ibid.

70. Mark Tungate, 'Analysis: Clifford and Bell Tussle for Victory in PR Debate', *PR Week*, 23 September 1994; 'The Truth Hurts', p. 22.

71. Daniel Rogers, 'Opinion: Honesty on Display at Ethics Debate', *PR Week*, 21 February 2007.

CHAPTER 3   THE HIDDEN HISTORY
OF CORPORATE PROPAGANDA, 1911–30

1. Jacquie L'Etang, 'State Propaganda and Bureaucratic Intelligence: The Creation of Public Relations in 20th Century Britain', *Public Relations Review*, 24(4), 1998, pp. 413–42.

2. Christopher Andrew, *Her Majesty's Secret Service*, London: Heinemann, 1985, p. 22, cited in Mark Hollingsworth and Charles Tremayne, *The Economic League: The Silent McCarthyism*, London: Liberty, The National Council for Civil Liberties, 1989, p. 1.

3. Mike Hughes, *Spies at Work*, 1 in 12 Publications, 1994. http://www.1in12.go-legend.net/publications/library/spies/spies.htm, chapter 1, p. 9.

4. EEF minute book 13, cited in J.A. Turner, 'The British Commonwealth Union and the General Election of 1918', *English Historical Review*, July 1978, p. 537.

5. Ray Eldon Hiebert, *Courtier to the Crowd: The Story of Ivy Lee and the Development of Public Relations*, Ames, IA: Iowa State University Press, 1966, p. 8.
6. Walter Lippmann, *The Phantom Public*, New York: Harcourt, Brace and Company, 1927, p. 155.
7. Gustav Le Bon, *The Crowd: A Study of the Popular Mind*, London: Unwin Fisher, 1921 (first published in 1896), pp. 45, 74–5.
8. Gabriel Tarde, 'The Public and the Crowd', in Gabriel Tarde, *On Communication and Social Influence*, Selected papers, Edited and with an introduction by Terry Clark, Chicago: University of Chicago Press, 1969 (original version published in 1901), p. 281.
9. Gabriel Tarde, 'Opinion and Conversation', in Tarde, *On Communication and Social Influence*, ibid., p. 304.
10. Tarde, 1901, p. 282.
11. Tarde, 1901, p. 287.
12. Tarde, 1901, p. 294.
13. Walter Lippmann, *Public Opinion*, London: Allen and Unwin, 1922, p. 248.
14. Edward Bernays, *Propaganda*, New York: Horace Liveright, 1930, originally published 1928, p. 9.
15. Lee, cited in Stuart Ewen, *PR! A Social History of Spin*, New York: Basic Books, 1996, p. 132.
16. As we have already noted, Bernays hired A.A. Brill to advise him on how best to promote cigarettes to women, one of his early successes in manipulation. See Larry Tye, *The Father of Spin: Edward L. Bernays and the Birth of Public Relations*, New York: Crown, 1998, p. 28.
17. Walter Lippmann, *Essays in the Public Philosophy*, Boston: Little, Brown, 1955, pp. 39–40. Cited in Sharon Beder, *Free Market Missionaries: The Corporate Manipulation of Community Values*, London: Earthscan, 2006, p. 2.
18. Anthony Sampson, *The Seven Sisters: The Great Oil Companies and the World they Shaped*, London: Hodder and Stoughton, 1975, p. 43.
19. Cited in Scott M. Cutlip, *The Unseen Power: Public Relations. A History*, Hillsdale, NJ: Lawrence Erlbaum Associates, 1994, pp. 47–8.
20. Roland Marchand, *Creating the Corporate Soul: The Rise of Public Relations and Corporate Imagery in American Big Business*, Berkeley: University of California Press, 1998, p. 2. See also Joel Bakan, *The Corporation*, London: Constable, 2004, p. 18.
21. Marchand, p. 139.
22. Marchand, p. 4.
23. H.M. Gitelman, 'Management's Crisis of Confidence and the Origin of the National Industrial Conference Board', *Business History Review*, 58(2), Summer 1984, p. 156.
24. Cited in Beder, p. 5.
25. Conference Board, History of the Conference Board, http://www.conference-board.org/aboutus/history.cfm (accessed March 2007).
26. Quotations from Industrial Relations Counselors, Inc. 'The Science and Art of Labor–Management Relations', History of IRC, http://ircounselors.org/history/history05.html (accessed March 2007).

27. Ibid.
28. Gitelman, p. 153.
29. Gitelman, p. 154.
30. David Vogel, *Fluctuating Fortunes: The Political Power of Business in America*, New York: Basic Books, 1989, p. 4.
31. Bernays, p. 75.
32. Frank Cobb, cited in Lippmann, 1922, pp. 217–18.
33. Cutlip, p. 119.
34. The Interchurch World Movement, Commission of Inquiry, 'Public Opinion and the Steel Strike', New York: Harcourt Brace, 1921, cited in Alex Carey, *Taking the Risk out of Democracy*, New South Wales: University of New South Wales Press, 1995, p. 22.
35. Carey, p. 23.
36. Interchurch World Movement, Commission of Inquiry, p. 22.
37. Robert Murray, *The Red Scare: A Study in National Hysteria 1919–1920*, Minnesota: University of Minneapolis Press, 1955, p. 17.
38. Joel Kovel, *Red Hunting in the Promised Land: Anticommunism and the Making of America*, London: Cassell, 1997, p. 22.
39. *Editor and Publisher*, 1937, cited in Sigmund Diamond, *The Reputation of the American Businessman*, New York: Harper and Row, 1955, p. 109.
40. *Independent Magazine*, 1921, cited in Elizabeth Fones-Wolf, *Selling Free Enterprise: The Business Assault on Labor and Liberalism, 1945–60*, Chicago: University of Illinois Press, 1994, p. 16.
41. Cited in Terence H. Qualter, *Graham Wallas and the Great Society*, New York: St Martin's Press, 1979, p. 134.
42. Graham Wallas, *Human Nature in Politics*, Lincoln: University of Nebraska Press, 1962 (original 1908), p. 29.
43. Carey, 1995.
44. Ronald Steel, *Walter Lippmann and the American Century*, New York: Vintage Books, 1980, p. 28.
45. Graham Wallas, *The Great Society: A Psychological Analysis*, New York: Macmillan Company, 1914.
46. Cited in Gary Messinger, *British Propaganda and the State in the First World War*, Manchester: Manchester University Press, 1992, p. 219.
47. Ibid., p. 219.
48. Charles Frederick Higham, *Looking Forward: Mass Education through Publicity*, London: Nisbert and Co., 1920, p. 22.
49. Ibid., p. 35.
50. Ibid., p. 12.
51. Ibid., pp. 104, 105.
52. Ibid., pp. 102–3, 110.
53. Messinger, p. 220.
54. R.P.T. Davenport-Hines, *Dudley Docker: The Life and Times of a Trade Warrior*, Cambridge: Cambridge University Press, 2002, p. 74.
55. Ibid., p. 70.
56. J.A. Turner, 'The British Commonwealth Union and the General Election of 1918', *English Historical Review*, July 1978, p. 529.
57. Ibid., p. 529.

58. Minutes of the General Purposes committee of the BCU, 13 June 1918, cited in Turner, p. 538.
59. Although Hughes suggests the numbers were 26 and 20 (chapter 1).
60. Hughes, chapter 1.
61. Hughes, chapter 1.
62. Cited in Keith Middlemass, *Politics in Industrial Society: The Experience of the British System Since 1911*, London: Andre Deutsch, 1979, p. 131.
63. Ibid., p. 132.
64. Ibid., p. 352.
65. Ibid., p. 153.
66. Ibid., p. 132.
67. Turner, p. 259.
68. Economic League, *Speaker's Notes*, No. 56, 16 July 1926, cited in Labour Research Department, *What is the Economic League?*, revised edn, London, 1937, p. 5.
69. Economic League, *Fifty Fighting Years*, Economic League Central Council, 1969, cited in Hughes, chapter 1, p. 8.
70. *Fifty Fighting Years*, cited in Hughes, chapter 1, p. 8.
71. John Hope, cited in Hughes, chapter 2, p. 4.
72. Ron Bean, cited in Hughes, chapter 2, p. 4.
73. Richard C. Thurlow, *The Red Menace: British Communism and the State 1920–51*, http://www.socialsciences.manchester.ac.uk/chnn/CHNN05TRM.html (accessed March 2007).
74. Cited in Hughes, chapter 1.
75. Middlemass, 1979, p. 131.
76. But see Hughes, *Spies at Work*.
77. Hughes, chapter 1.
78. Davenport-Hines, p. 72.
79. Davenport-Hines, p. 81.
80. Davenport-Hines, p. 82.
81. Davenport-Hines, p. 70.
82. Davenport-Hines, p. 76.
83. Davenport-Hines, p. 74.
84. Andrew Marrison, *British Business and Protection, 1903–1932*, Oxford: Oxford University Press, 1996, p. 299.
85. Patrick Beesly, *Room 40: British Naval Intelligence 1914–18*, London: Hamish Hamilton, 1982, p. 34.
86. Ibid., pp. 35, 36, 37.
87. Ibid., pp. 37–8.
88. Ibid., p. 39.
89. The diary entries include explicit details that recorded Casement's frequent gay sexual activities. The leaking of extracts was intended to discourage any calls for clemency that may have spared Casement from the gallows. The authenticity of the diaries is still disputed, though their effect is unquestionable.
90. Bernard Porter, *Plots and Paranoia*, London: Unwin Hyman, 1989, p. 141.

91. Cited in Christopher Andrew, *Her Majesty's Secret Service: The Making of the British Intelligence Community*, New York: Viking Penguin, 1986, pp. 247–8.
92. Hollingsworth and Tremayne, *The Economic League: The Silent McCarthyism*, London: Liberty, The National Council for Civil Liberties, 1989.
93. Hollingsworth and Tremayne, p. 6.
94. John Baker White, *True Blue: An Autobiography, 1902–1939*, London: Muller, p. 128, cited in Hollingsworth and Tremayne, p. 8.
95. John Baker White, 'It's Gone for Good', London: Vacher and Sons, 1941, pp. 122–3, cited in John Hope, 'Fascism, the Security Service and the Curious Careers of Maxwell Knight and James McGuirk Hughes', *Lobster*, No. 22, November, 1991, pp. 1–5. http://members.lycos.co.uk/mere_pseud_mag_ed/History/Hope1.htm.
96. Ibid.
97. John Baker White, *Dover–Nuremburg Return*, London: Burrup, Mathieson and Co., 1937, p. 32, cited in Hollingsworth and Tremayne, p. 9.
98. This paragraph based on Hollingsworth and Tremayne, pp. 9–10.
99. Hughes, chapter 3.
100. Cited in Hughes, chapter 4, p. 11.
101. Hughes, chapter 4, p. 2.
102. Margaret Morris, *The General Strike*, London: Pelican, 1976, p. 139.
103. Hughes, chapter 4.
104. Cited in Hughes, chapter 4, p. 6.
105. Middlemass, p. 195.

CHAPTER 4   THE SECOND WAVE
OF CORPORATE PROPAGANDA, 1936–50

1. Cited in David Vogel, *Fluctuating Fortunes: The Political Power of Business in the United States*, New York: Basic Books, 1989, p. 4.
2. See Stuart Ewen, *PR! A Social History of Spin*, New York: Basic Books, 1996; Richard Tedlow, *Keeping the Corporate Image: Public Relations and Business, 1900–1950*, Greenwich, CT: JAI Press, 1979, chapter 3.
3. Cited in Alex Carey, *Taking the Risk Out of Democracy: Corporate Propaganda Versus Freedom and Liberty*, Sydney: University of New South Wales Press, 1995, p. 25.
4. US Department of Labor, Office of the Assistant Secretary for Administration and Management, Glossary, http://www.dol.gov/oasam/programs/history/glossary.htm (accessed March 2007).
5. D.W. Chapman, 'Industrial Conflict in Detroit', in George Hartmann and Theodore Newcombe (eds), *Industrial Conflict: A Psychological Interpretation*, New York: Cordon Company, 1939, pp. 43–102, cited in Carey, p. 25.
6. Cited in Robert G. Rodden, *The Fighting Machinists: A Century of Struggle*, Washington, DC: Kelly Press, Inc., 1984. http://www.iamawlodge1426.org/hisupdate39.htm.

5 5 5 5 5 5 55 5 5 5 55 555555555555 5 5 5

7. Hill & Knowlton is one of the world's leading agencies today. It is owned by WPP. Selvage went on to form the company Manning Selvage & Lee which is now known as MS&L and owned by communication conglomerate Publicis. Ketchum is now owned by conglomerate Omnicom. For more detail on the ownership and conglomeration of the PR business see Chapter 7.
8. Cited in Scott Cutlip, *The Unseen Power: Public Relations. A History*, Hillsdale, NJ: Lawrence Erlbaum Associates, 1994, p. 243.
9. Cited in ibid., p. 468.
10. Cited in Tedlow, p. 75.
11. Cited in Cutlip, p. 470.
12. 'Self-Evident Subtlety', *Time*, 1 August 1938. http://www.time.com/time/magazine/article/0,9171,771150,00.html.
13. Albion G. Taylor, *Labor Policies of the National Association of Manufacturers*, Urbana: University of Illinois Press, 1928, pp. 175, 178, cited in Tedlow, p. 70.
14. Tedlow, pp. 209, 71.
15. John Hill, *The Making of a Public Relations Man*, Lincolnwood, IL: NTC Business Books, 1993 (original version published 1963), pp. 46, 51.
16. La Follette had noted only that he had 'taken measures' to 'stamp out' what he called 'influences within my own staff' from 'communist sympathisers'. Not a word about 'domination' or 'unfairness'.
17. Cited in Carey, p. 26.
18. John Streuben, *Strike Strategy*, New York: Gaer, 1950, p. 231, cited in Carey, p. 26.
19. Ibid.
20. See Seamus Milne, *The Enemy Within: The Secret War Against the Miners*, 2nd edn, London: Verso, 2004.
21. S.H. Walker and Paul Sklar, *Business Finds its Voice*, New York: Harper and Brothers, 1938, p. 1.
22. Carey, p. 18.
23. Cited in Ewen, p. 301.
24. Cited in Sharon Beder, *Free Market Missionaries: The Corporate Manipulation of Community Values*, London: Earthscan, 2006, p. 22.
25. Cited in Ewen, p. 306.
26. Daniel Bell, 'Industrial Conflict and Public Opinion', in A. Kornhauser, R. Dubin and A. Ross (eds), *Industrial Conflict and Public Opinion*, New York: McGraw Hill, 1954, p. 254, cited in Carey, p. 30.
27. Carey, p. 29.
28. Robert Griffith, 'The Selling of America: The Advertising Council and American Politics, 1942–1960', *Business History Review*, Autumn 1983, p. 401; Beder, p. 33.
29. Bell, cited in Carey, p. 30.
30. Beder, p. 41.
31. Beder, p. 41.
32. Cited in Carey, p. 34.
33. Carey, p. 32.

34. Elizabeth Fones-Wolf, *Selling Free Enterprise: The Business Assault on Labor and Liberalism, 1945–60*, Chicago: University of Illinois Press, 1994, p. 10.
35. Labour Research Department, *The Federation of British Industries*, London: LRD, 1950, p. 12; R.P.T. Davenport-Hines, *Dudley Docker: The Life and Times of a Trade Warrior*, Cambridge: Cambridge University Press, 1984.
36. Ron Noon, 'Goodbye, Mr Cube', *History Today*, 51(10), October 2001, p. 40.
37. Ibid., p. 40.
38. Cited in H.H. Wilson, 'Techniques of Pressure – Anti-Nationalization Propaganda in Britain', *Public Opinion Quarterly*, Summer 1951, pp. 231–2.
39. Ibid., p. 231.
40. Cited in Richard Kisch, *The Private Life of Public Relations*, London: MacGibbon and Kee, 1964, p. 35.
41. A.A. Rogow, with the assistance of Peter Shore, *The Labour Government and British Industry, 1945–51*, Oxford: Basil Blackwell, 1955, p. 143.
42. Noon, p. 40.
43. Cited in Rogow, p. 139.
44. Labour Research Department, p. 17.
45. Labour Research Department, p. 18.
46. H.H. Wilson, *Pressure Group: The Campaign for Commercial Television*, London: Secker and Warburg, 1961.
47. Cited in ibid., p. 165.
48. Ibid., p. 170.
49. Ibid., p. 175.
50. Ibid., p. 174.
51. Ibid., p. 172.
52. Kisch, p. 35.
53. Cited in Richard West, *PR: The Fifth Estate*, London: Mayflower Books, 1963, p. 65.
54. Ronald Steel, *Walter Lippmann and the American Century*, New York: Vintage, 1981, p. 323.
55. John Bellamy Foster, 'Contradictions in the Universalization of Capitalism', *Monthly Review*, April, 1999. http://findarticles.com/p/articles/mi_m1132/is_11_50/ai_54517443/pg_1.
56. Richard Cockett, *Thinking the Unthinkable: Think-Tanks and the Economic Counter-Revolution, 1931–83*, London: HarperCollins, 1994.
57. American Enterprise Institute, 'AEI's Diamond Jubilee, 1943–2003'. This essay appeared in AEI, Annual Report, 2003. http://www.aei.org/about/contentID.20031212154735838/default.asp (accessed March 2007).
58. Ibid.
59. Ibid.
60. Sidney Blumenthal, *The Rise of the Counter Establishment: From Conservative Ideology to Political Power*, New York: Harper and Row, 1988, p. 32.
61. Ralph Harris, 'The Plan to End Planning – the Founding of the Mont Pelerin Society', *National Review*, 16 June 1997. http://www.highbeam.com/library/docFree.asp?DOCID=1G1:19517834.

62. Ibid.

63. Hayek, cited in Harris.

64. Cited in Cockett, pp. 116–17.

65. Radhika Desai, 'Second-Hand Dealers in Ideas: Think-Tanks and Thatcherite Hegemony', *New Left Review*, No. 203, January–February 1994, p. 46.

66. Peter Jay interviewed on *Tory! Tory! Tory!*, Part 1, BBC4, 8 March 2006.

CHAPTER 5   THE CASE FOR CAPITALISM –
THE THIRD WAVE, TO THE 1980s

1. Cited in Richard Cockett, *Thinking the Unthinkable: Think-Tanks and the Economic Counter-Revolution, 1931–83*, London: HarperCollins, 1994, p. 173.

2. Organised through the Stockholm Network (http://www.spinprofiles. org/index.php/Stockholm_Network) and the Economic Freedom Network (http://www.spinprofiles.org/index.php/Economic_Freedom_ Network) amongst others. Both accessed March 2007.

3. Michael Ivens, 'Preface', in Michael Ivens and Reginald Dunstan (eds), *The Case for Capitalism*, London: Michael Joseph in association with Aims of Industry, 1967, p. 7.

4. Brian Crozier, *Free Agent: The Unseen War 1941–1991: The Autobiography of an International Activist*, London: HarperCollins, 1993, p. 106.

5. IRIS was set up after a split in Common Cause. In 1995 it was revealed that IRIS had been funded in part from the 'secret vote' by the government, meaning that it was in part an intelligence service operation. See Robin Ramsay, *The Clandestine Caucus*, Hull: Lobster, 1996. Several right-wing trade union leaders associated with IRIS were implicated in undercover activities in the miners' strike of 1984/85. See Seumas Milne, *The Enemy Within: The Secret War Against the Miners*, London: Verso, 2004, p. 386.

6. John Whitehorn, Draft memo in letter marked 'Strictly private and confidential' to Brian Crozier, 24 January 1972, cited in Paul Lashmar and James Oliver, *Britain's Secret Propaganda War, 1948–1977*, Stroud, Gloucestershire: Sutton Publishing, p. 166.

7. Ibid.

8. Crozier, p. 108.

9. Stephen Dorril and Robin Ramsay, *Smear! Wilson and the Secret State*, London: Fourth Estate, 1991, p. 230.

10. John Booth, 'Harold Wilson: Elected by the People; Undone by the Plotters', *Spinwatch*, 20 March 2006, http://www.spinwatch.org/content/ view/224/8/ (accessed March 2007).

11. Dorril and Ramsay, pp. 282–90.

12. Radhika Desai, 'Second-Hand Dealers in Ideas: Think-Tanks and Thatcherite Hegemony', *New Left Review*, No. 203, January–February 1994, p. 52.

13. Cited in Cockett, p. 237.

14. Cited in Desai, p. 55.

15. The Road to Power, *Tory! Tory! Tory!*, Part 2, BBC4, 15 March 2006.
16. Cited in Cockett, p. 221.
17. Cockett's term, p. 221.
18. Ambalavaner Sivanandan, 'Grunwick', *Race & Class*, 19(1), Summer 1977. http://libcom.org/library/the-grunwick-strike-a-sivanandan.
19. Interviewed on *Tory! Tory! Tory!*, Part 2, BBC4, 15 March 2006.
20. Available at http://www.spinprofiles.org/images/0/03/Barriers_to_Privatisation.pdf
21. Cockett, p. 268.
22. Cited in Cockett, p. 270.
23. See Cockett, pp. 272–4.
24. Feulner had in turn studied in the UK at the LSE and at Edinburgh where he got his PhD.
25. Cockett, p. 282.
26. Ted Nace, *Gangs of America: The Rise of Corporate Power and the Disabling of Democracy*, San Francisco, CA: Berrett-Koehler Publishers, Inc., 2003, p. 137.
27. Ibid., p. 137.
28. Ibid., pp. 139, 140, 142.
29. G. William Domhoff, *The Powers That Be*, New York: Vintage Books, 1979, p. 79.
30. Philip Burch, 'The Business Roundtable: Its Make Up and External Ties', *Research in Political Economy*, Vol. 4, 1981, p. 116.
31. Cited in David Vogel, *Fluctuating Fortunes: The Political Power of Business in the United States*, New York: Basic Books, 1989, p. 197.
32. John McArthur, *The Selling of 'Free Trade': NAFTA, Washington and the Subversion of American Democracy*, Berkeley: University of California Press, 2001.
33. Sidney Blumenthal, *The Rise of the Counter Establishment: From Conservative Ideology to Political Power*, New York: Harper and Row, 1988.
34. Joseph G. Peschek, *Policy-Planning Organizations: Elite Agendas and America's Rightward Turn*, Philadelphia: Temple University Press, 1987, p. 29.
35. Cited in ibid., p. 29.
36. Ibid., p. 33.
37. Ibid., p. 32.
38. Ibid., p. 66.
39. Ibid., p. 27.
40. Blumenthal, p. 88.
41. Ibid., p. 112.
42. See http://www.atlasusa.org/V2/main/acc.php (accessed March 2007).
43. Ralph Harris, 'The Plan to End Planning – the Founding of the Mont Pelerin Society', *National Review*, 16 June 1997. http://findarticles.com/p/articles/mi_m1282/is_n11_v49/ai_19517834/pg_1.

CHAPTER 6   THE REAL RULERS OF THE WORLD

1. Christopher Meyer, address to the Scottish Financial Enterprise Annual Dinner, 11 November 2004, The Thistle Hotel, Glasgow.

2. Christopher Meyer, *DC Confidential*, London, Weidenfeld and Nicolson, 2005, pp. 222–3.
3. Caroline Anstey, 'The Projection of British Socialism: Foreign Office Publicity and American Opinion, 1945–1950', *Journal of Contemporary History*, 19(3), 1984, pp. 417–51.
4. Details in the previous paragraph from G. William Domhoff, *The Bohemian Grove and Other Retreats: A Study in Ruling Class Cohesiveness*, New York: Harper and Row, 1975; Domhoff, *Who Rules America Now? A View for the 1980s*, New York: Touchstone Books, 1983, p. 31.
5. Domhoff, 1975, pp. 34–9.
6. Domhoff, 1975, pp. 63–9.
7. David Nye, *Image Worlds: Corporate Identities at General Electric*, Cambridge, MA: MIT Press, 1985, pp. 95–100.
8. The New Club Website, http://www.newclub.co.uk/NEW_CLUB_HISTORY/new_club_history.html (accessed 9 June 2007).
9. Collins Dictionary definition.
10. G. William Domhoff, 'There are No Conspiracies', *Who Rules America?* March 2005, http://sociology.ucsc.edu/whorulesamerica/theory/conspiracy.html (accessed March 2007).
11. Steve John, *The Persuaders: When Lobbyists Matter*, Basingstoke: Palgrave Macmillan, 2002, pp. ix and 201.
12. Steve John, comments at ECPA conference in London, 'Public Affairs and the World Crisis: What has Changed since September 11th?', 9 January 2002.
13. Steve John, 'Radical Campaigners are Retreating', *The Public Affairs Newsletter*, February 2002, p. 9.
14. Kevin Craig, 'Public Policy Issues: How Lobbying Your MP Can Help', BioIndustry Association, Risk and Reputation Seminar, 2 April 2001, p. 14. http://www.bioindustry.org/biodocuments/RiskManagement.doc (accessed March 2007).
15. Jeffrey Birnbaum, *The Lobbyists: How Influence Peddlers Work their Way in Washington*, New York: Times Books, 1993, p. 197.
16. From September 2004 the RIIA changed its name to Chatham House. See 'About Chatham House', http://www.chathamhouse.org.uk/index.php?id=2.
17. See John Mackenzie, *Propaganda and Empire: The Manipulation of British Public Opinion 1880–1960*, Manchester: Manchester University Press, 1986; Robin Ramsay and Stephen Dorril, *Smear! Wilson and the Secret State*, London: Fourth Estate, 1991, p. 349. The Roundtable is a staple of far right conspiracy theorists who see it as part of the masonic conspiracy to impose world government and destroy liberty. Just for good measure they see Karl Marx, communism, and Zionism as part of the same global conspiracy. If you think that such ideas have some plausibility you should not be reading this book.
18. The Royal Institute of International Affairs, http://www.chathamhouse.org.uk/index.php?id=3 (accessed March 2007). See also Chatham House, The Royal Institute for International Affairs, http://politics.guardian.co.uk/thinktanks/page/0,,1538994,00.html (accessed March 2007).
19. For examples of such perspectives see Stephen Haseler, *The Unjust World of Global Capitalism*, London: Macmillan, 2000.

20. For more detail on these corporate lobby groups see Belen Balanya et al., *Europe Inc.: Regional & Global Restructuring and the Rise of Corporate Power*, London: Pluto Press, 2000.

21. Ibid., p. 36.

22. The EC was represented by Vice-President of the Commission and Commissioner for Trade, Sir Leon Brittan, and the Commissioner for Industrial Affairs, Martin Bangemann.

23. Cited in Balanya et al., p. 104.

24. *Opening World Markets for Services: Towards GATS 2000*, EU GATS-INFO website, http://gats-info.eu.int/gats-info/g2000.pl?NEWS=bbb. Cited in Erik Wesselius, *Liberalisation of Trade in Services: Corporate Power at Work*, GATSwatch – a joint project of Corporate Europe Observatory and Transnational Institute, Amsterdam. http://www.gatswatch.org/LOTIS/LOTIS.html (accessed March 2007).

25. The GATT Uruguay Round lasted from 1986 until 1994. The conclusion of the Marrakesh Agreements led to the establishment of the World Trade Organisation in January 1995.

26. 'What the General Agreement on Trade in Services can do', speech by David Hartridge, director of Trade in Services Division, World Trade Organisation, to the conference 'Opening Markets for Banking Worldwide: The WTO General Agreement on Trade in Services', 8 January 1997, London (organised by British Invisibles and the transnational law firm Clifford Chance). Cited in Sharon Beder, 'How Corporations Drive the Global Agenda', 29 May 2006, http://www.spinwatch.org/content/view/249/8/ (accessed March 2007).

27. Herman von Bertrab, *Negotiating NAFTA: A Mexican Envoy's Account*, Washington, DC: Greenwood / Center for Strategic and International Studies, 1997, cited in John R. MacArthur, *The Selling of 'Free Trade': NAFTA, Washington, and the Subversion of American Democracy*, Berkeley: University of California Press, 2001, pp. 76–7 and 92–3. This account is disputed by the US trade negotiator Carla Hills who claimed she instigated a discussion about a trade deal with the Mexicans in a bilateral meeting. Another version of the origins of the idea in MacArthur's excellent study of NAFTA claims that Helmut Kohl and Jacques Delors told the Mexican president that the only way to clinch a trade deal with the EU was by first entering into a trade deal with the US.

28. MacArthur, p. 101.

29. MacArthur, p. 133.

30. MacArthur, p. 168.

31. MacArthur, p. 169.

32. Fratelli Group, 'USA*NAFTA Media Strategy for Lee Iacocco', cited in MacArthur, p. 203.

33. MacArthur, p. 246.

34. MacArthur, p. 214.

35. Public Citizen, *The Ten Year Track Record of NAFTA*, Washington, 2004. http://www.citizen.org/trade/nafta/ (accessed March 2007).

36. They are not 'the' conspiracy that runs the world and nor, most emphatically, are they secret collectivist conspirators, carrying out the work of the communists, masons or – in some versions – the Devil.

37. G. William Domhoff, *The Higher Circles: The Governing Class in America*, New York: Vintage, pp. 302–3.

38. Frederick Keppel, 'The International Chamber of Commerce', *International Conciliation*, 1922, pp. 189–210.

39. Keppel, pp. 197–8.

40. Balanya et al., pp. 137–8.

41. For the full results of the election see: http://www.electionsireland. org/result.cfm?election=1973&cons=99 (accessed March 2007).

42. See *Spin Profiles*: http://www.spinprofiles.org/index.php/Peter_ Sutherland; Peter Sutherland, GATT and WTO Director-General, 1993 to 1995, Biographical note, http://www.wto.org/English/thewto_e/dg_e/ ps_e.htm (accessed March 2007).

43. William Carroll and Colin Carson, 'Forging a New Hegemony? The Role of Transnational Policy Groups in the Network and Discourses of Global Corporate Governance', *Journal of World Systems Research*, 9(1), Winter 2003, pp. 67–102.

44. Balanya et al., p. 145.

45. Peter Thompson, 'Bilderberg and the West', in Holly Sklar (ed.), *Trilateralism: The Trilateral Commission and Elite Planning for World Management*, Boston, MA: South End Press, 1980, p. 157.

46. Ibid.

47. Alan Armstrong with Alastair McConnachie, 'The 1998 Bilderberg Meeting', *The Social Creditor: Official Journal of the Social Credit Secretariat*, July/August 1998, cited in Balanya et al., p. 146.

48. Denis Healey, *The Time of My Life*, London: Penguin, 1989, p. 195.

49. Jon Ronson, *Them: Adventures with Extremists*, London: Picador, 2001, p. 299.

50. Ibid., p. 297.

51. Conal Walsh, 'The Greens Who Took the Corporate Shilling', *Observer*, CSR supplement, 2 February 2003, p. 5.

52. Simon Caulkin and Joanna Collins, *The Private Life of Public Affairs*, London: Green Alliance, 2003.

53. Jonathon Porritt, *Capitalism: As if the World Matters*, London: Earthscan, 2005.

54. Juliette Jowit, 'Porritt Warns Greens to Mend "Negative" Ways', *Observer*, 6 November 2005, http://observer.guardian.co.uk/politics/ story/0,6903,1635387,00.html (accessed March 2007). As with many of the other links we have noted in other parts of these elite networks, we have not chosen these particular links for a particular reason, other than that they are easily found connections to important networks. We could, given space and time, follow up on Porritt's other links and bedfellows. But, in our view, this would not present a substantially different picture.

55. Cited in Balanya et al., p. 148.

56. Daniel W. Drezner, 'Davos' Downhill Slide', *LA Times*, 21 January 2007. http://www.latimes.com/news/opinion/sunday/commentary/la-op-drezner21jan21,0,2666683.story?coll=la-sunday-commentary (accessed March 2007).

57. Kees van der Pijl, 'The International Level', in Tom Bottomore and Robert Brym (eds), *The Capitalist Class: An International Study*, London: Harvester Wheatsheaf, 1989, p. 259.
58. Ibid.
59. Reginald Dale, 'Thinking Ahead: Club Surveys the Global Economy', *International Herald Tribune*, 16 March 1999. http://www.iht.com/articles/1999/03/16/think.2.t_2.php (accessed March 2007).
60. Commission of the European Communities, Communication from the Commission, *A Sustainable Europe for a Better World: A European Union Strategy for Sustainable Development*, Brussels, 15.5.2001, COM(2001)264 final (Commission's proposal to the Gothenburg European Council). http://europa.eu.int/eur-lex/en/com/cnc/2001/com2001_0264en01.pdf (accessed March 2007).
61. Gardner G. Peckham, 'Guide to the Seattle Meltdown: A Compendium of Activists at the WTO Ministerial', BKSH: Black, Kelly, Scruggs & Healy, A Burson-Marsteller Company: Washington, DC, 14 January 2000. http://www.commondreams.org/headlines/031000–03.htm.
62. On the ICFTU see Harry Kelber, 'AFL-CIO's Dark Past (3): U.S. Labor Secretly Intervened in Europe, Funded to Fight Pro-Communist Unions', *Labor Educator*, 22 November 2004, http://www.laboreducator.org/darkpast3.htm (accessed March 2007); Robin Ramsay, 'The Influence of Intelligence Services on the British Left', a talk given by Robin Ramsay to Labour Party branches in late 1996, http://www.lobster-magazine.co.uk/articles/rrtalk.htm (accessed March 2007).
63. David Osler, 'Big Business and the Moderates', *Rank and File*, 1995, http://www.rainbow-web-design.co.uk/caucus/news/BigbusinessandtheModerates.doc (accessed March 2007); Seumas Milne, *The Enemy Within: The Secret War Against the Miners*, 3rd edn, London: Verso, 2004, p. 387.

CHAPTER 7 THE GLOBAL PR INDUSTRY

1. Bernard Ingham, 'Opinion: Defend Capitalism or the PR Industry Dies', *PR Week*, 10 December 1999. http://www.prweek.com/uk/search/article/102123// (subscription required; accessed March 2007).
2. Leslie Sklair, 'The Transnational Capitalist Class and Global Politics: Deconstructing the Corporate-State Connection', *International Political Science Review*, 23, 2002, pp.159–74.
3. Anthony Sampson, *The Seven Sisters: The Great Oil Companies and the World they Shaped*, London: Hodder and Stoughton Ltd, 1975, p. 82.
4. Ian Burrell, 'Lord Bell: I'd do anything for Margaret', *Independent*, 2 May 2005. http://news.independent.co.uk/media/article221377.ece (accessed March 2007).
5. Chime Communications, Annual Report 2005, p. 6. http://www.chime.plc.uk/pdfs/annual_report_2005/completereport.pdf (accessed March 2007).
6. Mark Hollingsworth, *The Ultimate Spin Doctor: The Life and Fast Times of Tim Bell*, London: Hodder and Stoughton, 1997.

7. WPP, Annual Report 2005, p. 159. http://www.wpp.com/NR/rdonlyres/ 2A8BD31E-0588–45BF-9DD3–8ED3762B51CE/0/download_1146.pdf (accessed March 2007).

8. 'Hill & Knowlton Beijing Named Consultancy of the Year', http://www. hillandknowlton.com/index/news/press_releases/49 (accessed March 2007).

9. The Congressional Human Rights Caucus is not an official committee of Congress, and therefore lying in testimony to this Caucus is not a criminal offence. A Caucus is akin to a cross-party group in the British parliamentary system. However the reporting of this testimony treated it as if it were an official hearing. See John MacArthur, *Second Front: Censorship and Propaganda in the Gulf War*, Berkeley: University of California Press, 1992.

10. Lou Morano, 'Propaganda: Remember the Kuwaiti Babies?', *United Press International*, 26 February 1992.

11. WPP, Annual Report 2005, p. 8.

12. See Nicholas Jones, *The Control Freaks: How New Labour Gets Its Own Way*, London: Politico's, 2002, pp. 271–303.

13. Dewe Rogerson handled over 90 of all the UK privatisations, by value. David Miller and William Dinan, 'The Rise of the PR Industry in Britain, 1979–98', *European Journal of Communication*, 15(1), 2000, pp. 14–21.

14. Andrew Gamble, *The Free Economy and the Strong State*, Houndmills: Macmillan, 1988.

15. Nicholas Jones, *Strikes and the Media*, Oxford: Basil Blackwell, 1986, p. 5.

16. Ibid., p. 12.

17. Ibid., p. 13.

18. Miller and Dinan, 2000, p. 18 (table 2). The trend is noticeable particularly in the cases of British Telecom, British Gas, British Rail and the Central Electricity Generating Board.

19. BDO Stoy Hayward, *The Public Relations Sector: An Analysis for the Department of Trade and Industry*, October, 93/BJKC/49335, London: BDO Stoy Hayward, 1994, p. 15.

20. Jeremy Tunstall, *The Advertising Man in London Advertising Agencies*, London: Routledge, 1964.

21. *PR Week*, 1998 Top 150 League Tables, pp. 19–26.

22. Aggregated from data produced in the *PR Week* Top 150 League Table, 21 April 2006, pp. 13–21.

23. M. Hingstone, 'A Decade of Growth', pp. 44–7 in Public Relations Consultants Association, *The Public Relations Year Book, 1990*, London: Financial Times Business Information, 1990, p. 44.

24. Miller and Dinan, 2000, p. 11.

25. Calculated from *PR Week* Top 150 League Table, 21 April 2006, pp. 13–21.

26. Reported in the Chartered Institute of Public Relations, *Reaching New Heights*, Annual Review 2005, p. 6. The research was carried out by the Centre for Economics and Business Research (CEBR).

27. Yeap Sung Beng, 'The State of Public Relations in Singapore', *Public Relations Review*, 20(4), 1994, p. 374.

28. J. Van Leuven and C. Pratt, 'Public Relations' Role: Realities in Asia and in Africa South of the Sahara', in H. Culbertson and N. Chen (eds), *International Public Relations: A Comparative Analysis*, Mahwah, NJ: Lawrence Erlbaum, 1998, p. 99.

29. Mike Okereke, 'Public Relations Growth in Developing Countries', Paper given at The Importance of Public Relations in the Changing Global Environment, International Public Relations Association Conference, Cairo, Egypt, 13–15 October 2002.

30. Morris Davis, *Interpreters for Nigeria: The Third World and International Public Relations*, Chicago: University of Illinois Press, 1977.

31. Rosaleen Smyth, 'The Genesis of Public Relations in British Colonial Practice', *Public Relations Review*, 27(3), 2001, pp. 149–62.

32. Susan L. Carruthers, *Winning Hearts and Minds: British Governments, the Media and Colonial Counter-Insurgency, 1944–1960*, Leicester: Leicester University Press, 1995, p. 266.

33. Okereke, 2002.

34. Okereke, 2002.

35. Interviews with the authors by Nigerian PR operatives at the International Public Relations Association Conference, Cairo, Egypt, 13–15 October 2002.

36. Jeffrey H. Birnbaum, 'The Road to Riches is called K Street – Lobbying Firms Hire More, Pay More, Charge More to Influence Government', *Washington Post*, 22 June 2005.

37. Siim Kallas, 'The Need for a European Transparency Initiative', The European Foundation for Management, Nottingham Business School, Nottingham, 3 March 2005. http://europa.eu/rapid/pressReleasesAction. do?reference=SPEECH/05/130&format=HTML&aged=1&language=EN &guiLanguage=en (accessed March 2007).

38. Cited in Ray Josephs, 'Hong Kong: Public Relations Capital of Asia?', *Public Relations Journal*, September, 1991, p. 21.

39. Ibid., p. 21.

40. Philip Hanson, *Advertising and Socialism*, London: Macmillan, 1974.

41. Sam Black, 'Chinese Update', *Public Relations Quarterly*, Vol. 37, 1992, p. 42.

42. James B. Strenski and Kung Yue, 'China: The World's Next Public Relations Superpower', *Public Relations Quarterly*, Vol. 43, 1998, p. 25.

43. R.C. Isham, 'The China Trade Show', *Sales & Marketing Management*, Vol. 135, October 1985, p. 7.

44. He Ming, 'The Chinese PR Industry and Occupational Qualification Examination System', Paper presented at the IPRA World Congress 15–16 October 2001 in Berlin.

45. Scott Kennedy, *The Business of Lobbying in China*, Cambridge, MA: Harvard University Press, 2005, p. 46.

46. Ibid., p. 49.

47. Ibid., pp. 51, 215. According to Kennedy the Chinese word for lobbying, *youshui*, is translated in PRC dictionaries as 'canvassing' or 'selling an idea' and in Taiwanese dictionaries as lobbying or 'to drum up support'. The original meaning, 'wandering persuader', derives from references to philosophers who travelled between the Warring States (475–221

BC) offering ideas and strategies in return for political patronage from rulers, something akin to a cross between direct lobbying and think tank policy analyses in the contemporary western world.

48. M.Y. Yu, 'Putting the PR in the PRC: Public Relations in China is Broader than you Think', Piset Wattanavitikul's Awakening Dragon, Asia Pacific Management Forum, July/August 2000. http://www.apmforum.com/columns/china5.htm (accessed March 2007).
49. Ibid.
50. Black, p. 42.
51. *China Daily*, 'Firms Regard China's WTO Entry as Stimulus', 6 June 2001. http://www1.chinadaily.com.cn/news/cb/2001–11–06/42285.html (subscription access).
52. John MacArthur, *The Selling of 'Free Trade'*, Berkeley: University of California Press, 2000; Patrick Woodall, Lori Wallach, Jessica Roach and Katie Burnham, *Purchasing Power: The Corporate–White House Alliance to Pass the China Trade Bill over the Will of the American People*, Washington, DC: Public Citizen's Global Trade Watch, 2000.
53. *China Daily*, 2001.
54. *China Daily*, 2001.
55. E. Trickett, 'Global Rankings: Universal Picture', *PR Week*, 29 July 2002. http://www.hoffman.com/inthenews/articles/prweek_jul2902.htm.
56. Joe Studwell, *The China Dream: The Elusive Quest for the Greatest Untapped Market on Earth*, London: Profile Books, 2002.
57. *China Daily*, 2001.
58. *PR Week*, Global Special 2006, 'Markets of Tomorrow', p. 17.
59. *PR Week*, Global Special 2006, 'Markets of Tomorrow', p. 16.
60. Armand Mattelart (trans), *Advertising International: The Privatisation of Public Space*, London: Comedia, 1991, p. 25.
61. *Jack O' Dwyer's Newsletter*, 'Many Independents Grow 20%+', 7 March 2007.
62. Jack O'Dwyer, PR Opinion, *Jack O' Dwyer's Newsletter*, 39(35), 6 September 2006, p. 8.
63. Ibid.
64. The Lord Saatchi, http://www.conservatives.com/tile.do?def=people.person.page&personID=21892 (accessed March 2007).
65. Craig Endicott, *Advertising Age*, 22 April 2002, p. 1.
66. Bradley Johnson, 'Ad Holding Companies on Brink of New Order; WPP poised to overtake Omnicom by year's end; Interpublic could fall to 4th', *Advertising Age*, 4 September 2006, p. 4.
67. Jack O'Dwyer, September 2006.
68. http://www.odwyerpr.com/members/archived_stories_2004/june/0601comm_od_ethics.htm (subscription required; accessed March 2007).
69. About the Trilateral Commission, http://www.trilateral.org/annmtgs/trialog/trlglist.htm (accessed March 2007).
70. World Economic Forum, Strategic Partners, http://www.weforum.org/en/about/Members%20and%20Partners/StrategicPartners/index.htm?id=20866&reid=459290; http://www.weforum.org/site/homepublic.nsf/

Content/Members+and+Partners%5CStrategic+Partners (both accessed March 2007).

71. World Economic Forum Blog, 2006, http://www.forumblog.org/blog/2006/02/boardroom_talk__2.html (accessed March 2007).

72. 'Blair's Son to Experience Financial PR Firm', *Reuters*, 13 January 2006. http://www.spinwatch.org/content/view/2387/9/ (accessed March 2007).

73. 'Blair the Younger does Work Experience with City Spin Doctors', *Private Eye*, Issue 1150, 6 February 2006.

74. See the Britain in Europe website at the Web Archive: http://web.archive.org/web/*/http://www.britainineurope.org.uk/ (accessed March 2007).

75. IBLF, Supporters, http://www.iblf.org/supporters.jsp.

76. Business in the Community, http://www.bitc.org.uk/document.rm?id=4623 (accessed March 2007).

77. EACA /WFA, 2002, *Industry as a Partner for Sustainable Development: Advertising*, p. 6, http://www.aacc.fr/documents/advertising2002.pdf (accessed March 2007).

78. Ibid., p. 25.

79. Ibid., p. 29.

80. Fulton was exposed as an intelligence agent when he was working inside Glasgow University's Lockerbie commission. It was set up to assist in the inquiry into the Lockerbie disaster in which the Libyan suspects are widely believed to have been framed by the intelligence agencies. His last intelligence posting was as an MI6 representative in the Washington Embassy, from which he went straight to the Lockerbie job. BBC Online, *Lockerbie 'MI6' Man Dropped*, Monday 22 May 2000, http://news.bbc.co.uk/1/hi/scotland/758952.stm; Sophie Brodie, '"Spy in Washington" Takes Security Role', *Telegraph*, 21 August 2006, http://www.telegraph.co.uk/money/main.jhtml?xml=/money/2006/08/21/cnfulton21.xml. See also Terry Murden, 'The Spy Who Eluded Me', *Scotland on Sunday*, 16 April 2006. http://scotlandonsunday.scotsman.com/business.cfm?id=575922006 (accessed March 2007).

81. Joseph Nye, *Soft Power: The Means to Success in World Politics*, New York: Public Affairs, 2004.

82. Renaissance Weekend, Advisory Board, http://www.renaissanceweekend.org/AdvisoryBoard_25thNEW.htm (accessed March 2007).

83. See Chapter 8.

84. Sandra Laville and Matt Born, 'BBC Says Sorry to Tearful US Envoy', *Daily Telegraph*, 14 September 2001. http://www.telegraph.co.uk/news/main.jhtml;jsessionid=REPCPQROBXIUVQFIQMGSFFWAVCBQWIV0?xml=/news/2001/09/15/ntime15.xml (accessed March 2007).

85. Ibid.

86. WPP, Who We Are, WPP Leadership, http://www.wpp.com/WPP/About/WhoWeAre/Leadership.htm#name6 (accessed April 2007).

87. Carrie Kirby, 'Electronic Frontier Foundation: Online Freedom Fighters: Free-speech group returns to its roots, battles studios over DVD program', *San Francisco Chronicle*, 27 May 2001. http://www.mindfully.org/Reform/Electronic-Frontier-Foundation.htm (accessed March 2007).

88. The Eurasia Foundation, 'Engaging Citizens, Empowering Communities', http://www.eurasia.org/(ztkgr245ld1jppel34edlq55)/about/ (accessed March 2007).

89. The Eurasia Foundation, Publications, http://www.eurasia.org/ (xn00o555jjsswr3zexf1afrg)/publications/2002/trainwoman.aspx (accessed April 2007). For background on Yukos oil company see Marshall I. Goldman, *The Piratization of Russia: Russian Reform Goes Awry*, London: Routledge, 2003.

90. Richard Wray, 'The Clean-up Queen: Esther Dyson, Internet Guru', *Guardian*, Saturday 31 January 2004. http://business.guardian.co.uk/ story/0,3604,1135938,00.html (accessed March 2007).

91. Markle Foundation, *Protecting America's Freedom in the Information Age 2006*, http://www.markle.org/markle_programs/policy_for_a_ networked_society/national_security/projects/report1_overview.php (accessed March 2007).

92. David Osler, 'Big Business and the Moderates', CPSA Rank and File report, *Inside the Moderates*, 1995. http://www.spinprofiles.org/index. php/Big_Business_and_the_Moderates.

93. 'David Cameron Gains Support of City Figures', *Financial Times*, 8 September 2005. http://news.ft.com/cms/s/d809ef9a-2006–11da-853a-00000e2511c8.html (accessed April 2007).

CHAPTER 8   PULLING LABOUR'S TEETH

1. Cited in Andy Beckett, 'Friends in High Places', *Guardian*, Saturday 6 November 2004. http://www.guardian.co.uk/weekend/story/ 0,,1343578,00.html (accessed March 2007).

2. See the Claremont Hotel website: http://www.claremontresort.com/.

3. Beckett, 2004.

4. Duncan Parrish, 'The British-American Project: Right-wing Conspiracy or Right-on Broker of the Special Relationship? – The British-American Project for the Successor Generation', *New Statesman*, 17 May 1999. http://www.newstatesman.com/199905170015.

5. Beckett, 2004.

6. Parrish, 1999.

7. Parrish, 1999.

8. Parrish, 1999.

9. Gabriele Zamparini, 'The BBC, Iran and the Bomb', *The Cat's Blog*, Wednesday 12 April 2006, http://www.thecatsdream.com/blog/2006/04/ bbc-iran-and-bomb.htm.

10. Maurice Chittenden and Nicholas Rufford, 'MI6 "Firm" Spied on Green Groups', *Sunday Times*, 17 June 2001. http://www.commondreams.org/ cgi-bin/print.cgi?file=/headlines01/0617–01.htm.

11. Beckett, 2004.

12. Between 1978 and 1980, Phillips was president of the National Union of Students. He became Head of Current Affairs at LWT in 1992.

13. John Reid and Trevor Phillips, *The Best Intentions? Race, Equity and Delivering Today's NHS*, London: Fabian Society, July 2004. http://www.fabian-society.org.uk/press_office/display.asp?cat=24&id=342.

14. Cited in Beckett, 2004.

15. Cited in Beckett, 2004.

16. As shown in Chapter 4. See also G. William Domhoff, *Fat Cats and Democrats: The Role of the Big Rich in the Party of the Common Man*, Englewood Cliffs, NJ: Prentice Hall, 1972.

17. Caroline Anstey, 'The Projection of British Socialism: Foreign Office Publicity and American Opinion, 1945–1950', *Journal of Contemporary History*, 19, 1984, p. 424.

18. Frank Evans to J. Balfour, 25 August 1947. FO 371/61050 AN 3094/28/45, cited in Anstey, p. 438.

19. William Crofts, *Coercion or Persuasion? Propaganda in Britain after 1945*, London: Routledge, 1989, p. 245.

20. Anstey, p. 427.

21. Cited in Anstey, p. 431.

22. Anstey, p. 425.

23. Crofts, pp. 244–5.

24. Anstey, p. 425.

25. Cited in Paul Lashmar and James Oliver, *Britain's Secret Propaganda War: Foreign Office and the Cold War, 1948–77*, Stroud, Gloucestershire: Sutton Publishing, 1998, p. 27.

26. Ibid., p. 28.

27. Robin Ramsay, *The Rise of New Labour*, Harpenden, Herts: Pocket Essentials, 2002, p. 33.

28. Brian Crozier, *Free Agent: The Unseen War 1941–1991: The Autobiography of an International Activist*, London: HarperCollins, 1993, p. 147.

29. Ibid., p. 147.

30. See Tom Easton, 'Who Were They Travelling With?', Review of Ivor Crewe and Anthony King's *SDP: The Birth, Life and Death of the Social Democratic Party* (Oxford: Oxford University Press, 1995), *Lobster*, 31, June 1996, http://www.lobster-magazine.co.uk/articles/l31whowh.htm (accessed March 2007). Williams remains on the Ditchley Foundation Council of Management in 2007; Ditchley Foundation, 'The Council of Management', http://www.ditchley.co.uk/page/63/the-council.htm (accessed August 2007). On Williams' recent Ditchley activities see her entry in the Register of Lords Interests, 'Williams of Crosby, Baroness', http://www.publications.parliament.uk/pa/ld/ldreg/reg26.htm (accessed August 2007).

31. Easton, 1996.

32. Ramsay, 2002, p. 35.

33. Crozier, p. 147.

34. Crozier, pp. 147–8.

35. Ramsay, 2002, p. 36.

36. Neville Sandelson, MP, *Sunday Telegraph* 1996, cited in Robin Ramsay, *Prawn Cocktail Party: The Hidden Power Behind New Labour*, London: Vision, 1998, p. 92.

37. Seumas Milne, *The Enemy Within: The Secret War Against the Miners*, 3rd edn, London: Verso, 2004.
38. Seumas Milne, 'A Different Kind of Britain', *Guardian*, 6 March 2004. http://www.guardian.co.uk/Columnists/Column/0,5673,1163502,00. html.
39. Victor Allen, 'How MacGregor's Men Broke the US Miners' Union', *Guardian*, 5 November 1984.
40. Cited in Mark Hollingsworth, *The Ultimate Spin Doctor: The Life and Fast Times of Tim Bell*, London: Hodder and Stoughton, 1997, p. 117; cited in Jones, 1986, p. 136.
41. Cited in Nick Jones, *Trading Information: Leaks, Lies and Tip-Offs*, London: Politico's Publishing Ltd (an imprint of Methuen Publishing Ltd), 2006.
42. Cited in Hollingsworth, p. 132.
43. Crozier, p. 253.
44. Hollingsworth, p. 121.
45. Hollingsworth, p. 121.
46. Milne, *The Enemy Within*, p. 324.
47. Cited in Hollingsworth, p. 121.
48. Crozier, p. 253.
49. Jones, 1986, pp. 136–8.
50. Nicholas Jones, 'Reporting the Miners' Strike', *Free Press*, No. 140, May 2004. http://keywords.dsvr.co.uk/freepress/body.phtml?category= &id=707.
51. Andy McSmith, *John Smith: A Life, 1938–94*, London: Mandarin, 1994, cited in Ramsay, 2002, p. 52.
52. Davies then became chairman of Fulcrum Asset Management, a $1.35 billion hedge fund.
53. David Osler, *Labour Party Plc: New Labour as a Party of Business*, Edinburgh: Mainstream, 2002.
54. Tom Pendry, 'The Labour Finance and Industry Group: A Memoir', *Lobster*, 51, Summer 2006, p. 7.
55. Ibid.
56. The media has been surprisingly reluctant to investigate this issue, despite the unfolding cash-for-peerages scandal in 2006, and the brief arrest of Lord Levy in July 2006. Equally little attention is being paid to the funding of David Cameron's Shadow Cabinet.
57. Ramsay, 2002, p. 52.
58. McSmith, p. 209, cited in Ramsay, 2002, p. 54.
59. Ramsay, 2002, p. 54.

CHAPTER 9   BLAIR AND THE BUSINESS LOBBY

1. Cited in Francis Wheen, 'Social Justice – That's so Old Labour', *Guardian*, Wednesday 7 February 2001. http://www.guardian.co.uk/Columnists/ Column/0,5673,434619,00.html.
2. Muhammad Idrees Ahmad, 'Labour Friends of Israel in the House', *Spinwatch*, 21 March 2005, http://www.spinwatch.org/content/ view/97/8/.

3. David Osler, cited in 'Lord Levy: Labour's Fundraiser', BBC Online, 17 March 2006, http://news.bbc.co.uk/1/hi/uk_politics/4816692.stm.
4. Cited in Mark Hollingsworth, *MPs for Hire*, London: Bloomsbury, 1991, p. 177.
5. Tom Pendry, 'The Labour Finance and Industry Group: A Memoir', *Lobster*, 51, Summer 2006, p. 7.
6. Cited in David Osler, *Labour Party plc*, Edinburgh: Mainstream, 2002, p. 22.
7. See the profile of Hamilton on the 'Now You're Talking' website: http://www.nyt.co.uk/neilhamilton.htm. Information on Neil being thrown in for free in an email from Jane French, The Right Address, 9 July 2006.
8. See Hollingsworth, 1991; S.E. Finer, *Anonymous Empire*, Pall Mall, 2nd edn, 1966, originally published 1958.
9. Margaret Thatcher, *The Downing Street Years*, London: HarperCollins, 1993, pp. 677–8.
10. K. Wiltshire, *Privatisation – The British Experience*, Melbourne: Committee for Economic Development of Australia/Longman, 1987.
11. M. Forsyth, *Reservicing Health*, London: Adam Smith Institute, 1982.
12. M. Forsyth, *Reservicing Britain*, London: Adam Smith Institute, 1980.
13. Kate Ascher, *The Politics of Privatization: Contracting Out Public Services*, Houndmills, Basingstoke: Macmillan, 1987, pp. 27, 36.
14. Labour Research Department, 'Lobbying and MPs' Interests', *Labour Research*, July 1984, pp. 175–7.
15. Ascher, p. 49; Hollingsworth, pp. 70–6.
16. Labour Research Department, 1984.
17. Ascher, p. 75.
18. Ascher, p. 75.
19. Grant Jordan (ed.), *The Commercial Lobbyists: Politics for Profit in Britain*, Aberdeen: Aberdeen University Press, 1991, pp. 20–1.
20. Hollingsworth, p. 90.
21. Register of Members' Interests, 14 January 1991, cited in Hollingsworth, 1991.
22. Rob Baggott, *Alcohol, Politics and Social Policy*, London: Gower, 1990, pp. 67–8, cited in Hollingsworth, p. 119.
23. Letter to Labour Research, July 1984, cited in Hollingsworth, p. 120.
24. See David Leigh and Ed Vulliamy, *Sleaze: The Corruption of Parliament*, London: Fourth Estate, 1997.
25. Hollingsworth, pp. 127, 129.
26. Jamie Wilson, 'Who will listen to his story now? Media-hungry couple face ruin after libel loss', *Guardian*, Wednesday 22 December 1999. http://www.guardian.co.uk/hamilton/article/0,,195592,00.html.
27. Leigh and Vulliamy, pp. 57–8.
28. For examples see Hollingsworth, 1991.
29. Info-Dynamics Research Associates, *Where Are They Now? The 1997/1998 Special Advisers to the Labour Government*, Report for the GMB, April 2006, published June 2006. http://www.gmb.org.uk/Shared_ASP_Files/UploadedFiles/5D3DCAA1–15AB-4CF0-B7A5-EB449C165AF2_ListofAdvisersApril2006congressFINAL.pdf.

30. David Miller and William Dinan, 'The Rise of the PR Industry in Britain, 1979–98', *European Journal of Communication*, 15(1), 2000, pp. 5–35.
31. David Hencke, 'Tough New Code on Lobbyists', *Guardian*, 28 July 1998, p. 3.
32. As Greg Palast tried to tell the House of Commons Committee on Standards and Privileges in his memo titled 'Systemic Corruption, Systemic Solutions', 18 August 1999. http://www.spinprofiles.org/index.php/Systemic_Corruption%2C_Systemic_Solutions.
33. Ibid.
34. *Living With the Enemy*, BBC2, 23 September 1998.
35. Director of Public Affairs, Centrica.
36. Mark Hollingsworth, 'An infestation of lobbyists: The PR people have flocked into Labour's headquarters to offer their services – absolutely free', *Guardian*, Wednesday 6 June 2001. http://politics.guardian.co.uk/election2001/comment/0,9407,502322,00.html.
37. Hollingsworth, 1991, pp. 177–8.
38. Register of Members' Interests, 6 November 2005, http://www.publications.parliament.uk/pa/cm/cmregmem/051101/memi02.htm; http://www.publications.parliament.uk/pa/cm/cmregmem/regmem.pdf.
39. See http://www.cis.org.au/.
40. UK Defence Forum, http://www.ukdf.org.uk/members_area.asp.
41. Andrew Denham and Mark Garrett, *British Think Tanks and the Climate of Opinion*, London: UCL Press, 1998, pp. 180–1.
42. Nick Cohen, 'The New Statesman Profile – IPPR; What real influence does the voice of the centre left and Labour's favourite think-tank wield?' *New Statesman*, 21 August 2000.
43. Colin Hughes and Patrick Wintour, *Labour Rebuilt: The New Model Party*, London: Fourth Estate, 1990, p. 173.
44. Nick Cohen, 'IPPR', *New Statesman*, 21 August 2000; Info-Dynamics Research Associates.
45. Stuart Hall and Martin Jacques, *Thatcherism*, London: Lawrence and Wishart, 1983.
46. D. Aitkenhead, 'These aged teenagers at Marxism Today guiltily shuffling their feet', *Guardian*, 23 October 1998. http://www.guardianunlimited.co.uk/Archive/Article/0,4273,3785863,00.html.
47. Peter Oborne, *The Rise of Political Lying*, London: Free Press, 2005.
48. Geraldine Bedell, 'Geoff and Martin's Big Idea', *Independent on Sunday*, Sunday Review, 24 January 1993, p. 2.
49. Ibid.
50. Geoff Mulgan, 'Thinking in Tanks: The Changing Ecology of Political Ideas', *Political Quarterly*, 77(2), April–June 2006, pp. 147–55.
51. Brian Micklethwait, Review of 'The Parenting Deficit, Amitai Etzioni', Demos, Paper No. 4, London, 1993, *Free Life*, Issue 23, August 1995. http://www.libertarian.co.uk/freelife/fl023.pdf; http://www.seangabb.co.uk/freelife/flhtm/fl23etzi.htm.
52. Charles Leadbetter, *Living on thin Air*, London: Viking, 1999, pp. 96–7.
53. Ibid.

54. 'Re-elected Blair Triggers Furor over Appointments', Agence France Presse, 10 May 2005.

55. Sense About Science, 'Peer Review: The Arbiter of Scientific Quality', http://www.senseaboutscience.org.uk/peerreview/.

56. Michael White, 'On May 1 Paul Drayson was given a peerage. On June 17 he gave Labour a £500,000 cheque', *Guardian*, Wednesday 25 August 2004. http://politics.guardian.co.uk/funding/story/0,11893,1290153,00. html.

57. Michael White, 'Blair Defies Critics in Reshuffle: Promotions Court Controversy', *Guardian*, Tuesday 10 May 2005. http://politics.guardian. co.uk/labour/story/0,9061,1480353,00.html.

58. Billy Clark is the former editor of *Variant*, an extraordinary radical 'arts' magazine given away free throughout Britain and Ireland which has somehow managed to survive the New Labour period (http://www. variant.randomstate.org/). His research on Demos and Stevenson are discussed in his 'The Atlantic Semantic', in William Dinan and David Miller (eds), *Thinker, Faker, Spinner, Spy: Corporate PR and the Assault on Democracy*, London: Pluto Press, 2007.

59. Dennis Stevenson, 'I'm No Crony', *Independent*, 8 July 2003, p. 15.

60. John Gapper, 'Pearson to End Political Party Donations', *Financial Times*, 8 April 1998, p. 10.

61. See the list of financial supporters on the archive of the Demos site circa 1998, http://web.archive.org/web/19980613031138/www.demos. co.uk/A_funder.htm.

62. 'People's Peers: The Strange Case of the Missing Lollipop Ladies', BBC Online Open Politics, 2001 (no date specified), http://news.bbc. co.uk/hi/english/static/in_depth/uk_politics/2001/open_politics/lords/ peoples_peers.stm.

63. Cited in Bedell, p. 2.

64. Cited in Matthew Lynn, 'Patter Merchant with a Power Base', *Sunday Times*, 20 October 1996.

65. Andrew Grice, 'Labour's Red-rose Guru to Help True-blue Firms', *Sunday Times*, 19 August 1990.

66. Cited in Eleanor Mills, 'Doing the Business with Blair and Co', *Sunday Times*, 21 June 1998.

67. Ibid.

68. Cited in Lynn, 1996.

69. Rob Blackhurst, 'The Sad Decline of the Policy Wonks', *New Statesman*, Monday 31 January 2005. http://www.newstatesman. com/200501310024.

70. Neil Hume, 'Break up BT, says Demos. Its sponsor? C&W', *Guardian*, Monday 4 November 2002. http://business.guardian.co.uk/story/ 0,3604,825381,00.html.

71. Solomon Hughes, 'Judge Bread', *Red Pepper*, April 2004, http://www. redpepper.org.uk/KYE/x-kye-Apr2004.html.

72. Information in the foregoing paragraph from 'Purnell's Progress', *Guardian*, Monday 23 May 2005. http://politics.guardian.co.uk/ interviews/story/0,11660,1490315,00.html.

73. The work for Portland was registered on 23 July 2003. See the Register at http://www.theyworkforyou.com/regmem/?p=11176.
74. Barclay Sumner, 'Former No 10 Union-buster Nailed over Asda Link Again', *Tribune*, 3 March 2006.
75. Kevin Maguire, 'Such Cheek by Jowell and Allan', *Daily Mirror*, 1 March 2006. http://www.mirror.co.uk/news/kevinmaguire/tm_column_date=01032006-name_index.html
76. Cited in Sumner, 2006.
77. Jolyon Kimble, 'Interview with Alan Donnelly, Executive Chairman of Sovereign Strategy', *Euractiv*, Tuesday 10 May 2005. http://www.euractiv.com/en/pa/interview-alan-donnelly-executive-chairman-sovereign-strategy/article-139242.
78. Registered 28 January 2005.
79. As recorded on the Sovereign website via the Web Archive: http://web.archive.org/web/20051227234744/http://www.sovereignstrategy.com/news.asp#40 (archived 27 December 2005, accessed 9 June 2007); 'DCMS Freedom of Information Requests Meetings Between Ministers and Sovereign Strategy 19/09/2005', http://www.culture.gov.uk/global/foi_requests/archive_2005/case_23000.htm?properties=archive_2005%2C%2Fabout_dcms%2FQuickLinks%2Ffoi_requests%2Fdefault%2C&month=.
80. Robert Winnett, 'Revealed: Minister's Links to Nuclear Lobby, *Sunday Times*, 14 May 2006. http://www.timesonline.co.uk/article/0,,2087-2180107,00.html.
81. In September 2007, Sovereign indicated they might join the APPC. David Singleton, 'Agencies Bow to APPC Membership Pressure', *PR Week*, 6 September 2007, http://www.brandrepublic.com/News/736023/Agencies-bow-APCC-membership-pressure/www.prweek.co.uk.
82. David Hencke, 'Ex-ministers Cleared to Work for Lobbying Firm', *Guardian*, Tuesday 24 May 2005. http://politics.guardian.co.uk/funding/story/0,11893,1490857,00.html.
83. Ibid.

CHAPTER 10   CAMERON AND THE NEO-CONS

1. Ravi Chandiramani, 'After Blair', *PR Week*, 16 February 2006. http://www.prweek.com/uk/home/article/541392/.
2. Anthony Browne and Andrew Pierce, 'Secretive Guru Behind the New Dave Project', *The Times*, 5 October 2006. http://www.timesonline.co.uk/tol/news/politics/article660820.ece.
3. S. Hilton and G. Gibbons, *Good Business: Your World Needs You*, London: Texere, 2002, pp. 232–3.
4. Ian Beaumont, 'From ITV to PLC: Merge, Merge, Merge and Miss the Boat', ITV at Fifty, Transdiffusion Broadcasting system, http://www.transdiffusion.org/emc/itv50/itvplc/ (accessed 3 April 2007).
5. Cited in Brian Wheeler, 'The David Cameron Story', BBC Online, 6 December 2005, http://news.bbc.co.uk/1/hi/uk_politics/4502656.stm.

6. UTEK Corporation, Directors, http://www.utek.co.uk/files/directors. asp?pageID=15 (accessed April 2007).
7. Meg Carter, 'The Art of Spinning: From PR to Parliament', *Independent*, 8 January 2007. http://news.independent.co.uk/media/article2132894. ece.
8. Brian Wheeler, 'Profile: George Osborne', BBC Online, 10 May 2005, http://news.bbc.co.uk/1/hi/uk_politics/4534107.stm.
9. http://www.theyworkforyou.com/regmem/?p=11905.
10. Its website is http://www.henryjacksonsociety.org.
11. David Morrison, 'David Cameron: Blair Mark II?' *Spinwatch*, 21 November 2005, http://www.spinwatch.org/content/view/4145/8/.
12. Neil Clark, 'Cameron is no moderate: He supports the Iraq war and tax cuts, opposes EU social policies and has neocon associations', *Guardian*, Monday 24 October 2005. http://www.guardian.co.uk/comment/ story/0,3604,1598988,00.html.
13. *Private Eye*, 15–29 March 2007.
14. Cited in Ravi Chandiramani, 'British politics is hotting up at last and PA professionals are preparing for the change in leadership and policy', *PR Week* 16 February 2006.
15. http://www.cchange.org.uk.
16. John Elliot, 'Top Tory Aide is King of the Urban Swingers', *Sunday Times*, 22 June 2003. http://www.freerepublic.com/focus/f-news/933338/ posts.
17. Fever Parties website, http://www.feverparties.com/cgi-bin/template. cgi?content=home.
18. Vincent Moss, 'Tory Dave's Latest Aide,' *Sunday Mirror*, 6 August 2006, p. 33.
19. Politeia, About Us, http://www.politeia.co.uk/AboutUs/tabid/52/Default. aspx (accessed 2 April 2007).
20. http://www.openeurope.org.uk/about-us/ (accessed 9 June 2007).
21. http://www.openeurope.org.uk/about-us/supporters.aspx (accessed 9 June 2007).
22. See the list of UK members at http://www.stockholm-network.org/ network/details.php?id=1 (accessed 2 April 2007).
23. http://www.stockholm-network.org.
24. Corporate Europe Observatory, 'Covert Industry Funding Fuels the Expansion of Radical Rightwing EU Think Tanks', July 2005, http:// www.corporateeurope.org/stockholmnetwork.html.
25. Ibid.
26. http://www.consespain-usa.org/intro/biografias/ing/18.html; http:// www.stockholm-network.org/pubs/Agenda70203.htm; http://www.cne. org/about2.htm#3. All cited in Corporate Europe Observatory, 2005.
27. http://www.atlanticpartnership.org/index.php?fuseaction=about.
28. Alice Thomson, 'The Camp David Team', *Daily Telegraph*, 7 December 2005. http://www.telegraph.co.uk/news/main.jhtml?xml=/news/2005/ 12/07/ncam707.xml.
29. http://www.theatlanticbridge.com.
30. *Spectator*, 28 February 2004, cited in Morrison, 2005.

31. Matthew Parris, 'Welcome to Cameron's Europe-hating and Pentagon-loving Party', *The Times* Online, 20 May 2006, http://www.timesonline.co.uk/tol/comment/columnists/matthew_parris/article722056.ece.
32. Ibid.
33. Jeff Randall 'CBI CONFERENCE Passionless Davies Should Try Orgasmic Chocolates', *Daily Telegraph*, 30 November 2005, p. 4.
34. Ibid.
35. Wheeler, 'David Cameron Story', 2005.
36. Hellier on Sport, 'Unsportsmanlike Spinning', *Sunday Express*, 10 October 1999.
37. Solomon Hughes, 'Cameron the Compassionate', *Red Pepper*, May 2006, http://www.redpepper.org.uk/KYE/x-kye-may2006.htm.
38. Ibid.
39. Ibid.
40. For more on Renwick see 'Robin Renwick', *Spin Profiles*, http://www.spinprofiles.org/index.php/Robin_Renwick.
41. Tobias Buck, David Buchan, Krishna Guha and Sheila McNulty, 'Oiling the Political Engine', *Financial Times*, 1 August 2002.
42. House of Commons Register of Members' Interests, David Willetts, http://www.publications.parliament.uk/pa/cm199899/cmregmem/memi29.htm (accessed January 2007); Sadiq Khan MP, Blog, 24 January 2006, http://www.sadiqkhan.org.uk/blog/archive/2006_01_01_archive.htm.

CHAPTER 11   CONCLUSION: COMMUNICATION AND POWER

1. For a discussion of this issue see G. Philo and D. Miller, *Market Killing*, London: Longman, 2001.
2. Philip Mirowski and Dieter Plehwe, *The Making of the Neoliberal Thought Collective*, Harvard University Press, forthcoming, 2008.
3. J.M. Keynes, *The General Theory of Employment, Interest and Money*, New York: Harcourt and Brace, 1936, p. 383.
4. Madsen Pirie, *Micropolitics: The Creation of Successful Policies*, Wildwood House, 1988, p. 267, cited in Richard Cockett, *Thinking the Unthinkable: Think-Tanks and the Economic Counter-Revolution, 1931–83*, London: HarperCollins, 1994, p. 283.
5. Karl Marx and Friedrich Engels, *The German Ideology*, Part 1, Feuerbach. Opposition of the Materialist and Idealist Outlook, A. Idealism and Materialism, 1845/6. http://www.marxists.org/archive/marx/works/1845/german-ideology/ch01a.htm.
6. Radhika Desai, 'Second-Hand Dealers in Ideas: Think-Tanks and Thatcherite Hegemony', *New Left Review*, No. 203, January–February 1994, p. 62.
7. Ibid., p. 62.
8. Cited in Paul D'Amato, 'Imperialism and the State: Why McDonald's Needs McDonnell Douglas', *International Socialist Review*, Issue 17, April–May 2001. http://www.isreview.org/issues/17/state_and_imperialism.shtml.

9. Richard Tedlow, *Keeping the Corporate Image: Public Relations and Business, 1900–1950*, Greenwich, CT: JAI Press, 1979, p. 208.
10. As summarised by Karen Miller, *The Voice of Business: Hill and Knowlton and Postwar Public Relations*, Chapel Hill: University of North Caroline Press, 1999, p. 193.
11. Ibid.
12. Douglas Rushkoff, *Coercion: Why We Listen to What 'They' Say*, New York: Riverhead Books, 1999, p. 270.
13. See David Miller, 'Media Power and Class Power: Overplaying Ideology', in L. Panitch and C. Leys (eds), 'A World of Contradictions', Socialist Register 2002, London: Merlin Press, US, Monthly Review Press, Canada, Fernwood Publishing, 2001.
14. For example: 'an understanding of bourgeois class rule as based to a large extent on the consent of the ruled, rather than based on force'. Dorothee Bohle and Gisela Neunhoffer, 'Why Is There No Third Way?' in Dieter Plehwe, Bernhard Walpen and Gisela Neunhoffer (eds), *Neoliberal Hegemony: A Global Critique*, London: Routledge, 2006, p. 90.
15. Colin Leys, 'Still a Question of Hegemony', *New Left Review* I/181, May–June 1990, pp. 119–28.
16. Ibid., p. 127.
17. Alex Carey, 'Reshaping the Truth: Pragmatists and Propagandists in America', *Meanjin Quarterly*, 35(4), 1976, pp. 370–8.
18. Steven Lukes *Power: A Radical View*, Basingstoke: Palgrave Macmillan, 2nd edn, 2004.

Index